The American Century

THE
AMERICAN CENTURY

ART & CULTURE
1950–2000

Lisa Phillips

Whitney Museum of American Art, New York

in association with

W. W. Norton & Company   New York   London

**The American Century
Art & Culture 1900–2000**

Organized by the
Whitney Museum
of American Art
Presented by
Intel Corporation

Additional support for this exhibition
is provided by
the National Endowment for the Arts,
the National Committee of the
Whitney Museum,
Booth Ferris Foundation, and
The Lauder Foundation, Evelyn and
Leonard Lauder Fund.
Educational and Public Programs are
funded by a generous grant from
The Brown Foundation, Inc., Houston.

This publication is made possible by a gift
from Susan and Edwin Malloy.

Research for Museum publications is
supported by an endowment established
by The Andrew W. Mellon Foundation
and other generous donors.

This book was published on the occasion of the exhibition
The American Century: Art & Culture 1900–2000
at the Whitney Museum of American Art.
Part I, 1900–1950
April 23 to August 22, 1999, and
Part II, 1950–2000
September 26, 1999, to February 13, 2000.

A complete list of works in the exhibition is available at www.whitney.org.

Library of Congress Cataloging-in-Publication Data
Phillips, Lisa.
      The American century : art & culture, 1950-2000 / Lisa Phillips.
          p. cm.
      Completes the history begun with: The American century : art & culture,
1900-1950 / Barbara Haskell.
      Includes bibliographical references and index.
      ISBN 0-393-04815-2 (Norton)
      1. Art, American. 2. Art, Modern—20th century—United States.
3. Arts, American. 4. Arts, Modern—20th century—United States.
I. Haskell, Barbara. American century. II. Whitney Museum of American Art.
III. Title.
N6512H355 1999 Suppl.
709' .73'0747471—dc21   99-24969
                                        CIP

ISBN 0-393-04815-2 (Norton cloth)
ISBN 0-87427-123-1 (Whitney paper)

W. W. Norton & Company, Inc.
500 Fifth Avenue, New York, NY 10110
www.wwnorton.com

W. W. Norton & Company Ltd.
10 Coptic Street, London WC1A 1PU

1 2 3 4 5 6 7 8 9 0

Cover: **Jasper Johns**, *Three Flags*, 1958. Encaustic on canvas, 30 7/8 x 45 1/2 x 5 in. (78.4 x 115.6 x 12.7 cm).
Whitney Museum of American Art, New York; 50th Anniversary Gift of the Gilman Foundation, Inc., The Lauder
Foundation, A. Alfred Taubman, an anonymous donor, and purchase 80.32
© Jasper Johns/Licensed by VAGA, New York, NY

Frontispiece: **Robert Smithson**, *Spiral Jetty*, 1970 (fig. 338).

Statement of Collaboration

Organized by the Whitney Museum of American Art
Presented by Intel Corporation

Intel Corporation is honored to collaborate with the Whitney Museum of American Art in presenting *The American Century: Art & Culture 1900–2000*, a sweeping exhibition that explores the forces of immigration and technology in the context of America's social and cultural landscape during the past one hundred years. Within this landscape, it is the spirit of inventiveness, the openness to new ideas and technologies, and the intellectual rigor found in the work of American artists which speak to us. These are the same dynamics that gave birth to and continue to propel the American high-technology industry.

The American Century is also a record of the evolution and growth of our modern visual culture, from silent film to television to the visual computer. Modern American artists have a tradition of standing in the vanguard—of tackling tough issues and creating new visual languages that force us to look at how new technology impacts our society.

As visual computers, connected to the Internet, change the way we learn and communicate, Intel looks to artists to help our industry develop a new visual and interactive literacy in order to make PCs even more useful to more people. In that spirit, Intel and the Whitney Museum will be working together over the course of *The American Century* to design a range of new interactive and educational tools that will enrich the museum experience and extend the exhibition into homes and classrooms around the world.

We commend the Whitney Museum of American Art for undertaking this ambitious and important exhibition and are pleased to help bring it to the American public.

Andrew S. Grove
Chairman, Intel Corporation

Contents

Sidebar Texts

Foreword

Maxwell L. Anderson
Director
Whitney Museum of American Art

Jackson Pollock
Number 17, 1950, 1950
Enamel and aluminum
paint on board, 22¼ x
22¼ in. (56.5 x 56.5 cm)
Whitney Museum of
American Art, New York;
Gift of Mildred and
Herbert C. Lee 99.59

The second half of the twentieth century in America has been a time of change so rapid as to defy the imagination. Cycles of creativity are now so accelerated that barely has an art movement been charted by the critical, museological, and academic establishments than its energy seems spent. Demographic changes also differentiate the art of the past fifty years. According to the Internal Revenue Service, hundreds of thousands of Americans today describe themselves as artists—an exponential increase in the population of artists that greeted American museums at the time of the Whitney's charter in 1930. It should not be surprising to find that artistic life in these last five decades has been a contradictory and kaleidoscopic affair, one characterized by concurrent but diverse impulses that cannot be chronicled in a straightforward, linear progression. Reading an account of this period therefore requires patient agility on the part of the reader.

In keeping with the dizzying pace of these decades, this second part of *The American Century: Art & Culture 1900–2000* represents a history of the avant-garde. This focus is warranted not only by the complexity of the task facing the museum world at the end of the century, but as well by the leading role American art has played on the international scene since 1950. The vanguard concentration of this volume and of the exhibition it accompanies also reflects the Whitney's own history in these years as a leader in identifying and championing the avant-garde—despite the indignant stance of some critics, for whom the Museum is too connected to contemporary artistic milieus rather than to the more mainstream creative landscape. Many of the works included in Part II are by artists who received their first or early-career exhibitions at the Whitney, and who subsequently achieved renown. The selection of artists will no doubt irritate some and win favor with others, but such dissension in the critical ranks is also part of the Whitney tradition—as attested by the controversies that attend every one of our Biennial exhibitions. Ultimately, however, the aim of this project is not to create a definitive "A-list" of vanguard artists during the past fifty years, but rather to peg their work to the society and culture in which they flourished.

The story begins with Abstract Expressionism and the New York School, whose proponents set a new course for American art. This sustained burst of individual creativity launched an art that affirmed America's emergence from the shadow of the Old World. The second generation of New York School artists are then given their due, even as the text charts their ineluctable descent into the last phase of a revolutionary artistic cycle: the perceived ossification of what was once seen as daring and innovative. The need to overthrow the hegemony of Abstract Expressionism spawned a series of responses, including the resurgence of figurative art and the broader acceptance of women artists.

The decade of the 1950s was also defined by the Beat generation and the introduction of assemblage and junk sculpture as well as environments and Happenings—all representing an openness to nontraditional media and an interdisciplinary enterprise that marked a decisive break from the norms of European art. These works, in a time-honored *épater le bourgeois* sensibility, offered pastiches of contemporary life that challenged the complacency of establishment America during the Eisenhower years. Photographers weaned on photojournalism exposed the surreality of Main Street and the urban jungle and made America see itself in ways that undermined the pristine Technicolor picture promoted by mainstream media. By the 1960s, the hip, ironic language of Pop culture coexisted with this impassioned resentment of the stern moral and political center.

In the fertile collision of Pop art and Minimalism, the disconnection of art-making from social concerns and from the Abstract Expressionist model of the heroic artist was complete, and a new vanguard of activist, anti-modernist artists took the stage. In the later 1960s and into the 1970s, Minimalism was followed by Eccentric Abstraction,

Postminimalism, Earthworks, and Conceptual art. A section on the influence of feminism sheds light on the use of pattern and decoration as well as craft, while the discussions of performance, body art, video, and the founding of alternative spaces reinforce the complex picture of this period. Painting and sculpture were also reconceived—in expressionist and superrealist modes, among others—which allowed these traditional media to continue alongside the myriad assaults on conventional art.

In the 1980s, the emergence of street culture, graffiti art, and other forms that rejected the art establishment as the arbiter of quality kindled a younger generation of artists. Meanwhile, Ronald Reagan's election in 1980 gave rise to a conservative culture—small but vocal—that declared war on the avant-garde, even as the art market boomed in an explosion of record-breaking auction prices. The prosperous economy of the eighties produced a materialist sensibility that made art collectible once again, and it is surely no coincidence that the appropriation-rich styles of postmodernism held sway during the decade.

In the closing decade of this century, the manifestations of high culture that demand our attention are more difficult to identify than ever. Although challenging the authority of a solipsistic art world has always been a prerogative of the avant-garde, in the 1990s the number and diverse character of the artists tilting their lances almost defy analysis in the short view. Artistic responses in a media-saturated world and a largely affluent and self-congratulatory America are extraordinarily multifaceted, which makes the mining of today's art as formidable and potentially rewarding a task as ever.

We are grateful to the scores of lenders from the United States and around the globe who parted with their treasures to make this exhibition possible. The staff of the Whitney was exemplary at every turn in bringing this highly ambitious enterprise to fruition. Everyone worked tirelessly to plan and implement the project, from the Museum's senior managers to the Publications and New Media Department to the art handlers. I single out here only Lisa Phillips, curator of the exhibition and author of this catalog, and Susan Harris and Karl Willers, associate curators for Part II of *The American Century* project.

We have been fortunate in attracting major support from the National Endowment for the Arts, the National Committee of the Whitney Museum, Booth Ferris Foundation, and The Lauder Foundation, Evelyn and Leonard Lauder Fund. The Brown Foundation, Inc., of Houston funded the educational and public programs in conjunction with the exhibition. The book itself was made possible by a gift from Susan and Edwin Malloy.

On behalf of the Whitney's Board of Trustees and its president, Joel S. Ehrenkranz, I thank Andrew S. Grove, chairman of Intel Corporation. Intel and the Whitney have embarked on an unprecedented collaboration which marries the latest advances in high technology with the finest examples of American art. Our association allows the masterworks and related educational resources from *The American Century* to reach a broad, global audience. I would like to add my personal thanks to Leonard A. Lauder, chairman of the Whitney Museum, and to my predecessor, David A. Ross, now director of the San Francisco Museum of Modern Art, who played key roles in securing Intel's support for the exhibition. This collaboration testifies to the Whitney's rightful place as a primary arbiter of American culture and to Intel's as a visionary company dedicated to the support of the technological and artistic vanguard.

The story of American art in the twenty-first century will begin in the aftermath of *The American Century* with the Whitney's 2000 *Biennial*. We look forward to welcoming back readers and visitors who want to participate in the "research and development" phase of art history, in which we are justifiably proud of our contribution.

America Takes
Command
1950–1960

The chronological halfway mark of the twentieth century may be 1950, but a more decisive turning point is the end of World War II in 1945. The war was a watershed in American life and culture. Though there were heavy death tolls, America emerged politically and economically victorious and physically intact.

This was exactly the outcome Henry Luce had envisioned when he penned his historic February 1941 editorial for *Time* magazine, "The American Century," from which this book takes its title. Lamenting American isolationist tendencies, Luce exhorted his readers to throw aside their moral and intellectual confusion and to support American involvement in the war then raging in Europe. He wanted Americans to accept responsibility for the "world-environment" and to embrace a "vision of America as a world power which...will guide us to the authentic creation of the 20th Century—our Century."

The immediate postwar years met Luce's expectations. While most of Europe and part of Asia suffered extensive physical damage during the war, the United States was untouched. It thus emerged in 1945 with its manufacturing capacity intact and a strong economy generated by years of war production. Going into the war, America had been one of the world's great powers; by 1945, it was militarily, politically, and economically without equal. By 1947, for instance, America was producing half the world's manufactured goods: 57 percent of its steel; 43 percent of its electricity; 62 percent of its oil; and 80 percent of its automobiles. In addition, America had a monopoly on the atomic bomb, the most dangerous weapon the world had ever seen.

But the postwar period was politically and socially complex. These years of victory and supremacy also brought a perceived threat to the safety and indeed the existence of the United States from the Soviet Union, which acquired atomic weapons in 1949 and soon controlled the governments of most nations in Eastern and Central Europe. The once vocal left in American politics was nearly silenced as the nation became committed to an ideology of anti-Communism.

The postwar years also saw the rise of new social conditions. Vast numbers of poor blacks and whites from the South migrated to urban centers in the North— a population movement comparable in numbers to the immigration from Europe to the United States between the Civil War and World War I.[1]

In 1940, ten out of thirteen million African Americans still lived in the South, where they were segregated, denied access to justice and the political process, and deliberately kept in a state of social and economic inferiority. But with the economic boom of the war years, rural blacks flocked to cities in search of jobs in burgeoning industries. This radical change in the nation's demographics inflamed racial issues that had been smoldering for almost a century.

There were other important demographic shifts. The postwar baby boom produced a million more Americans each year, a birthrate that vastly exceeded that of the Depression and the war years. Increased postwar employment opportunities led to rising incomes and a growth in the middle class. Higher education became cheaper and more available through the GI Bill of Rights, which helped veterans with loans for college tuition, as well as for home construction and business initiatives. A flourishing economy also enabled other Americans to afford tuition costs, and a college education thus became a possibility for many, instead of the privilege of a few.

The dramatic changes following the war are crucial to understanding the art of the last fifty years. America's ascendance on the geopolitical stage and the new social order irrevocably altered art and culture no less than daily life. In examining these five decades, however, we should remember that neither history nor art progresses in a straight line—at any point, multiple, shifting, and often contradictory tendencies coexist.

This book therefore provides an array of perspectives that reflect the complexity of this period, the heterogeneity that is America. As a new century dawns, it is essential to take both a retrospective and a prospective view—to look back at the past with an eye to the future. Today we are inclined to question Luce's ideal of American hegemony—a monolithic entity at the dynamic center of an ever-widening sphere of influence. Instead, it seems more relevant to challenge each word of "The American Century." Is there only one story, one uniform identity, one center, as implied by the definitive "the"? How has the meaning of "American" changed over the past fifty years? And is the notion of a "century" the best way to delineate history?

The Postwar American Art Community

"If [Picasso] drips, I drip," said the Armenian-born American painter Arshile Gorky in the 1930s.[2] His statement epitomizes the condition of American art before World War II as essentially a province of European art. While Americans customarily looked to Paris for the latest developments in art, Europeans did not look at American art at all. It was the prevailing critical view that until the late 1940s America "had not yet made a single contribution to the mainstream of painting or sculpture."[3] Even American modernists were considered too parochial to provide a model for the international mainstream.

As America became a world leader after the war, however, American artists wanted to take the initiative and create something new—something that would express aspiration, risk, freedom, and, in keeping with the new anti-isolationist spirit, "cultural values on a global scale."[4] Though these general goals for art coincided with America's larger political agenda, the artists did not see their work as ideological. Freedom, to them, was best communicated through unconstrained individual expression; their break with tradition represented risk, and their epic scale spoke of ambition. Their form of abstraction, they believed, could transcend national boundaries and the specificity of particular cultures.

With Europe still rebuilding after the devastation of war, New York replaced Paris as the capital of the art world and would dominate the American and international art scene for the next two decades. A few hundred artists, a half dozen dealers devoted to contemporary art, and a couple of supportive museums formed the basis of what became by 1950 an explosive vanguard—the "New York School," an umbrella term that encompassed a variety of styles, primarily, but not exclusively, Abstract Expressionism.

Many New York School artists had come to the city from elsewhere. Several had immigrated from abroad—Mark Rothko (in 1913), Willem de Kooning (in 1926), Hans Hofmann (in 1930), and Arshile Gorky (in 1920)—while Jackson

1. **Hans Hofmann**
Equipoise, 1958
Oil on canvas, 60 x 52 in.
(152.4 x 132.1 cm)
Los Angeles County
Museum of Art; Gift of
Marcia Weisman
©Estate of Hans
Hofmann/Licensed by
VAGA, New York, NY

Pollock, Clyfford Still, and Philip Guston had come from other parts of the country. Though they had different cultural backgrounds and styles of working, they did share alliances, friendships, and certain goals for art. They bonded together in a vital community in Greenwich Village, and the dynamic, cosmopolitan environment of New York fueled their desires and ambitions.

Three factors helped solidify the New York School. The first was sociological: during the Depression, many of the artists had worked together on federally supported relief programs such as the Federal Art Project, an officially sanctioned form of employment that lent legitimacy to the art profession. The second factor was the German-immigrant artist Hans Hofmann (fig. 1) who in the 1930s had founded the Hans Hofmann School of Fine Arts in Greenwich Village. Hofmann's

CORPORATE HEGEMONY: THE PUBLIC TRIUMPH OF MODERNITY

By the early 1950s, American corporate culture had seized upon and thoroughly transformed the architectural interest in transparency that had been developing since Joseph Paxton built the Crystal Palace for London's 1851 World Exposition. Glass was, and remains, a kind of architectural talisman and projection screen: all the conflicting desires and contradictory thoughts that constitute the modern tradition can be read in its reflective, translucent, and opaque surfaces. In 1950, Ludwig Mies van der Rohe broke ground on 860 Lake Shore Drive

(fig. 2) in Chicago for an apartment building that used the repetitive and modular schema of the curtain wall—in which the exterior wall of a building serves no structural purpose—not only to realize his dream of a glass tower, first sketched in 1919, but to establish a universalizing logic of architectural expression and production. As the vitreous structure absorbed reflected images of the surrounding area into its surface, the distinction between the object and its context broke down, producing instead a conceptually infinite terrain. This ever-proliferating and expanding field was further stretched by the fact that Mies' Lake Shore Drive project comprises two buildings. This doubling initiated an almost endlessly repeating series of curtain-wall structures throughout the world.

The effects of the glass tower were created by machine modes of manufacture, which produced an infinitely applicable and universalizing logic of production and anonymous exchange. This logic was that of the postwar, increasingly international, corporation—Skidmore, Owings & Merrill's Lever House of 1950–52 (fig. 3), designed by Gordon Bunshaft, typifies the elegant, relentless form of the curtain-wall building that dismantled barriers not only between solid and void, object and context, but between public and private, one nation and another, making the world the potential site of a new American hegemony. —S. L.

2. **Ludwig Mies van der Rohe**
Lake Shore Drive Apartments, Chicago, 1952, photograph by Ezra Stoller
© Esto. All Rights Reserved

3. **Gordon Bunshaft (Skidmore, Owings & Merrill)**
Lever House, New York, 1950–52, photograph by Ezra Stoller
© Esto. All Rights Reserved

teachings, which combined Cubist structure and space with German Expressionist and Fauvist feeling and color, influenced a generation of artists who emerged in the 1950s, including his former students Larry Rivers, Lee Krasner, and Ray Eames. But most important to the momentum of the New York School was the influx of European vanguard artists to New York during the war—from Fernand Léger, Piet Mondrian, Marc Chagall, and Walter Gropius to the Surrealists (Matta, Yves Tanguy, Salvador Dalí, André Breton, Max Ernst, André Masson), who arrived practically en masse in 1939. This firsthand contact with the European avant-garde during the war is widely considered to be one of the most significant developments in the history of American art.[5]

In the 1940s, the burgeoning community of young American artists in New York had frequent contact with the Surrealists through Peggy Guggenheim's Art of This Century gallery, among other professional and social venues. They absorbed the Surrealists' emphasis on mythic content and on the unconscious, including their use of automatic writing and other techniques that gave precedence to intuitive process over rational conception. Toward the end of the decade, however, New York artists began to move away from Surrealist-inspired biomorphism and mythic references to forge their own independent styles. By 1948, after many of the Surrealists had left New York or returned to Europe, most American artists had abandoned even the allusive imagery of the Surrealists in favor of the radical abstract styles that would become famous under the banner of Abstract Expressionism.

Abstract Expressionism: The New York Vanguard

The aesthetic breakthrough of the New York School rested on two concepts: spontaneous process and a dramatic increase in scale. The very method of painting was direct and confrontational, reflecting America's new, emboldened identity as the most powerful country in the world. Despite Willem de Kooning's warning that "it is disastrous to name ourselves," this radical new aesthetic was called Abstract Expressionism[6]—the first American art movement to win international acclaim as central to the development of contemporary art. De Kooning was not alone in his resistance to constricting labels, for Abstract Expressionism championed the primacy of individual expression. In this pursuit, a collective style was as abhorrent as a single name. By 1950, most of the original Abstract Expressionists had arrived at their individual signature styles. And the bold images that would become trademarks of the new American painting were visibly different from one another: Jackson Pollock's drip paintings (1947); Mark Rothko's floating, rectangular expanses of color (1950); Clyfford Still's excoriated dark fields (1947); Franz Kline's architectonic black-and-white gestures (1949).

The critical penchant for categorization, however, has left us not only with the term "Abstract Expressionism," but with subdivisions. The work of the first generation of Abstract Expressionists is generally divided into two strains: the gestural and energetic Action Painters (Jackson Pollock, Willem de Kooning, Franz Kline) and the Chromatic Abstractionists (Barnett Newman, Mark Rothko, Adolph Gottlieb, Clyfford Still, Ad Reinhardt), with Robert Motherwell, Philip Guston, and Bradley Walker Tomlin in between. Whatever the nomenclature—and no matter how idiosyncratic their individual styles—all these artists shared a desire to do away with the conventions of easel painting and eliminate representation or the use of forms borrowed from Cubism, Surrealism, and other sources. They often adopted generic or numbered titles to help purge allusions to imagery and subject matter from the real world.

Newman said that he wanted to be free from "the impediments of memory, association, nostalgia, legend, myth."[7] Rothko rejected the obstacles of "memory, history, or geometry," and Still wanted no "outworn myths or contemporary alibis."[8] This collective will to abandon subject matter was a final attempt to break free from the weight of European culture—to seek something indigenous to the American experience. Even if, as in the case of de Kooning and, by 1951, Pollock, a personal aesthetic impulse led some artists to retain or reintroduce figurative references, large-scale abstraction became a fresh new language of individual expression and invention—one in which iconoclasm could be linked to innovation. The scale of these works, unprecedented in American art, may have been an outgrowth of the public mural painting in which many artists engaged while working on government projects during the 1930s. Translated to private canvases a decade later, such scale reflected the ambitiousness of the American self-image. But it also bespoke the experience of America's dramatic landscape, which had led nineteenth-century artists and philosophers to pantheism and transcendentalism. To American artists at the mid-twentieth century, this indigenous history could be transmitted through epic scale and rhythmic processes—"I *am* nature" was Pollock's famous declaration.[9] To the critic Clement Greenberg, writing in 1950, the monumental size of Abstract Expressionist painting was one of its defining characteristics.[10] One Pollock work of that year, *Number 27* (fig. 4), was 106 inches wide; another, *Autumn Rhythm: Number 30* (fig. 5), stretched to 207 inches—more than 17 feet long.

Rothko, Newman, and Still were also making wall-scale pictures at that time. In fact, Still was the first to expand his paintings to gargantuan scale, which he did in 1944, even before Pollock. The large scale subsumed viewer and artist alike, and it allowed the artist to "be" in the picture, to be inside the work. As Rothko described it:

> I paint very large pictures. I realize that historically the function of painting large pictures is painting something very grandiose and pompous. The reason I paint them, however—I think it applies to other painters I know—is precisely because I want to be very intimate and human. To paint a small picture is to place yourself outside your experience, to look upon an experience as a stereopticon view with a reducing glass. However you paint the larger pictures, you are in it. It isn't something you command.[11]

Abstract Expressionists relished the drama of the encounter. The large-scale canvas enabled them to have a more direct connection with their work—as Pollock

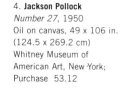

4. Jackson Pollock
Number 27, 1950
Oil on canvas, 49 x 106 in.
(124.5 x 269.2 cm)
Whitney Museum of
American Art, New York;
Purchase 53.12

said, "When I am *in* my painting, I'm not aware of what I'm doing . . . because the painting has a life of its own."[12] The artists' physical immersion allowed for emotional immersion, which was further assisted by spontaneous processes.

Abstract Expressionists, particularly the gestural painters, who used their whole arm or body, not just the wrist, prized immediacy. They worked spontaneously—dripping, pouring, slashing, the artist's hand serving as conduit for unconscious, unpremeditated feelings. The picture's "life of its own" was, in fact, the unconscious revealed.

5. **Jackson Pollock**
Autumn Rhythm:
Number 30, 1950
Oil on canvas, 105 x 207 in.
(266.7 x 525.8 cm)
The Metropolitan Museum
of Art, New York; George A.
Hearn Fund, 1957

ACTION PAINTING

With the introduction of his "drip" paintings of 1947–52, Jackson Pollock made a radical break with pictorial conventions of the past. He painted his canvases on the floor, standing over them, dripping and splashing turpentine-thinned enamel paint in rhythmic formations, using sticks, dried-out brushes, and basting syringes (fig. 6). He was not painting in the conventional sense: his brush never touched the canvas. Instead, he used the movements of his body and the density of the paint to create intricate webs of lines that filled the field (fig. 5). The painting was a trace of a process, a performance, a dance. It was explosive and direct.

As if to suggest the action of a bullfight, Pollock called his floor-bound canvas "the arena." In his defining essay of 1952, "The American Action Painters," the critic Harold Rosenberg went on to describe all the large canvases of the Abstract Expressionists as "an arena in which to act." Painting was not a "space in which to reproduce, redesign, analyze or 'express' an object, actual or imagined. What was to go on the canvas was not a picture but an event. . . . Form, color, composition, drawing, are auxiliaries any one of which . . . can be dispensed with. What matters always is the revelation contained in the act. . . . The act-painting is of the same metaphysical substance as the artist's existence. The new painting has broken down every distinction between art and life."[13]

In compositional terms, there was no hierarchy in these "all-over" paintings, which dispensed with the conventional figure-ground relationship, illusionistic space, and central focus. Instead, there was an atmosphere that Pollock's critical champion, Clement Greenberg, described as "pulverized value contrasts in a vaporous dust of interfused lights and darks."[14] There were implications of cosmic space in these optical paintings, but the unprimed canvas also asserted itself as literal, raw material, with hair, fingerprints, sand, broken glass, string, and cigarette butts embedded in the paint, bringing the viewer back to the material "here and now." Some important precedents for this all-over painting include Joan Miró's "constellation" paintings, where the field was filled with a network of delicate con-

6. *Jackson Pollock Painting in His Studio,* 1950, photograph by Hans Namuth

necting spheres and lines, and Claude Monet's *Water Lilies,* where the entire surface was covered with brushstrokes that represented not only flowers but light and atmosphere—the effect approached total abstraction. Pollock's painting was also quickly compared to the abstractions of the Dutch Neoplasticist Piet Mondrian and to Cubist collage in terms of their nonhierarchical compositions. The legacy of Cubism was strong, and the most influential critics of the time sought to connect Cubism and Abstract Expressionism, declaring that the latter had realized the revolutions implied by Synthetic Cubism.[15] But no one before Pollock had ever reoriented the picture plane horizontally, from the vertical easel to the floor. Even when the final painting was hung on the wall, it bore evidence of its horizontal vector in the pooling and scabbing of paint congealed into tarry pockets or flowing in bleeding rivulets. This reorientation, Pollock himself suggested, may have been inspired by the paint-spattered floor of his studio or by the ceremonial sand paintings of the Navajo Indians he admired.[16]

Pollock also liberated line from any descriptive function of contour and form, instead creating a calligraphy of fluid, undulating rhythms. An artist of great formal intelligence, he merged drawing and painting, line and color. The rhythmic layering of great skeins of color, plane over plane, represented a new way of depicting pictorial space.

Pollock and his Abstract Expressionist colleagues contributed more than art to American culture in the 1950s. The premium they placed on originality, autonomy, and individual actions led to one of the most enduring myths of the decade—the idea of the artist as the romantic, alienated genius. Photographs of Pollock, particularly those by Hans Namuth, have abetted this myth. In a remarkable sequence of still and filmed images, we see Pollock alone in his studio, confronting the canvas and, through his rhythmic actions, creating a painting (fig. 6). Though Pollock had pioneered a new kind of space and process, his background, painting style, and personal manner contributed to his ascendance as an "American hero"—as did his premature death in an automobile accident at the age of forty-four in 1956.

Pollock was the virile and rugged man of the American West. Born in Cody, Wyoming, and raised in California and Arizona, he was hard-drinking and physical and, like the cinematic persona of John Wayne, an anti-intellectual man of action.

The idea of frontier America, where heroic acts and individual freedom prevailed, continued to ignite the American imagination. The Western—consoling stories about independence, individualism, open spaces, self-reliance, discovery, and man against nature—enjoyed enormous popularity in the 1950s. The frontier myth was part of the larger Cold War "us and them" spirit, and Abstract Expressionism both originated from and contributed to this mythology.

7. **Willem de Kooning**
Woman, 1953
Oil and charcoal on paper mounted on canvas, 25⅝ x 19⅝ in. (65.1 x 49.8 cm) Hirshhorn Museum and Sculpture Garden, Smithsonian Institution, Washington, D.C.; Gift of Joseph H. Hirshhorn, 1966

The Abstract Expressionist credo of free individual expression through direct action was epitomized by Willem de Kooning, who achieved a sense of power through brash and raw virtuoso brushwork. De Kooning began his career in the Netherlands, where his academic training gave him prodigious drafting skills that enabled him to continually synthesize tradition and modernism. He arrived in the United States at the age of twenty-three in 1926, and during the 1930s worked on Works Progress Administration (WPA) murals with Arshile Gorky and Pollock. After an early figurative period, his work became increasingly abstract, and by 1950 the brushwork had loosened considerably as the scale of the paintings increased. Like Pollock's, his paintings had an all-over quality, but there was more compositional planning to his interwoven biomorphic forms. The brushwork was robust and muscular and soon took on a powerful life of its own.

In de Kooning's renowned Woman series, begun in 1950, high-intensity color mixed with aggressive brushstrokes produced charged works that were as startling when first shown in 1953 at the Sidney Janis Gallery in New York as Pollock's drip paintings had been (figs. 7, 8). These large, confrontational canvases, dominated by fragmented human figures, are fierce. De Kooning retained figurative references throughout his work (and Pollock eventually returned to figuration), demonstrating that abstraction and figuration need not be polarized. In de Kooning's paintings, the fluidity of the space, the unpremeditated brush slashing, and the disjunctive syntax result in an ever-shifting quality that brilliantly communicates the flux and velocity of modern life (fig. 9).

Franz Kline took another approach to gestural abstraction in his grand-scale architectonic black-and-white paintings. His conversion to abstraction came in 1949, when de Kooning suggested that he put one of his small ink drawings in a Bell-Opticon opaque projector that de Kooning had been using to enlarge his own

8. **Willem de Kooning**
Woman and Bicycle,
1952–53
Oil on canvas, 76½ x 49 in.
(194.3 x 124.5 cm)
Whitney Museum of
American Art, New York;
Purchase 55.35

sketches onto big canvases. Suddenly, Kline's little ink drawing of a rocking chair "loomed in gigantic black strokes," obliterating the image.[17] The strokes became entities in themselves, monolithic forms divorced from any external reality. Kline went on to create dynamic, enveloping paintings, such as *Mahoning*, that began their lives as intimate gestures on paper (fig. 10). Still, the directness and vigor of the paint handling conveyed immediacy—these works were not merely reproductions of originals in another scale.

The primacy of the act, epitomized in Abstract Expressionist painting, was also one of the central tenets of existentialism—the most influential philosophical movement to emerge in the postwar period. In an uncertain world, where the A-bomb and the H-bomb made the future seem tenuous, one could reaffirm one's existence only by acting in the here and now. The distinct possibility that there would be no tomorrow demanded an existential view. Thus artists who had been political activists in the 1930s turned to personal acts of free will as a means of self-liberation and as an expression of anxiety.

SCULPTURE OF THE NEW YORK SCHOOL

Even sculptors of this period developed working methods that allowed for greater spontaneity and relied on unconscious and aleatory effects. The direct metal process, for instance, was a three-dimensional analogue to Action Painting. Thanks to the improvement of welding technology during the war and the introduction of the portable oxyacetylene torch, sculptors could weld, braze, and model durable metals to create textured effects that paralleled expressionist painting surfaces. Using a combination of Constructivist and expressionist approaches, sculptors freed themselves at last from the relatively static, monolithic tradition of carving and modeling. Artists like Theodore Roszak, Herbert Ferber, Seymour Lipton, Ibram Lassaw, and David Smith forged raw, open, penetrating forms that were often more about line and surface than about volume and mass (figs. 12–17).

In describing the connection between materials and intentions, David Smith observed that "metal possesses little art history, what associations it does possess are those of this century: power, structure, movement, progress, suspension, brutality."[18] Also implicit, though unacknowledged, were associations of male conquest and domination. Theodore Roszak recognized the brutal, violent content of direct metal and used it to explain his abrupt shift of imagery following the war. Having abandoned his earlier Constructivist ideals as innocent illusions, he was now turning to highly expressionist, mythic images in welded and brazed steel because "the

9. **Willem de Kooning**
Door to the River, 1960
Oil on canvas, 80 x 70 in.
(203.2 x 177.8 cm)
Whitney Museum of American Art, New York; Purchase, with funds from the Friends of the Whitney Museum of American Art
60.63

forms [he found] necessary to assert are meant to be blunt reminders of primeval strife and struggle, reminiscent of those brute forces that not only produced life, but in turn threaten to destroy it" (fig. 12).[19]

Sculptures of this era often had repellent surfaces that suggested scorched and excoriated skin and alluded to the devastation of war—particularly atomic devastation. The drama of the possible extinction of the human race is as much in evidence in sculpture of the fifties as in the popular science fiction novels and films of the time. Like many monsters of science fiction, new sculptural images were imaginative crossbreeds of dinosaurs, predatory plants, pods, and blobs— nature gone berserk, grotesque mutations that represent an attempt to exorcise unbearable terrors by invoking and then subduing them. Resonant as these images were of death, however, they also suggested a natural cycle moving from birth, death, and decay to rebirth—the process of natural growth was visualized as a momentous, primordial event.

18. **Mark Rothko**
Orange and Yellow, 1957
Oil on canvas, 91 x 71 in.
(231.1 x 180.3 cm)
Albright-Knox Art Gallery,
Buffalo; Gift of Seymour
H. Knox, 1956

CHROMATIC ABSTRACTION

The second group of Abstract Expressionist painters who achieved prominence in the early 1950s was the Chromatic Abstractionists, foremost among them Mark Rothko, Barnett Newman, Ad Reinhardt, and Clyfford Still. Their work was as nonrelational as Pollock's all-over paintings, but they concentrated on the physical sensations generated by large color fields, producing what have been called "single image" paintings. Enveloping and atmospheric, their large canvases yielded luminous, optical effects. But the Abstract Expressionist label never really fit, because the Chromatic Abstractionists were not gesturally expressive and their enormous surfaces were usually thinly painted. Unlike those of the Action Painters, their canvases showed little evidence of brushwork.

The empty expanses of the Chromatic Abstractionists suggested to some the vastness of the American landscape: Rothko's exalted light emanating from ethereal fields of color (figs. 18, 19); Newman's simple, vast spaces (fig. 67); the sense of solitude and emptiness in Reinhardt's painting (fig. 68). All these works allude to the awe that generations of Americans had experienced before the seemingly boundless expanse of nature. An enveloping, operatic statement about nature is given in Clyfford Still's jagged, flamelike vertical contours that suggest crags and fissures (fig. 20) or in Philip Guston's shimmering clusters of brushstrokes (fig. 21).

19. **Mark Rothko**
Four Darks in Red, 1958
Oil on canvas, 102 x 116 in.
(259.1 x 294.6 cm)
Whitney Museum of American
Art, New York; Purchase, with
funds from the Friends of the
Whitney Museum of American
Art, Mr. and Mrs. Eugene M.
Schwartz, Mrs. Samuel A.
Seaver, and Charles Simon
68.9

20. **Clyfford Still**
Untitled, 1957
Oil on canvas, 112 x
154 in. (284.5 x 391.2 cm)
Whitney Museum of
American Art, New York;
Purchase, with funds from
the Friends of the Whitney
Museum of American Art
69.31

21. **Philip Guston**
Dial, 1956
Oil on canvas, 72 x 76 in.
(182.9 x 193 cm)
Whitney Museum of
American Art, New York;
Purchase 56.44

In their search for an American identity, artists found themselves drawn to the dramatic sensations of the American landscape, as they were attracted by its huge scale. It was this scale as well as the emotion-laden imagery of the Abstract Expressionists that suggested to some the eighteenth-century European concept of the sublime—the intermingling of beauty and terror before the majesty of natural phenomena.[20]

The detonation of the atomic bomb at the end of World War II and subsequent nuclear tests conducted throughout the 1950s (fig. 28) may have contributed another, more contemporary dimension to the "sublime." We have already seen how the threat of nuclear extinction produced an existential climate and how sculptors in particular created works with apocalyptic themes. Yet artists were also affected by the beauty of these cataclysmic explosions. The light-emanating works of Rothko, for instance, may refer not only to the magnificence of the natural world but to the threat that science posed to the world's very existence. As technology seemed to be returning humankind to a primal state of mythic awe and vulnerability before the universe,[21] it is no accident that we find this primal condition expressed not just in the overwrought, rough-hewn manner of Action Painting but also in the titles of such Chromatic Abstractions as *Day One* and *The Beginning* (both by Newman), and *Primeval Landscape* (Rothko).

Born of growing confidence, yet tempered by the anxieties of the age, Abstract Expressionism was an art of paradoxical extremes—one that could evoke anger, aggression, fragmentation, and angst—as well as joy, liberation, and lyricism.

Vanguard Art and Cold War Politics

If Abstract Expressionism conveyed both confidence and anxiety, it perfectly mirrored the contradictions and conflicted longings that defined America in the 1950s.

On the positive side, as the economy surged, upward mobility seemed attainable to most Americans. The private home and automobile were the most conspicuous symbols of the new affluence. Suburbs like Levittown, New York (fig. 24) proliferated, and a vast new interstate highway system knit together far-flung forms and cities into one national community. Television also unified the nation, and by the end of the 1950s people would spend more time watching it than they would spend at work (fig. 26). In 1950, only 9 percent of American families owned television sets; by 1960, over 50 million homes (or 87 percent) were receiving images of the good life and American "family values" into their homes.[22] There was another revolution in the home as increasingly affordable modern appliances cut housework in half. The postwar house embodied a golden age of domesticity. A rising standard of living produced more money, more leisure time, and a richer cultural life. The "American dream" seemed to be a tangible reality.

President Dwight D. Eisenhower, who was elected in 1952 and served two terms, watched over this growing economy. His campaign motto was "peace and prosperity," and the public responded with "I like Ike," voting in the first Republican president in twenty years (fig. 27). Under Eisenhower's paternalistic leadership, stability and complacency reigned. His moderation had a powerful appeal to a nation ready for peace and tranquillity. Under his tenure, Americans came to believe that the U.S. economic system was sound and that the capitalist free-enterprise system would provide social harmony and prosperity at home and prestige abroad.

Materialism prevailed and, with it, fantasies of modernization and progress. This was the period of Disneyland Park, drive-in movies, McDonald's, and flamboyant car tail fins (fig. 25). The decade's abundance also produced a more supportive

NEW LANDSCAPES OF DOMESTICITY: THE PRIVATE TRIUMPH OF MODERNITY

American residential architecture and domestic furnishings of the 1950s are, at this turn of the century, the object of an extraordinary revival and nostalgia. The covers of lifestyle magazines have moved from the flounces and fusses of chintz and Wedgwood to the simple lines and once new materials of Florence Knoll's lounge (1954) and Russell Wright's plastic dinnerware. Suburban patterns of life established after World War II are now being redeployed by late twentieth-century city planners; domestic situation comedies of the 1950s can be viewed at any time of day or night on revival television; even Martha Stewart now lives in an important modernist building completed by Gordon Bunshaft in 1962.

This revival can be best understood as a longing for domesticity itself, for it was in 1950s America that the idealized standards of family life that still prevail were established. Indeed, the American postwar house not only encapsulated for many the golden age of domesticity (which never was) but realized European fantasies of modern living that had been developing since the turn of the preceding century. An important exemplar of this private triumph of modernity was the Case Study House Program, initiated by John Entenza, editor of *Arts & Architecture*. Between 1945 and 1966, the journal sponsored the construction of thirty-six middle-class houses intended to serve as prototypes not only for future mass production but for a new mode of domestic life. The houses had open plans which, the architects felt, would promote happier family lives with less reliance on domestic servants; the slick materials used and contemporary "look" of the design were meant to gain a place for these homes in an emerging suburban utopia. Although initially thought of as a regional development local to Southern California and its architects, including Richard Neutra, Charles and Ray Eames, Pierre Koenig, and Craig Ellwood, the program caused a tidal wave in domestic architecture that was felt from Sarasota, Florida, to Sydney, Australia.

The Case Study houses might be profitably seen as wish fulfillments: actualizing the dismantling of barriers between inside and outside, developing new forms of transparency, eliminating Victorian domestic formality, and mobilizing machine production that had been only dreamed of by the "masters" of European modernism. Yet the very success of this program introduced a significant change in the cultural reception of modernity: with the widespread popularity of an architect such as Richard Neutra (fig. 22), who in the postwar period built an enormous number of houses for a broad range of clients and appeared on the cover of *Time* magazine in 1949, this postwar American modernism gave to the avant-garde the character of victor rather than renegade.

An important aspect of this change in cultural status was the way in which the Case Study program—and indeed much of the American domestic apparatus of the period—

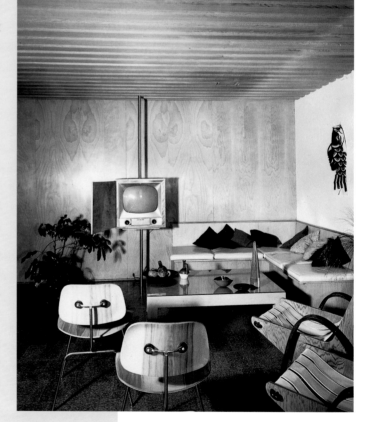

22. **Richard Neutra**
Goodman Residence,
1952, photograph by
Julius Shulman

23. **Charles Eames**
*Exterior of Charles Eames
House, Pacific Palisades,
California,* 1949

entered the new and burgeoning logic
of consumer culture. Not only did high
modernist houses incorporate advanced
technologies, as in Raphael Soriano's
steel frame houses or in the increasingly
common use of mullionless, insulated,
large-expanse glass, but they came replete
with an entire menagerie of domestic
technologies, such as televisions, washers,
dryers, refrigerators, and central heating.
This equipment, which perhaps trans-
formed the American house into more of a machine for living than Le Corbusier ever
imagined, was produced by retooling the massive production facilities developed during
the war for civilian use. Military command-and-control techniques were quickly transformed into consumer operations of supply and demand.

While such proliferating creature comforts were readily absorbed into this new economic and domestic logic—and are a primary reason for today's nostalgia for the good
life, when TV was free and vacuum cleaners exciting—they propelled architecture into a
new relationship with the marketplace. Instead of being conceived of as permanent and
monumental, houses of the 1950s were expected to last only as long as the mortgage
amortization period; instead of containing attics in which to store family treasures, flat-
roofed and often basementless postwar houses encouraged the acquisition of increasingly disposable goods; and through the invasion of picture windows, television, and
other media, the privacy of the postwar house entered a new and more public arena.

One of the most interesting features of these combined developments is the way in
which they eroded conventional distinctions between high and low culture. The Case
Study Program generated buildings that can be easily assimilated to the category of progressive modernism; the Eames House of 1949 (fig. 23), for example, was built in a
matter of weeks, was constructed out of prefabricated elements, and rigorously avoided
formal stylization and organization. The same can be said of the millions of ranch-style
houses, of suburban developments based on the model of Levittown, and of trailer
houses—all of which suddenly covered the United States with a promise of happiness.
Most of these structures were in significant part factory-made, incorporated innovative
construction methods, and contained countless domestic machines. The sudden and
seemingly infinite proliferation of these modern houses created a new suburban landscape, which in turn generated the possibility of its own critique and hyperextension. In
1955, Walt Disney opened his first theme park, which, like much of the new American
domestic scene, deployed the most advanced devices of modernity, such as mass transit systems developed for large cities, yet packaged them in rural nostalgia to suggest
that one could simply opt out of the processes of modernization. In this totally paradoxical environment, apparently private but plugged into the media and markets of the
public realm, the tools of modernism triumphed while being domesticated in new and
still strangely unsettling ways. —S. L.

24. *Levittown Houses, Long Island, New York*, 1954
UPI/Corbis-Bettmann

25. *Sleeping Beauty Castle, Disneyland Park*, Anaheim, California

27. *Gen. Dwight D. Eisenhower with Women from the Republican National Committee*, 1952
UPI/Corbis-Bettmann

28. *Atomic Bomb Explosion in Nevada*, 1951

environment for art. Framed reproductions of Impressionist works or replicas of Old Master paintings were popular additions in the home. Though the vast majority of Americans remained mistrustful of advanced art and preferred the anecdotal realism of Norman Rockwell or Andrew Wyeth (fig. 59), prosperity and greater disposable income still translated into greater sales for the emerging vanguard.

In response to this growing interest in art, a number of new dealers opened their doors. In New York alone, the handful of thirty respectable galleries at the start of the decade had mushroomed to three hundred by 1960. Visionary dealers such as Sam Kootz, Betty Parsons, and Charles Egan, who had been supporting vanguard artists throughout the forties, were joined by many more, among them Sidney Janis (1948), Tibor de Nagy (1950), Martha Jackson (1952), Eleanor Ward (1953), and Leo Castelli (1957).

The exhibition opportunities brought by the new galleries were further increased by the artists themselves, who met in active groups to discuss mutual concerns. This dialogue peaked in the early 1950s around meetings at the Artists' Club. The Club, located in Greenwich Village, was a forum for lectures and discussions for artists throughout the decade. It had grown out of earlier meetings at Subjects of the Artists, a school founded by Clyfford Still, Mark Rothko, Robert Motherwell, William Baziotes, and David Hare in 1948, where weekly discussions under Motherwell's leadership helped define the New York School. After the meetings, they would go over to the Cedar Tavern, the social epicenter of downtown culture (fig. 29). Protests against the exclusionary practices of The Metropolitan Museum of Art toward contemporary vanguard American art were organized by a group of eighteen painters and ten sculptors (from Studio 35, another short-lived group, formed in 1949). Dubbed "The Irascibles," they garnered attention from the press and credibility as serious contenders (fig. 30).[23]

29. *Cedar Tavern*, New York, 1959 Photograph © Fred W. McDarrah

30. "The Irascibles," from *Life*, January 15, 1951, photograph by Nina Leen From left to right, top row: Willem de Kooning, Adolph Gottlieb, Ad Reinhardt, Hedda Sterne; middle row: Richard Pousette-Dart, William Baziotes, Jackson Pollock, Clyfford Still, Robert Motherwell, Bradley Walker Tomlin; bottom row: Theodoros Stamos, Jimmy Ernst, Barnett Newman, James Brooks, Mark Rothko

The growing public interest in art also engendered expanding forums for arts coverage, both in specialized journals and in the mainstream press. Several critics emerged as articulate and powerful spokesmen for this new American vanguard:

Clement Greenberg and Harold Rosenberg, as we have seen, both wrote important defenses of Abstract Expressionism. For the first time, writers with literary credentials were publishing essays about advanced American art for an enlightened public: Greenberg wrote for the *Partisan Review* (mid-1940s) and then *The Nation* (late 1940s); Robert Goldwater became editor of the *Magazine of Art* in 1948; Manny Farber started writing on art for *The New Republic* in 1945; Thomas Hess took over as managing editor of *Art News* in 1948. The arrival of eloquent advocates and serious critical voices championing the new American art was inestimable in widening its sphere of influence. Even the popular press was taking notice of vanguard developments. Often cited examples include *Life* magazine's 1949 article on Jackson Pollock—headlined "Is He the Greatest Living Painter in the United States?"—and a *Vogue* magazine spread photographed by Cecil Beaton where models were posed in front of a drip painting (figs. 31, 32).[24]

31. "Jackson Pollock: Is He the Greatest Living Painter in the United States?" from *Life*, August 8, 1949 Photograph copyright © Arnold Newman

32. *Model Wearing Baby Blue Ball Gown Against Backdrop Art by Jackson Pollock, at Betty Parsons Gallery*, from *Vogue*, March 1, 1951, photograph by Cecil Beaton

But expansive as the climate for art seemed, it was simultaneously stifling. The vanguard painters and sculptors in New York had banded together partly as a refuge from the prevalent anti-intellectual and chauvinist sentiments of the public at large. The idyllic picture of the 1950s as a time of abundance masks the underlying tensions of the Cold War, which created the stagnant atmosphere of timid conformity that permeated American life.

Conformity was born of fear that all might be lost. Many Americans were still haunted by memories of the Depression, but for most the threats of the postwar era came from Communism and the bomb. Both Communism and nuclear radiation were invisible threats that fomented tensions and insecurities. Mao Tse-tung ousted Chiang Kai-shek's Nationalists in 1949, and installed a Communist government in China; that same year, the Soviet Union detonated an atomic bomb. Senator Joseph McCarthy, who, as a member of the House Committee to Investigate Un-American Activities (HUAC), had conducted a Communist witch-hunt in Hollywood and in the State Department, was at the peak of his popularity in 1950; the Hollywood Ten, who refused to testify before his committee about alleged Communist affiliations or denounce colleagues in the film industry, began serving prison sentences in 1950; and Julius and Ethel Rosenberg, accused of passing nuclear secrets to the Russians, were sentenced to

HOLLYWOOD AT TWILIGHT

It was the best of times for America, the worst of times for Hollywood—and a great time for movies. As the nation marched from World War II into unprecedented economic prosperity, fortress Hollywood endured continual assault and barely survived.

No sooner did the House Committee to Investigate Un-American Activities (HUAC) begin to purge suspected Communists from Hollywood in 1947 than the Supreme Court ordered studios to divest themselves of their movie theaters, an antitrust action that dammed up a revenue stream. In 1948, moreover, moviegoers began defecting to television. An unintended result of the GI Bill was that veterans used loans to buy homes in the suburbs, where there were no movie theaters. Yet like many civilizations at twilight, Hollywood's colors shone their most brilliant—literally and figuratively.

To compete with the black-and-white box, movies increasingly were made in color. And to distinguish themselves from that squarish TV frame, movies expanded from portrait to panorama, thanks to new wide-screen processes—all the better to accommodate biblical spectacles such as *Ben-Hur* (1959, William Wyler), musicals such as *Funny Face* (1957, Stanley Donen), and Westerns such as *Rio Bravo* (1959, Howard Hawks).

Many of the period's memorable films analogized the end of an epoch. *Sunset Boulevard* (1950, Billy Wilder), *Singin' in the Rain* (fig. 33), and *Splendor in the Grass* (1961, Elia Kazan) each eulogized the twenties. Wilder's Hollywood gothic profiled a silent star (Gloria Swanson) projecting her grand delusions on the walls of her decaying mansion. Kelly's bouncy musical focused on Hollywood's transition from silents to sound. Kazan's drama with Natalie Wood and Warren Beatty showed teens on the cusp of sexuality in a country on the cusp of the Depression. *The Man Who Shot Liberty Valance* (1962, John Ford) and *Cleopatra* (1963, Joseph Mankiewicz) are the ultimate twilight films, one set in the frontier West and the other in the Roman Empire, and mark the last gleaming of great directors. Both star legends (John Wayne and James Stewart in *Valance*, Elizabeth Taylor in *Cleopatra*) and explore the paradox of our need to create legends—and to destroy them.

While worrying about its own extinction, Hollywood produced compelling dramas about human dinosaurs—among them, the aging Broadway diva (Bette Davis in *All About Eve*, 1950, Joseph Mankiewicz), the washed-up Hollywood hoofer (Fred Astaire in *The Band Wagon*, 1953, Vincente Minnelli), and the remorseless bigot (John Wayne in *The Searchers*, fig. 34).

Prewar Hollywood leading men such as Humphrey Bogart, Gary Cooper, and James Stewart continued to play leading roles in the fifties, but Katharine Hepburn was virtually alone among the female icons to make the transition (*The African Queen*, 1951,

33. Gene Kelly, Debbie Reynolds, and Donald O'Connor in *Singin' in the Rain*, directed by Gene Kelly and Stanley Donen, 1952
Courtesy Metro-Goldwyn-Mayer

34. John Wayne, Natalie Wood, and Jeffrey Hunter in *The Searchers*, directed by John Ford, 1956
Courtesy Warner Brothers

57. **Bob Thompson**
Triumph of Bacchus, 1964
Oil on canvas, 60 x 72⅟₁₆ in.
(152.4 x 183 cm)
Whitney Museum of
American Art, New York;
Purchase, with funds from
The Lauder Foundation,
Evelyn and Leonard Fund
and the Painting and
Sculpture Committee
98.19

58. **Larry Rivers**
*Washington Crossing the
Delaware*, 1953
Oil, graphite, and charcoal
on linen, 83⅜ x 111⅝ in.
(212.4 x 283.5 cm)
The Museum of Modern
Art, New York; Anonymous
gift
©Larry Rivers/ Licensed
by VAGA, New York, NY

59. **Andrew Wyeth**
Christina's World, 1948
Tempera on panel,
32¼ x 47¾ in. (81.9 x
121.3 cm)
The Museum of Modern
Art, New York; Purchase

60. **Edward Hopper**
People in the Sun, 1960
Oil on canvas,
40⅜ x 60⅜ in. (102.6 x
153.4 cm)
National Museum of
American Art,
Smithsonian Institution,
Washington, D.C.;
Gift of S.C. Johnson &
Son, Inc.

61. **David Park**
Four Men, 1958
Oil on canvas, 57 x 92 in.
(144.8 x 233.7 cm)
Whitney Museum of
American Art, New York;
Purchase, with funds from
an anonymous donor
59.27

62. **Richard Diebenkorn**
Girl Looking at Landscape,
1957
Oil on canvas, 59 x 60¼ in.
(149.9 x 205.7 cm)
Whitney Museum of
American Art, New York;
Gift of Mr. and Mrs. Alan H.
Temple 61.49

ensuing decades (fig. 63). Like other Chicago artists, he communicated the irrationality and baser instincts of human behavior through crusty surfaces and rendered the body as distorted or mutilated—a penchant for pictorial violence that earned the group the label Monster Roster.

By the mid-1950s, art communities in major urban centers such as Los Angeles, San Francisco, and Chicago had expanded to include a yeasty brew of jazz musicians, poets, independent filmmakers, performers, and photographers—a multidisciplinary mix that encouraged artists to cross boundaries and experiment with other media. As a new era of hybridity loomed, mainstream defenders of modernism clamped down to ensure that the traditional boundaries were preserved. Clement Greenberg, the critic who had championed Pollock early on and whose opinion had been ratified by Pollock's subsequent acclaim, had in 1940 given another verdict in support of his formalist credo: that every art form must be true to its particular properties. In the case of painting, this meant attention to the irreducible elements of surface, edge, color, and shape. Any reference to the outside world was prohibited.[44]

63. **Leon Golub**
Fallen Warrior (Burnt Man),
1960
Lacquer on canvas, 81 x
73 in. (205.7 x 185.4 cm)
Collection of Mr. and Mrs.
Ulrich Mayer

In the 1950s, the austere, nonreferential work of Clyfford Still, Mark Rothko, Ad Reinhardt, and particularly Barnett Newman proved useful to Greenberg's line of thinking. These artists, who had never really fit into the categories of Abstract Expressionism and Action Painting, became, at the end of the fifties, exemplars of an alternative to expressionist abstraction. They offered a way out of de Kooning-style imitations—while still adhering to the abstract mode. Their kind of painting had no self-revelatory brushstrokes, and the most ascetic work approached monochromes. It was said that "Newman had closed the door, Rothko had pulled down the shades, and Reinhardt had turned out the lights"—a statement that created a vivid image for their reductive process.[45]

Newman, who had his first show in 1950, at the Betty Parsons Gallery, was a well-known speaker and provocateur at the Artists' Club. He was more valued for his ideas than for his canvases of single, unmodulated colors punctuated by a few vertical lines of contrasting color—"zips," as he called them (fig. 67). His work had been somewhat neglected during the fifties, but was resurrected when Clement Greenberg arranged for a show in 1959 at French and Co. and praised Newman's painting for its formal simplicity, rigor, and transcendent capacity. His work prefigured much of the classic hard-edge and geometric abstraction that was developed

69. Helen Frankenthaler
Mountains and Sea, 1952
Oil on canvas,
86⅞ x 117¼ in.
(220.6 x 297.8 cm)
Collection of the artist;
On loan to the National
Gallery of Art, Washington,
D.C.

corporate headquarters and government buildings. This purportedly advanced abstract art was far less threatening in the early sixties than art with obvious content and subject matter.

Greenberg fiercely defended his purist position. He was less perceptive than he had been with Abstract Expressionism, however, and his pronouncements became increasingly formulaic, exclusionary, and dogmatic. His authoritative declarations nevertheless propelled a new generation of critics in the sixties, many of whom would rigorously and zealously defend their positions with an unparalleled moral fervor. Greenberg's hard line was provoked in part by what he saw as an impending crisis—the threat of popular art invading and polluting the domain of "high" or "pure" art.

70. **Kenneth Noland**
Song, 1958
Synthetic polymer on canvas, 65 x 65 in. (165.1 x 165.1 cm)
Whitney Museum of American Art, New York; Purchase, with funds from the Friends of the Whitney Museum of American Art 63.31
©Kenneth Noland/ Licensed by VAGA, New York, NY

Redefining
the American
Dream
1950–1960

Truth Tellers and Rebel Angels

The "impurities" that disturbed Clement Greenberg were already apparent in Pollock's work, as the young artist Allan Kaprow was quick to recognize: "Pollock . . . left us at the point where we must become preoccupied with and even dazzled by the space and objects of our everyday life, either our bodies, clothes, rooms, or if need be, the vastness of 42nd Street."[48]

Kaprow's advocacy of what can be called street-level realism reflects another take on America in the 1950s. If many Americans seemed to be realizing the American dream, others either could not grasp it or did not care to. Groups that fell outside of consensus culture had different values and a different vision that eventually redefined the American dream. This was the period in which civil rights protests set the groundwork for the cultural revolution of the 1960s: boycotts against racial segregation in Montgomery, Alabama (fig. 71); the emergence of Martin Luther King, Jr., as a civil rights leader; protests against school segregation in Little Rock, Arkansas (fig. 72).

71. *Rosa Parks Sitting in the Front Seat of a Montgomery, Alabama, Bus After Supreme Court Ruling Banning Segregation on the City's Public Buses*, 1956
UPI/Corbis-Bettmann

72. *Elizabeth Eckford, Age 15, One of Nine Black Students Whose Admission to Central High School in Little Rock, Arkansas, Was Ordered by a Federal Court, Following Legal Action by NAACP Legal Defense Fund Attorneys*, 1957
UPI/Corbis-Bettmann

As dissident voices gathered force, they were bolstered by an explosion of youth culture. By the end of the 1950s, the baby boomers born shortly after World War II were swelling the ranks of teenagers. Before the war, teens had often worked on the farm or in other family businesses. In the affluent fifties, they had more leisure time, education, and money to spend. Teenagers were becoming important consumers, enjoying jive, junk, and jazz music, and fast cars. They also began to investigate adult activities such as drinking and sex at an earlier age, the latter made more accessible through skin magazines like *Playboy*, which started publication in 1953. But teenagers also took part in important civil rights boycotts, and it was a group of African American teenagers who, in 1957, forced the issue of school integration by walking into segregated Central High School in Little Rock.

Teen role models were also polarized. While some teens bought into the clean-cut Ozzie and Harriet or Mouseketeer image broadcast on television, others were identifying with young literary protagonists such as Holden Caulfield in J. D. Salinger's *Catcher in the Rye* (1951), young rebels like Marlon Brando in *The Wild One* (fig. 73) and James Dean in *Rebel Without a Cause* (fig. 74), the gyrating rock 'n' roller Elvis Presley, who debuted on TV's *Ed Sullivan Show* in 1956, and Allen Ginsberg and Jack Kerouac, the cool nonconformist Beats. These youthful heroes—or anti-heroes—defined the restlessness and dissatisfaction that American youth felt toward the status quo.

In an age that brought us David Riesman's *The Lonely Crowd* (1950), an examination of suburban conformity that introduced new terms for social alienation,

73. Marlon Brando in
The Wild One, directed by
Stanley Kramer, 1954

74. *James Dean*, 1950s

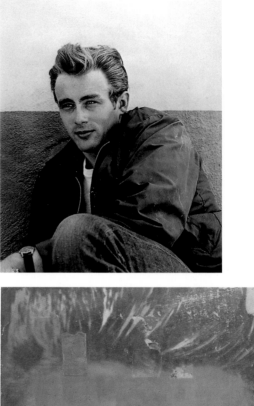

75. Cover of *Free Jazz*, by
the Ornette Coleman
Double Quartet, featuring
Jackson Pollock's *White
Light* (1954)
Atlantic Records, 1960

76. **Ray Johnson**
Elvis Presley #2, 1957
Collage, 15⅜ x 11½ in.
(39.1 x 29.2 cm)
Collection of William
Wilson

William H. Whyte's *The Organization Man* (1956), a commentary on the sacrifice of individuality for corporate norms, and Vance Packard's *The Hidden Persuaders* (1957), a critical dissection of advertising and consumerism, a large segment of a new generation was understandably "sickened on the inside and rebellious on the outside at having seen human existence being squeezed into organized molds of conformity."[49] Many artists, musicians, and writers gave strong voice to these concerns about timid conformity by creating art that offered another American reality—the radical experiments of free jazz (fig. 75), the emergent sounds of rock 'n' roll, and the openly gay lyrics of Beat poetry. In this revisionist spirit, the liberal Greenwich Village newspaper *The Village Voice* began publication.

ROCK 'N' ROLL: THE CRAFT BEHIND THE CRAZE

Bold, brash, and uncompromised music was the soundtrack to American life in the 1950s. Jazz musicians broke free from conventional forms to find a level of self-expression unheard-of in popular culture. The segregated genres of rhythm & blues and country & western fused to form rock 'n' roll. And the idea of the "teen" wreaked havoc in the social structure of the country. It was as if all the energy spent and lost in World War II had come home to roost with a vengeance—fueled by fast cars, cheap electricity, affordable middle-class housing, and the explosion of radio, television, and portable record players.

But there is also another story here, more obscure, but perhaps as significant. Using techniques intrinsic to the recording studio like multitracking and electronic manipulation of sound such as reverberation, popular music began to evolve from merely capturing low fidelity folk performances to sophisticated sonic compositions that manipulated, edited, and altered what was played. This was both a technological advance that permitted high-fidelity recordings for the first time and an artistic achievement in the hands of certain performers and producers who took advantage of recording methods unavailable before.

In 1954, Sam Phillips was a struggling music producer with a label in Memphis, Tennessee, called Sun Records. He had been recording local blues legends like B.B. King, Howling Wolf, and Junior Parker for a few years. According to legend, he boasted, "If I could find a white performer who could sing like [them] I'd make a million dollars." As fate would have it, a young man named Elvis Presley walked into the studio shortly thereafter to cut a record for his mother (fig. 78). Phillips' secretary overheard his voice and suggested that they record Presley. After a few weeks of tepid rehearsals, Phillips heard Elvis and his guitarist Scotty Moore cut loose with a crazy version of Arthur Crudup's "That's All Right Mama." Phillips recorded the sound on the big half-inch tape machine he bought from a local radio station, adding a dollop of reverb that would become the signature of the Sun Records sound for Elvis, Jerry Lee Lewis, Carl Perkins, Roy Orbison, Johnny Cash, and others. Together they changed not only music but the basic fabric of American society.

On the other end of the Mississippi River, two brothers in Chicago (Leonard and Phil Chess) owned another independent label, named Chess Records after themselves. During the early fifties they also made great recordings of blues artists, with the help of Willie Dixon, who supervised recordings, played bass, and wrote most of the best songs. Chess concentrated on musicians who had migrated north after World War II—Muddy Waters, Little Walter, and Howling Wolf. These artists had grown up in the Mississippi Delta and transformed the blues from acoustic guitar and voice to powerhouse electric bands that rocked the crowded bars on Chicago's South Side. In 1954, a young beautician named Chuck Berry walked into the Chess studio, hoping to record some of his tasteful blues songs in the more sophisticated style of Nat King Cole and Charles Brown. He did, but on the back of one of those releases, there was a different type of track named after his days in the beauty parlor. It was called "Maybellene" and, like "That's All Right Mama," it defined the driving beat and controlled abandon that came to be known as rock 'n' roll.

77. *Ray Charles*, 1960s

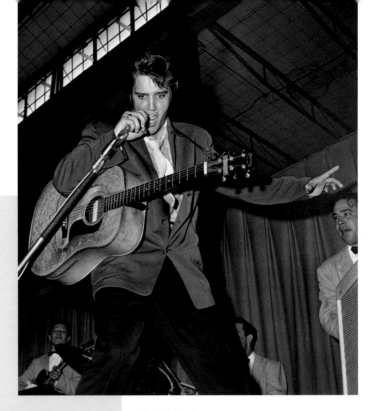

Interestingly enough, this story occurred many times and in many places in America between 1954 and 1957. Little Richard recorded "Tutti Frutti" in New Orleans for Specialty, while Clyde McPhatter and Ray Charles (fig. 77) invented soul music for Ahmet Ertegun and Jerry Wexler at Atlantic, Buddy Holly added his own unique spin for Coral, so-called girl groups, such as the Shirelles, reigned at Scepter, and Hank Ballard paved the way for James Brown on King. All over, America was exploding with regional artists bursting to encapsulate their energy in three-minute songs that were pressed on vinyl, played on AM radio, and bought by teens with more disposable income and leisure time than ever before.

By the late 1950s, rock music had not only captured the hearts, minds, and bodies of young Americans, it was beginning to grow into a remarkable medium for artistic expression. Rock did not just thrive on the libidinous charm of rising icons like Elvis. It galvanized the best creative talents of the age who filled the ranks of producers and songwriters. Two writers from New York's Brill Building, Leiber & Stoller, wrote many of Presley's best songs while transforming the disposable teen fluff of 1950s pop music into classic arias of romantic longing and social desperation. Meanwhile, producers like Phil Spector began to push the idea of the recording studio as a creative instrument through which they could craft little sonic symphonies. One of the ways that Spector did this was by making extensive use of multitracking, the practice of having a single instrument play the same part many times; these parts are then compressed and equalized to the point where they sound as uplifting on tiny AM radio speakers as would a live gospel choir. By thinking of the recording studio as an essential tool in the creation of music, Spector paved the way for the even more innovative and popular work of Berry Gordy, Brian Wilson, and John Lennon and Paul McCartney in the mid-sixties. —J. C.

JAZZ: THE BIRTH OF COOL

The 1950s were a remarkably fertile time in the history of American music. Rock 'n' roll, arguably the dominant form of mass expression in the late twentieth century, was born. Experimental musicians such as John Cage began to influence a wide range of artists in all media. And bebop jazz, begun by Charlie Parker, Dizzy Gillespie, and Thelonious Monk, in the forties crossed over into the mainstream.

At mid-century the Royal Roost was a popular New York City nightclub and Parker was the reigning star. By 1950, bebop had permanently transformed jazz from dance-oriented big band swing to contemplative abstract jams. The Royal Roost performances were broadcast on radio and later released on record. Careful listeners noticed that a teenage trumpet player named Miles Davis had replaced Dizzy in Parker's group. In these early performances Davis is remarkably self-assured, but still learning from the master. Within a few years, he grew to become the preeminent jazz musician of the fifties and the progenitor of a sound almost as important as bebop itself. It came to be known as cool jazz (fig. 79).

78. *Elvis Presley Singing with Country and Western Band*, 1956, photograph by Bruce Roberts

79. *'Round About Midnight*, by Miles Davis Columbia Records, 1955

Jazz itself was born at the turn of the century when black musicians in New Orleans began playing a new syncopated form of music that adapted African rhythms and "bent" or "blue" notes to European instruments like the trumpet, trap drum, and piano. Early composers such as Jelly Roll Morton, Eubie Blake, and James P. Johnson gave a form to these early experiments that was called ragtime. During the early 1920s, a remarkable trumpet player, Louis Armstrong, developed the idea of the jazz solo, one instrument taking the lead rather than tight-knit ensemble playing that had been the norm in both popular and classical groups. By the late 1920s, the great Duke Ellington began a more sophisticated style of ensemble playing that came to be known as swing. This became the dominant form of American music through the 1940s, popularized by bandleaders such as Benny Goodman, Glenn Miller, and Count Basie, and singers such as Frank Sinatra and Ella Fitzgerald.

By the mid-forties, a few innovative young musicians from popular swing bands, particularly Charlie Christian, Max Roach, Monk, Parker, and Gillespie began to jam together after-hours in a Harlem nightclub called Minton's. They abandoned the relatively conservative structure of the dance music they were paid to play, and experimented with a far more abstract form of music they called bebop. Bop was meant to be listened to carefully, not just treated as entertainment. For example, drumming in this new form of music implied the beat rather than emphasizing it, soloists played much longer than the standard eight bars, and references to popular tunes, notably by Cole Porter and George Gershwin, gave a sense of inspired play rather than studied virtuosity. The music still followed the jazz tradition of playing hot and wild, but abandoned the use of apparent formal structures to ground increasingly daring solos. Cool jazz built upon this radical shift in how music was played and listened to, but added an even greater emphasis upon aural atmospheres that provoked contemplation rather than melodies you could hum or rhythms you could dance to.

80. *Miles Davis and John Coltrane*, 1956

One can hear the birth of cool in Monk's "'Round Midnight," Parker's ballads such as "Embraceable You," and in the impressionistic tonality of his occasional bandmate, the pianist Lennie Tristano. Tristano, in turn, mentored another saxophone player, Lee Konitz, who helped inaugurate a jazz scene on the West Coast where the new cool style thrived and was popularized through the work of Chet Baker, Gerry Mulligan, and Stan Getz.

In the mid-fifties, Davis had found his own voice. He began to take his music in an entirely new direction by working with a brash young saxophonist named John Coltrane (fig. 80). The first Miles Davis Quintet recorded what many consider some of the finest

BEAT CULTURE

More than any other group in the 1950s, it was the Beats whose lives and literary creations rebelled against the conformity of American culture, which they took as a sign that the American promise had not been fulfilled. Poets and writers who started as a small underground in the early 1950s, the Beats believed that if you loved your country, you *had* to be a rebel. The Beat movement began in New York in the mid-forties, with the meeting of the writers William Burroughs and Jack Kerouac and the poet Allen Ginsberg. A decade later, the Beats overlapped with another underground movement, which had also been active since the forties—the San Francisco Renaissance. In 1955, San Francisco poet Michael McClure invited Ginsberg to give his first public reading of "Howl" (1956) at the Six Gallery, a vanguard artists' cooperative. The reading is now legendary: the artists and poets in the audience were riveted by the power of the poem, by Ginsberg's delivery of what would become the Beat anthem: "I saw the best minds of my generation destroyed by / madness, starving hysterical naked / dragging themselves through the negro streets at dawn / looking for an angry fix . . ."—and by Kerouac's gospel-like shouting refrains from the sidelines.[50]

ensemble jazz ever played, but broke up in 1957. Fortunately, they regrouped in 1959, adding saxophonist Cannonball Adderley and pianist Bill Evans, who built upon Tristano's style of combining abstract jazz with classical influences from Claude Debussy and Erik Satie. Together they recorded what is often regarded as the greatest jazz album of all time, *Kind of Blue* (1959).

Legend has it that Davis and Evans came up with the basic "modalities" for the session and then had the musicians perform directly on tape without extensive rehearsal. This was called "modal" jazz because improvisations were based on scales rather than on chord changes or harmonies. All the tracks, except one, were captured on the first take with no overdubs or edits. The result was an album with unique pace and atmosphere, different from anything heard before. On one hand, that sound is defined by the utter melodic simplicity of Davis' and Evans' approach, anchored by the subtle pulse of Paul Chambers and Jimmy Cobb's rhythm section. But Coltrane's arching solos take the record to another place: a kind of blues that is both hot and cool—beauty tempered with the tension of musicians relaxed within themselves, struggling to transcend. —J. C.

81. *On the Road*, by Jack Kerouac, 1951 Original manuscript on teletype paper scroll, 120 ft. (36.6 m) length Collection of the Sampas Family

In coffeehouses in San Francisco, as well as in New York's Greenwich Village and the canyons of Los Angeles, the Beats stood opposed to censorship, the arms race, corporate values, and consumerism. Repudiating bourgeois culture, with its materialism and work ethic, they found ecstasy and wonder in the ordinary and the debased. Beat poetry drew on a vast range of sources and experience: Walt Whitman and slang, drug culture and Zen Buddhism, Hollywood movies and the garbage dump—all were fused in a confrontational but redemptive realism. The Beats redeemed the commonplace by incorporating found objects, words, and sounds to celebrate the subject matter of America itself. In an introduction to Robert Frank's photographic essay *The Americans*, a brilliant, gritty portrait of real-life America (figs. 108–11), Jack Kerouac hailed the vibrant inclusiveness of the images:

> The humor, the sadness, the EVERYTHING-ness and American-ness of these pictures! Tall thin cowboy rolling butt outside Madison Square Garden New York for rodeo season, sad, spindly, unbelievable—Long shot of the night road arrowing forlorn into immensities and flat of impossible-to-believe-America in New Mexico under the prisoner's moon—under the whang whang guitar star—Haggard old frowsy dames of

THE BEAT GENERATION

"America demands a poetry that is bold, modern and all-surrounding and kosmical, as she is herself," wrote Walt Whitman. Although he made his observation soon after the Civil War, Whitman's prescription also applies to the period immediately following World War II, when the Beat generation came of age. The range of figures frequently described as Beat includes writers, artists, filmmakers, and coffeehouse devotees in goatees and T-shirts, but there were only a handful of founding members in the 1940s and early 1950s. The term "Beat generation" was coined by Jack Kerouac in 1948. A decade later, the movement became a national phenomenon, popularly known, in the columnist Herb Caen's coinage, as "beatniks" (Allen Ginsberg considered Caen's shorthand to be the "Frankenstein" version of the Beat generation). Setting the model for dress, drugs, and youth culture, Beat poets were treated like rock stars rather than like ivory tower academics (fig. 82).

The Beats were drawn together by personal intimacy and social rebellion as well as by literary aesthetics, and this was apparent from the moment in 1944 when Columbia University student Lucien Carr introduced the three seminal figures of the Beat generation to one another: William Burroughs (age thirty), Jack Kerouac (age twenty-two), and Allen Ginsberg (age eighteen). They served one another as sexual partners, literary agents, mentors, and, above all, developing writers who read and encouraged each other's work when it had not yet found support in the literary establishment. Ginsberg's description of their "New Vision" in the mid-1940s characterizes their later output: (1) uncensored self-expression is necessary to creativity; (2) creativity is expanded through nonrational means and derangement of the senses—hallucinations, visions, drugs, and dreams; (3) art supersedes the dictates of conventional morality.

In the mid-1950s, the Beat generation overlapped with poets associated with Black Mountain College in North Carolina (Robert Creeley, John Weiners) and a group in San Francisco who initiated what became known as the San Francisco Renaissance (including Lawrence Ferlinghetti, Bob Kaufman, Philip Lamantia, Michael McClure, Peter Orlovsky, Gary Snyder, and Philip Whalen; figs. 83, 84). For a period of about five years, the San Francisco Renaissance flourished in tandem with the Beat generation, in coffeehouses and in bookstores such as City Lights. From that stimulating West Coast environment

82. Hal Chase, Jack Kerouac, Allen Ginsberg, and William Burroughs, Morningside Heights, New York, 1944

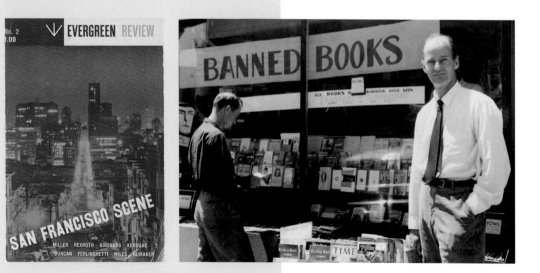

83. Evergreen Review, 1, no. 2, 1957

84. Lawrence Ferlinghetti in Front of City Lights Bookstore, San Francisco, 1957, photograph by Harry Redl

came Lawrence Ferlinghetti's *A Coney Island of the Mind* (1958), which became the twentieth century's best-selling book of American poetry, as well as connections to underground filmmakers (Bruce Conner, James Broughton) and the artists George Herms and Wallace Berman. Like the Beat generation, members of the San Francisco Renaissance were bound together by a sense of collective embattlement in a world that seemed more materialistic than spiritual, more conformist than creative.

The literature of the Beat generation was deeply intertwined with autobiography. The events of their lives—transcontinental car trips, homosexual companionship, and heroin addiction—became sources for three key Beat texts: Kerouac's *On the Road*, Ginsberg's *Howl and Other Poems*, and Burroughs' *Naked Lunch*. Personal candor was essential to these writings, and the books exploded the tight literary conventions in America during the age of New Criticism, which focused on literary themes, language, and imagery and excluded consideration of biographical or historical perspectives. Confronting Beat writers, many critics described them as juvenile delinquents who were set on destroying literature and morality. This shortsighted view ignored the Beats' voracious interest in authors both classical (e.g., William Blake) and contemporary (e.g., William Carlos Williams, Thomas Wolfe) and their desire to forge a new morality based on candid human relationships. Moreover, the Beats' conception of poetry as public performance, often incorporating jazz accompaniment in San Francisco's North Beach clubs (fig. 85), harked back to the ancient tradition of the wandering bard. Beat poetry could evoke the spirituality of the natural environment (Michael McClure), Buddhism and the rigor of meditation (Gary Snyder and Philip Whalen), and the presence of indigenous peoples (Snyder). Using vernacular language, these poets pioneered the rhythms that reflected the improvisations of jazz.

The Beat generation opened many doors for later generations in pop and literary culture. Some have been commercial; as Burroughs observed, "Kerouac opened a million coffee bars and sold a million pairs of jeans to both sexes." More lastingly, by defeating obscenity charges against *Howl* and *Naked Lunch*, the Beats helped defeat America's laws of literary censorship, while providing models and directives for future generations to experiment with language and life, to reinvent the idea of being an American and simultaneously a citizen of the cosmic world. —S. W.

85. *Last Gathering of the Beat Poets and Artists, City Lights Bookstore, San Francisco*, 1965, photograph by Larry Keenan

Los Angeles leaning peering out the right front window of Old Paw's car on a Sunday gawking and criticizing to explain Amerikay to little children in the spattered back seat—tattooed guy sleeping on grass in park in Cleveland, snoring dead to the world on a Sunday afternoon with too many balloons and sailboats. . . .[51]

And Ginsberg, poet laureate of the Beats, exclaimed in "Howl" that everything is holy, "The world is holy! The soul is holy! The skin is holy! The nose is holy! The tongue and cock and hand and asshole are holy!"

The Beat exaltation of the lowly and discarded had parallels in the new realist novel and in the confrontational experimental theater of the Living Theater and other groups. It signaled an integral connection between art and life, best seen perhaps in Kerouac's *On the Road*, published in 1957 (fig. 81), which became a manifesto of the Beat generation. *On the Road* was written in one mad, intense session—typed more or less continuously for three weeks on a 120-foot-long roll of paper. This method reflected Kerouac's motto "first thought, best thought." His style was also inspired by the improvisational rhythms and fast-paced riffs of bebop jazz and was called "spontaneous bop prosody."[52] For Kerouac, writing, like

REALISM IN THE NOVEL

American writers of the fifties bared the dark side of national affluence. The postwar economic boom had supposedly landed Americans in a placid valley filled with consumer goods: pastel pedal pushers, self-cleaning ovens, and cheeseburgers delivered by waitresses on roller skates. Yet the illusion that economic prosperity had left everyone fulfilled was splintered by American authors who doggedly undermined the prevailing assumption that prosperity guaranteed happiness. In fact, they delivered the opposite message: too much prosperity left people grasping for more, blind to their own immorality, and far from the ideals for which American soldiers had fought and died in World War II.

As Saul Bellow warns in *Seize the Day* (fig. 86), "You want to avoid catching the money fever. This type of activity is filled with hostile feeling and lust. You should see what it does to some of these fellows." Unfortunately, Tommy Wilhelm, Bellow's main character, does catch the money fever. The novel's final scene shows him weeping at a stranger's funeral, mourning the death of genuine human connections in a harsh and victimizing world.

Tommy's grief and isolation ennoble him, since fifties novelists agreed that those who succeeded in this mercenary culture were, in the words of *Catcher in the Rye*'s Holden Caulfield (fig. 87), "phony bastards." Like Tommy, Holden is a misfit because he cannot aspire to the conventional consumerist attitudes of his peers. Yet, like Huckleberry Finn, his predecessor in vernacular realism, Holden fights hypocrisy with a highly developed talent for seeing the cracks in America's seemingly smooth surfaces. Like other fifties misfits, Holden will be ushered into analysts' offices, tranquilized, and made to adapt. For doing so, he will earn the dubious privilege of joining the ranks of America's upwardly mobile.

The achievement of wealth and upper-class status proves to have its pitfalls in several important novels of the fifties. As Mary McCarthy's *The Group* (1963) coldly reports, money and class position only serve to reinforce the prison bars of conformity and compliance, which for women of the decade began to take on frightening dimensions. Those who subordinated themselves to their husbands, abandoning their education and skills, would end up like McCarthy's heroine Kay, beautiful and pedigreed, but institutionalized and suicidal. Indeed, the sordid domestic scene of Kay's marriage, her husband's abuse, the black walls of their friends' apartment, their anxiety about money—all provide a stark contrast to the pictures of the happy homemakers peopling American advertisements. The sexual frankness of this book also startled Americans, who either praised or protested McCarthy's discussions of impotence and orgasm, psychoanalysis and homosexuality, adultery and divorce.

Marital discord occupies center stage in many novels of the fifties, with writers presenting relationships that cannot survive the economic realities the characters must

86. *Seize the Day*, by Saul Bellow
New York: Viking Press, 1956
Harry Ransom Humanities Research Center at The University of Texas at Austin

everything else, was a kind of performance. Art and life were intertwined, part of one carnivalesque mélange of music, conversation, drinking, reading, working, smoking, sex, and traveling.

Though the Beats formed a literary movement, their all-embracing attitude promoted synergy among disciplines. This produced works ranging from jazz poetry performances at the Five Spot, a New York jazz club, or the Living Theater, and independent films such as *Pull My Daisy* (fig. 90), a collaboration between Robert Frank and the painter Alfred Leslie, which featured performances by the poet and Hansa gallery director Richard Bellamy, the poet Gregory Corso, and the painters Alice Neel and Larry Rivers, among others. This film marked the beginning of a new avant-garde film genre, the New American Cinema, which included Bruce Conner, Shirley Clarke, and John Cassavetes. In other cross-disciplinary enterprises, poets wrote about visual artists, and visual artists illustrated many of the books of Beat writers or designed sets for the Beats' experimental plays.

face. In John Updike's *Rabbit, Run* (1960), the hero, Harry "Rabbit" Angstrom, goes to war instead of college and thus can barely manage to support his wife, a heavy drinker, and his children. Eventually, the couple's unhappiness leads to the drowning of their daughter. The novel's conclusion offers no closure and no solution to Rabbit's spiritual malaise; instead of moral pronouncements, Updike renders, with his close descriptions of rural Pennsylvania and its inhabitants, a grim slice of American life.

Updike's brand of social realism had at its root the desire to tell the truth about all segments of the American population. For Philip Roth, that meant focusing his attention on that class of Americans who had just devoured their piece of the expanding economic pie. *Goodbye, Columbus* (fig. 88) cautions against such appetites, finding that ruthless pursuit of wealth defiles the American character and desecrates American values. In Roth's novel, the main character, Neil Klugman, pursues his golden girl, the spoiled, nouveau riche Brenda Patimkin. In her father's suburban mansion, Neil gratifies his materialistic and carnal desires, gorging himself on the summer fruit that falls from the Patimkins' bursting refrigerator. Such cornucopia blinds him to the truth about Brenda. Finally confronting her moral dissolution, and his own, he wonders, "What was it that had turned pursuit and clutching into love, and then turned it inside out again?"

Under the scrutiny of these writers, the facade of a robust and productive America collapses, and behind it rears the wasteland of the national spirit. In John Cheever's premier story, "The Enormous Radio" (1953), a well-to-do couple, living in a Manhattan apartment, buys a radio that receives, instead of planned programming, the conversations of their neighbors. Listening ceaselessly, the wife hears sounds of men and women fighting, wife-beating, drunkenness, anxiety about money, and parental cruelty. Cheever, too, exposed the disparity between the image and the reality of America. For just behind the external signs of prosperity, the shiny new Formica of dinette sets and kitchen counters, lay the neglected: the outcasts, the alcoholics, the poor, the impotent, the abused. Paradoxically, however, in the eyes of these novelists, those who reaped the benefits of economic abundance fared the worst. Blind to the misery just next door, devoted to meretricious values, and seduced by advertisements for the American dream, the greedy suffer the flimsiness of their purchases and the hollowness of their own ideals. —H. F.

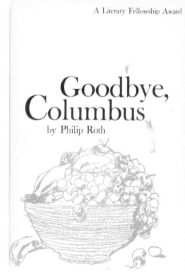

87. *Catcher in the Rye*, by J. D. Salinger Boston: Little, Brown, 1951 Harry Ransom Humanities Research Center at The University of Texas at Austin

88. *Goodbye, Columbus*, by Philip Roth Boston: Houghton Mifflin, 1959 Harry Ransom Humanities Research Center at The University of Texas at Austin

THE NEW AMERICAN CINEMA

During the late 1950s, a new generation of experimental filmmakers emerged from the bohemian subcultures of New York and San Francisco. Influenced by Beat culture, the anti-narrative experiments of Abstract Expressionist painting, Eastern religion, the radical sound pieces of John Cage, and the new dance forms of Merce Cunningham, this group rebelled against the European-based Surrealist "trance film" model of the 1940s, inspired by Jean Cocteau, which had characterized the groundbreaking work of Maya Deren, Kenneth Anger, and others. Both generations rejected conventional cinema's use of a narrative structure based on the novel, and drew on painting, music, poetry, and popular culture to create a new cinematic language. But whereas the avant-garde film of the 1940s aligned itself to poetry, during the end of the 1950s a new sensibility began to take hold. Stan Brakhage, Ken Jacobs, Jonas Mekas, Jordan Belson, Bruce Conner, and Shirley Clarke developed a new film language, using home-movie techniques and experimenting with unconventional film speeds, color, multiple printing, montage, and special lenses—all of which were used to radically transform film space and subject matter.

Of all the filmmakers creating these new cinematic forms during the 1950s, the dominant, and most prolific, was Stan Brakhage. Producing several films each year between 1952 and 1958, he created what came to be known as the "lyrical" film. His highly subjective, personal form of filmmaking, which took his domestic life, his wife and children, and his own inner struggles as central subjects, greatly influenced the next generation of filmmakers. The key film that marked Brakhage's transition to this new genre was *Anticipation of the Night* (fig. 89); its fragmented images and transformation of film space into multilayered perspectival planes brought filmmaking to new territory. The camera became not an "objective" eye but a subjective expression of a personal vision.

During the 1950s, New York was one of two main hubs of avant-garde filmmaking, centered around the activity of Jonas Mekas, a poet and refugee from Lithuania. Mekas was to become the main champion, critic, distributor, and defender of avant-garde film in America for the next four decades, as well as a filmmaker in his own right. He first established himself in New York through his writing, founding the influential journal *Film Culture* in 1955 and beginning his weekly film column in the newly founded *Village Voice* in 1958. Much influenced by Cinema 16, a group established by Amos Vogel in New York in 1947 in order to present and distribute alternative film, Mekas was to erect a wide-ranging support structure for avant-garde film, creating the Film-makers' Cooperative in 1962 and the Anthology Film Archives in 1970.

It was in New York that another key figure in American avant-garde film, Ken Jacobs, made *Little Stabs at Happiness* (fig. 91), one of his earliest films, featuring the filmmaker Jack Smith. Shirley Clarke filmed the bridges of New York for her multiperspective

89. **Stan Brakhage**
Anticipation of the Night,
1958
16 mm film, silent, color;
40 min.
Anthology Film Archives,
New York

90. **Robert Frank** and
Alfred Leslie
Pull My Daisy, 1959
16 mm film, sound,
black-and-white; 28 min.
Anthology Film Archives,
New York

95. George Herms
The Librarian, 1960
Wood box, newspaper,
brass, books, and painted
stool, 57 x 63 x 21 in.
(144.8 x 160 x 53.3 cm)
Norton Simon Museum,
Pasadena, California; Gift
of Molly Barnes, 1969

98. Bruce Conner
*PORTRAIT OF ALLEN
GINSBERG*, 1960
Wood, fabric, wax, tin
can, glass, feathers,
metal, string, and spray
paint, 20 x 11¼ x 21⅜ in.
(50.8 x 28.6 x 54.3 cm)
Whitney Museum of
American Art, New York;
Purchase, with funds from
the Contemporary Painting
and Sculpture Committee
96.48

97. Bruce Conner
BLACK DAHLIA, 1960
Mixed-media assemblage,
26¾ x 10¾ x 2¾ in.
(67.9 x 27.3 x 7 cm)
Collection of Walter Hopps

96. Bruce Conner
LOOKING GLASS, 1964
Paper, cotton, cloth, nylon,
beads, metal, twine, glass,
leather, plastic, wood, and
masonite, 60½ x 48 x 14½ in.
(153.7 x 121.9 x 36.8 cm)
San Francisco Museum of
Modern Art; Gift of the
Modern Art Council

99. **Edward Kienholz**
The Illegal Operation,
1962
Mixed media, dimensions
variable
Collection of Betty and
Monte Factor

100. **Simon Rodia**
*Watts Towers, Los
Angeles, California*,
1921–54, photograph by
Julius Shulman

103. Richard Stankiewicz
Kabuki Dancer, 1954
Iron and steel, 84 in.
(213.4 cm) height
Whitney Museum of
American Art, New York;
Purchase, with funds from
the Friends of the Whitney
Museum of American Art
57.12

104. John Chamberlain
Velvet White, 1962
Painted and chromium-
plated steel, 80⅜ x 53 x
49⅜ in. (205.1 x 134.6 x
124.9 cm)
Whitney Museum of
American Art, New York;
Gift of the Albert A. List
Family 70.1579a–b

105. Mark di Suvero
Hankchampion, 1960
Wood and chains, 77½ x
149 x 105 in. (196.9 x
378.5 x 266.7 cm)
Whitney Museum of
American Art, New York;
Gift of Mr. and Mrs.
Robert C. Scull 73.85

full of humor and irreverence. Stankiewicz fashioned old car parts and metal pipes into figurative totems like *Kabuki Dancer* (fig. 103); Nevelson used found bits of wood to construct her abstract and atmospherically evocative environments like *Dawn's Wedding Chapel, II* (fig. 102). Chamberlain scavenged autobodies and fit them together in a three-dimensional extension of Action Painting (fig. 104), and di Suvero assembled mammoth timbers into dramatic constructions of gesture and balance (fig. 105). West Coast assemblagists—Conner, Edward Kienholz, and Berman—took a more political approach in their work, often addressing moral issues of the moment such as capital punishment and illegal abortions (fig. 99).

Assemblage artists worked without expectation of sales or institutional support and sometimes with open disdain for the art establishment. Their work was often ephemeral or made with materials that easily deteriorated. Some forward-looking museum curators, however, were not put off by the artists' indifference or by the fragility or commonness of the materials. Gradually, assemblage began to gain respect in the very world whose authority it challenged. In 1961, William Seitz gave it the highest institutional imprimatur when he organized the exhibition "The Art of Assemblage" at The Museum of Modern Art in New York.

A NEW LENS ON AMERICA

The photographers grouped in what is often called the New York School of photography, which paralleled the development of New York School painting in the postwar years, also had an unromanticized view of life and took to the streets in search of the "real" America. Although they built on the methods of documentary journalism, they rejected its anecdotal descriptiveness, instead forging a style that mingled the spirit of existentialism with Hollywood film noir.[53] And in place of the formal pretensions of earlier photographers, they developed a "snapshot aesthetic" analogous to the found materials of assemblage art and Beat writing. Their work, too, expressed the isolation, alienation, abrasiveness, and social malaise of the contemporary urban experience.

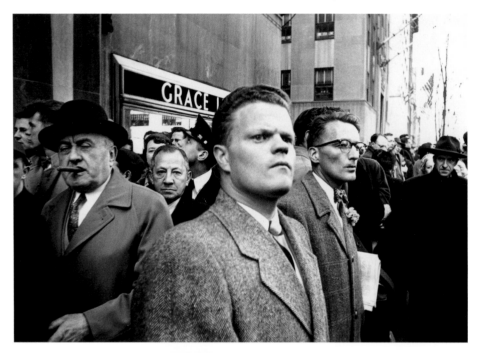

106. **William Klein**
St. Patrick's Day, 5th Avenue, 1955
Gelatin silver print, 10 x 12 in. (25.4 x 30.5 cm)
Courtesy Howard Greenberg Gallery, New York
© William Klein

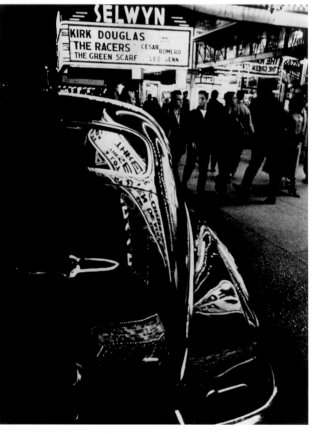

107. **William Klein**
Selwyn, New York 1955 (42nd Street), 1955
Gelatin silver print, 11⅛ x 9⁷⁄₁₆ in. (30.2 x 24 cm)
Whitney Museum of American Art, New York; Purchase, with funds from the Photography Committee 96.64
© William Klein

Robert Frank, Diane Arbus, Richard Avedon, William Klein, Lisette Model, Helen Levitt, and Weegee (figs. 106, 107, 114, 115) took spontaneous and candid shots of street and crime scenes, city subways, circus freaks, and Coney Island. Individually and together, their works portray the diversity of urban life, from high style to squalor.[54] Adding to this picture is the work of Roy DeCarava. Although not normally grouped with the New York School, DeCarava was socially affiliated with many of those photographers. He took straightforward, passionate photographs of life in New York, particularly in Harlem—portraits of great jazz musicians (John Coltrane, Lester Young, Billie Holiday) as well as ordinary people—creating a remarkable pictorial record that inspired Langston Hughes' story "The Sweet Flypaper of Life," which was published as a book with some of DeCarava's photographs.

The Swiss-born Robert Frank, although based in New York in the 1950s, surveyed the entire expanse of America with the blunt candor of his lens. In 1955, Frank received a Guggenheim Fellowship to travel across the country, documenting America's people. The resulting book (and series of photographs), *The Americans* (1958–59), is a brilliant portrait of the real life of America that celebrates the beauty in the everyday: the noble and sophisticated, the rich and poor, the common

108. **Robert Frank**
Parade: Hoboken, New Jersey, from the series *The Americans,* 1953–57
Gelatin silver print, 12¼ x 18¾ in. (31.1 x 47.6 cm)
Philadelphia Museum of Art; Purchase, with funds from Dorothy Norman
© Robert Frank

109. **Robert Frank**
Restaurant: U.S. 1 Leaving Columbia, South Carolina, from the series *The Americans,* 1953–57
Gelatin silver print, 9 x 13¼ in. (22.9 x 33.7 cm)
Collection of Barbara Schwartz
© Robert Frank

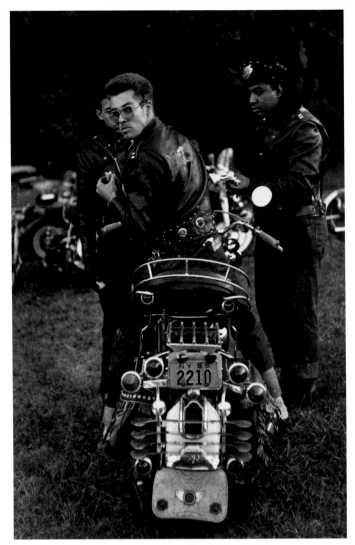

110. **Robert Frank**
Newburgh, New York, from the series *The Americans*, 1953–57
Gelatin silver print, 13⅜ x 8¹³⁄₁₆ in. (33.8 x 22.4 cm)
The Art Institute of Chicago, Photography Gallery Fund
© Robert Frank

111. **Robert Frank**
Charleston, South Carolina, from the series *The Americans*, 1953–57
Gelatin silver print, 8¹³⁄₁₆ x 13⅜ in. (22.4 x 33.8 cm)
Addison Gallery of American Art, Phillips Academy, Andover, Massachusetts
© Robert Frank

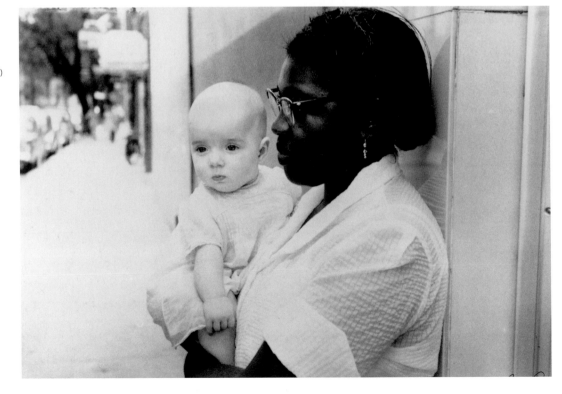

and exotic, the mix of races, the rural desolation and urban anomie (figs. 108–111). Frank crisscrossed the country, catching Yom Kippur in New York, a political rally in Chicago, a movie premiere in Hollywood, a navy recruiting station in Butte, Montana. His camera took in the transition from the old—log cabins and coal mining towns—to the new—jukeboxes and drive-ins. The candid character of Frank's photographs, their slice-of-life realism, owes much to the off-center, seemingly casual framing of each image, a technique some photographers regarded as a violation of professional photographic standards—just as assemblage and Beat literature violated the purist norms of art.

Frank represented the unvarnished diversity of America, and his realism inspired other artists. It was Edward Steichen, however, who represented the popular mainstream in *The Family of Man*, a 1955 photo-essay that accompanied an epochal exhibition at The Museum of Modern Art, New York. Steichen assembled 503 pictures by photographers from sixty-eight countries in an extravagant installation that he "conceived as a mirror of the universal elements and emotions in the everydayness of life—as a mirror of the essential oneness of mankind throughout the world" (fig. 112).[55] In the process of culling images from around the globe to make a grand, sentimental statement about the range of human experience, Steichen blurred cultural differences. Frank, on the other hand, was investigating a particular country in all its facets in order to produce a poetry of place—one tougher, more troubling, and nuanced. Frank's America was a country of carnivalesque urban rhythms and lonely barren expanses of open road.

Robert Frank initiated a kind of photographic realism that continued into the next decade. Breaking with conventional standards of pictorial composition, Garry Winogrand took pictures of crowded parties and street scenes with a random, almost accidental quality (fig. 113). Lee Friedlander's deadpan urban scenes—storefronts, display windows, and street signs—presented a view of America that was chaotic, disjointed, and often surreal. Diane Arbus cast an honest eye toward the ordinary and exotic in her memorable portraits of midgets, socialites, transvestites, and adolescents. Her pictures were immensely powerful in their dispassionate examination of lives and worlds that others overlooked (figs. 114, 115).

112. Installation view of "The Family of Man" at The Museum of Modern Art, New York, 1955

Closing the Gap Between Art and Life

RAUSCHENBERG, CAGE, JOHNS, CUNNINGHAM

The artist who most clearly redefined the boundaries of art in the 1950s by bringing real life into it was Robert Rauschenberg. "I don't want a picture to look like something it isn't. I want it to look like something it is. And I think a picture is more like the real world when it's made out of the real world."[56] One of the most prolific artists of the last fifty years, he began in 1953–54 to incorporate real objects into his assemblages and by 1955 was producing what he called "Combine" paintings—neither painting nor sculpture, but both (figs. 117–21, 134). No object was too lowly for his art. The cast-off and the discarded were redeemed through his energetic combinations and overlays that celebrated memory as well as the raw sense of everyday life. A shirt, a sock, a tire, a quilt, a parachute, a street sign, a Coca-Cola bottle, a stuffed goat—each found its way into his hybrid constructions. These works were a far cry from the iconic distillations of Abstract Expressionism.

In this spirit of redefinition, Rauschenberg had erased a de Kooning drawing in 1953, an act of tribute and oedipal defiance that wiped the slate clean (fig. 116). He had already executed a series of white paintings designed to register the play of shadows rather than make a pictorial statement. These works were shown at his first one-artist exhibition, at the Betty Parsons Gallery, New York, in 1951. That same year, he embarked on a series of black and then red paintings, applying newspapers to the canvas and then coating them in enamel, a buildup that evoked the urban decay and rawness of life in Lower Manhattan. Though clearly indebted to the work of earlier European collagists and the constructions of Joseph Cornell, Rauschenberg took the collage tradition into a new realm. In some works from the period, such as *Rebus* or *Factum I* and *II* (figs. 117, 118), he affixed differently scaled images and pieces of cloth to the picture in a montage-like fashion, overlaying them with brushstrokes.

Further merging collage with painting, Rauschenberg's later three-dimensional Combines, *Monogram*, *Satellite*, and *Canyon* (figs. 119–21), spill into the viewer's space, offering an experience of multiplicity and random order. Rauschenberg brought the world into his art, in content as well as form. His was an inclusive vision—generous, engaging, and physically extroverted. "Painting relates to both art and life," he said. "Neither can be made. (I try to act in that gap between the two.)"[57]

John Cage, the avant-garde musician and Rauschenberg's friend, would write, "These are the feelings Rauschenberg gives us: love, wonder, laughter, heroism (I accept), fear, sorrow, anger, disgust, tranquillity."[58] Like his Beat compatriots, Rauschenberg expressed the full range of human experience and emotions even if it violated social taboos. "Where does beauty begin and where does it end? Where it ends is where the artist begins," said Cage. He proclaimed Rauschenberg "the giver of gifts," someone who redefined beauty by looking at things that we thought were ugly or that had grown too familiar to be seen.[59] Rauschenberg's work transformed our everyday experience, sensitizing us to the beauty of a derelict sign or a crumbling wall.

Rauschenberg had learned much from Cage, whose aesthetic derived in part from Zen Buddhism. Zen philosophy valued chance over structured sequence and rejected the polarities of good and bad, ugly and beautiful. Everything is subsumed

116. **Robert Rauschenberg**
Erased de Kooning Drawing, 1953
Traces of ink and crayon on paper in gold-leaf frame, 25¼ x 21¾ in. (64.1 x 55.2 cm)
San Francisco Museum of Modern Art; Purchased through a gift of Phyllis Wattis
© Robert Rauschenberg/ Licensed by VAGA, New York, NY

117. **Robert Rauschenberg**
Factum I, 1957
Combine painting, 61½ x
35¾ in. (156.2 x 90.8 cm)
The Museum of
Contemporary Art,
Los Angeles; The Panza
Collection
© Robert Rauschenberg/
Licensed by VAGA, New
York, NY

118. **Robert Rauschenberg**
Factum II, 1957
Combine painting, 62 x
35½ in. (163.7 x 90.2 cm)
The Morton G. Neumann
Family Collection
© Robert Rauschenberg/
Licensed by VAGA, New
York, NY

119. **Robert Rauschenberg**
Monogram, 1955–59
Combine painting, 42 x
63¼ x 64½ in. (106.7 x
160.7 x 163.8 cm)
Moderna Museet,
Stockholm
© Robert Rauschenberg/
Licensed by VAGA, New
York, NY

120. **Robert Rauschenberg**
Satellite, 1955
Combine painting, 79⅜ x
43¼ x 5⅝ in. (201.6 x
109.9 x 14.3 cm)
Whitney Museum of
American Art, New York;
Gift of Claire B. Zeisler
and purchase with funds
from the Mrs. Percy Uris
Purchase Fund 91.85
© Robert Rauschenberg/
Licensed by VAGA, New
York, NY

121. **Robert Rauschenberg**
Canyon, 1959
Combine painting, 81¾ x
70 x 24 in. (207.6 x
177.8 x 61 cm)
Sonnabend Collection,
New York
© Robert Rauschenberg/
Licensed by VAGA, New
York, NY

MODERN DANCE: CHANCE AND IMPROVISATION

Modern dance had begun with the explorations of Americans such as Loïe Fuller, Isadora Duncan, and Ruth St. Denis at the turn of the century. By the thirties and forties, historical modern dance (by the choreographers Martha Graham, Doris Humphrey, and José Limón, among others) had crystallized its techniques to emphasize weight and breath, and had established its concerns with political themes and symbolic emotional expression.

In the 1950s, however, several choreographers began to move in new directions, using different dance techniques, employing compositional methods that paralleled innovations in visual art, music, and theater, and collaborating with avant-garde artists and composers. Merce Cunningham had danced with Martha Graham and studied ballet with George Balanchine in the 1940s. He developed his own dance technique, a marriage of the flexible upper body of modern dance and the verticality and brilliant footwork of ballet. In 1951, working closely with John Cage as well as with other avant-garde composers, Cunningham introduced into choreography the chance methods favored by Cage in his musical composition (fig. 126). The effect of these chance techniques was to decentralize the dance in time and space, since both phrasing and spacing were determined aleatorically. Formally, Cunningham's dances bore a resemblance to the work of Abstract Expressionist painters; unlike them, however, Cunningham wanted to eradicate all marks of self-expression.

In 1954, Cunningham commissioned a set from the painter Robert Rauschenberg, who became the company's resident designer for the next ten years (fig. 127). Like Sergei Diaghilev's Ballets Russes earlier in the century, the Merce Cunningham Dance Company became a site where the most advanced experiments in contemporary art,

Johns, more than any other American artist, extended the legacy of Duchamp into the area of painting. While Rauschenberg's work seemed spontaneous and exuberant, Johns' was much more studied and his choice of subjects more deliberate. He used public imagery—flags, targets, numbers, and letters—"things the mind already knows," as he said (figs. 131, 132, 135). Although Johns' cerebral work seemed contrary to the vibrant rough edges of the New York School, it nevertheless retained a handmade sensuality through carefully crafted encaustic surfaces, which he achieved by blending pigment into hot wax. The first review of his work noted that "the commanding sensuous presence of [the paintings'] primer-like imagery. . .has the rudimentary, irreducible potency of the best of Abstract Expressionism," but that there was added poignancy in the "beloved, handmade transcription of unloved, machine-made images."[64]

Jasper Johns first came to New York from South Carolina in 1948. Six years later, he met Robert Rauschenberg, a meeting that would irrevocably alter the course of American art history. From 1956 to 1961, the two shared loft space in lower Manhattan. During this period, they nourished and encouraged each other in many ways, producing exceptional bodies of work, opening up territory that would be mined by artists for decades.

music, and dance met on the stage. But in Cunningham's work all three arts retained their autonomy, coexisting without necessarily accompanying one another.

James Waring (fig. 128) was another experimental choreographer whose work in the 1950s diverged from mainstream modern dance. He applied collage techniques derived from visual art to his often witty or fantastical choreography, which made use of ballet technique as well as popular dance styles from earlier periods. He also collaborated with contemporary composers (Richard Maxfield and John Herbert McDowell), visual artists and Happenings makers (Jasper Johns, George Brecht, Robert Indiana, Robert Whitman, and Red Grooms), and poets (Diane DiPrima).

Cunningham and Waring were based in New York from the 1940s on. Anna Halprin, working in northern California, was another influential dancer, choreographer, and teacher during this time. Her analytic approach to anatomy and kinesiology and her use of free improvisation and natural settings (her students worked out-of-doors on a mountain platform) led to an intuitive, community-rooted form of dance that blurred boundaries between art and life (fig. 129). Halprin, too, collaborated with painters, musicians, and poets, as well as her husband, the architect Lawrence Halprin. In the early sixties, her students included Simone Forti, Yvonne Rainer, and Robert Morris.

Though different in many respects, Cunningham, Waring, and Halprin were all committed to experimentation—to regenerating dance through infusions of ideas from the broader culture. In this way, they made the fifties a hotbed of revolution. —S. B.

128. *James Waring*, late 1950s–early 1960s Cunningham Dance Foundation, New York

129. Anna Halprin's Dancers' Workshop Multiracial Company in *Parades and Changes*, choreographed by Anna Halprin, 1965, photograph by Paul Fusco/Magnum Photos

130. **Jasper Johns**
Flag, 1954–55 (dated on reverse 1954)
Encaustic, oil, and collage on fabric mounted on plywood, 42¼ x 60⅜ in. (107.3 x 154 cm)
The Museum of Modern Art, New York; Gift of Philip Johnson in honor of Alfred H. Barr, Jr.
© Jasper Johns/Licensed by VAGA, New York, NY

131. **Jasper Johns**
Green Target, 1955
Encaustic on newspaper and cloth over canvas, 60 x 60 in. (152.4 x 152.4 cm)
The Museum of Modern Art, New York; Richard S. Zeisler Fund
© Jasper Johns/Licensed by VAGA, New York, NY

132. **Jasper Johns**
Grey Alphabets, 1956
Beeswax and oil on
newsprint and paper on
canvas, 66⅛ x 48¾ in.
(168 x 123.8 cm)
The Menil Collection,
Houston
© Jasper Johns/Licensed
by VAGA, New York, NY

Rauschenberg was the better known of the two when he and Johns met. He had already shown at the Betty Parsons Gallery, and Leo Castelli had included him in the infamous "Ninth Street Show" in 1951—an exhibition in a vacant East Village storefront space that brought together older Abstract Expressionists with younger artists (fig. 133). The exhibition was so popular that it was continued as an annual salon-type event at Eleanor Ward's Stable Gallery, dominated by a New York School aesthetic. In 1955, Johns submitted work to the show and was rejected. In response, Rauschenberg made and exhibited *Short Circuit* (fig. 134). This altarlike assemblage contained works by artist friends of Rauschenberg: a small Johns flag painting, the first of this series; a painting by Rauschenberg's wife at the time, Susan Weil; as well as a program from a John Cage concert and Judy Garland's signature (a collage by correspondence artist Ray Johnson and a piece by Stan Vanderbeek were not finished in time). By including artists who had been rejected or neglected, Rauschenberg's entry was literally intended to "short-circuit" the selection process of the "Ninth Street Show."[65]

133. Installation view of the "Ninth Street Show" at Leo Castelli Gallery, New York, 1951

At the time of the exhibition, Johns, then only twenty-five, had already produced his breakthrough series of Flags and Targets. Dispensing with the emotional dramatics of the New York School, but retaining the mark of the hand or brushwork, he treated the painting as an object and allowed its literal qualities to dominate. In *Canvas*, for instance, he brought the stretcher bars to the front of the canvas, thus revealing the physical structure of the painting. In a work such as *Flag* (fig. 130), he presented the image-as-object—just as Rauschenberg was presenting the image-as-material. The flag's iconic form corresponds to its depicted shape. Johns' Flags, and the Targets as well, are thus spatial equivalents of their images (fig. 136).

134. **Robert Rauschenberg**
Short Circuit, 1955
Combine painting, 40¾ x 37½ in. (103.5 x 95.3 cm)
Collection of the artist
© Robert Rauschenberg/
Licensed by VAGA, New York, NY

By rejecting the traditional figure-ground relationship in painting—the relationship of a depicted form to the space it inhabits—Johns upset cherished notions about illusion versus reality: are we seeing a rendering of a flag, or a flag? He questioned what an object is and how we know it, and what an image is. His paintings stand as an inquiry into the paradoxical relationship between the object represented and its representation. Johns would later use broad painting strokes—streaks, smears, drips—in a variety of colors as images themselves to parody Abstract Expressionist heroics. But *Painting with Two Balls* (fig. 137) also introduces sexual imagery, another element that persists throughout Johns' work. Personal symbolic references abound, despite the visual air of cool detachment, and we are offered clues and codes that beg deciphering. Johns' layered symbolism was inherited from Duchamp, as was his frequent reference to the body through the inclusion of casts of body parts, handprints, and painted forms. The objecthood of Johns' work would reverberate for decades—in Minimalism, for instance; his use of popular symbols and common images became prototypes for Pop art; and his incorporation of the body established a framework for later generations.

Johns' seminal pieces, such as the Flags and Targets, and Rauschenberg's first Combines were executed around 1955, during the heyday of the Artists' Club and

135. Jasper Johns
Three Flags, 1958
Encaustic on canvas,
30⅞ x 45½ x 5 in.
(78.4 x 115.6 x 12.7 cm)
Whitney Museum of
American Art, New York;
50th Anniversary Gift of
the Gilman Foundation,
Inc., The Lauder
Foundation, A. Alfred
Taubman, an anonymous
donor, and purchase
80.32
© Jasper Johns/Licensed
by VAGA, New York, NY

136. Jasper Johns
Target with Plaster Casts,
1955
Encaustic and collage on
canvas with objects,
51 x 44 x 2½ in.
(129.5 x 111.8 x 6.4 cm)
Collection of David Geffen
© Jasper Johns/Licensed
by VAGA, New York, NY

137. Jasper Johns
Painting with Two Balls,
1960
Encaustic and collage on
canvas with plaster casts,
65 x 54 in. (165.1 x
137.2 cm)
Collection of the artist
© Jasper Johns/Licensed
by VAGA, New York, NY

Cedar Tavern. But neither artist came into wide public prominence until 1958, with their first one-artist exhibitions at the Leo Castelli Gallery. In January 1958, Johns' *Target with Four Faces* was on the cover of *Art News*, and Rauschenberg's *Bed* was reproduced in the *Newsweek* article "Trend to the 'Anti-Art.'" The Museum of Modern Art bought four works from Johns' first exhibition. These events took place as Abstract Expressionism was just beginning to receive broad, international recognition. But the instant notoriety Johns and Rauschenberg achieved in 1958 signaled that a change was already afoot in the American art world. Independently and together, they had transformed American art. Both had introduced things looked at but not really seen and had used literal objects of everyday life and blatant American imagery. The strategies in their hybrid works had reconceptualized traditional genres of art by challenging underlying assumptions about representation. Together with Cage and Cunningham, they initiated a new aesthetic, one based on cool detachment and one diametrically opposed to the emotive dramatics of Abstract Expressionism.

ENVIRONMENTS AND HAPPENINGS

Other artists brought real life into art through the creation of environments—actual spaces, often filled with real objects and materials. These artists, however, many of whom began as assemblage sculptors, used visual strategies that owe more to Abstract Expressionism than to the conceptual framework established by Johns and Rauschenberg. The environments of Allan Kaprow, George Segal, Lucas Samaras, Claes Oldenburg, Jim Dine, and Red Grooms are assembled with a spontaneity, visceral energy, and gestural expressiveness that create a three-dimensional assemblage extension of an Abstract Expressionist sensibility.

The environment had precedents in Kurt Schwitters' room-size *Merzbau* (1924–33), a Constructivist sculpture assembled in his own home out of junk, and in the radical, visionary architecture and exhibition design of Frederick Kiesler, whose works include *Endless House* (fig. 140), an unrealized project for proto-architectural sculpture, and exhibition installations such as "Blood Flames" (fig. 139), in which painted bands of color turned the gallery into a sculptural environment. Even the huge, mural-scale paintings of late Monet or the Abstract Expressionists could be construed as environments. But the environments created by the younger artists, such as Allan Kaprow, conveyed a strong sense of flux, disorder, and impermanence (figs. 141, 142), an effect ill suited to established galleries and museums.

The showcases for this burgeoning art were small, mostly newly formed experimental galleries. Among them, in New York, were the Hansa Gallery (1952), a co-op founded by former students of Hans Hofmann; the Reuben Gallery (1959); the Judson Gallery (1958), in the basement of the Judson Memorial Church; and Red Grooms' City Gallery (at first located in his studio and later transmuted into the Delancey Street Museum). On the West Coast, the Six, Batman, and Dilexi Galleries in San Francisco and the Ferus Gallery in Los Angeles were also hosting

139. **Frederick Kiesler**
Installation of "Blood Flames" at the Hugo Gallery, New York, 1947

140. **Frederick Kiesler**
Model for the Endless House, 1959
Cement and wire mesh with plexiglass,
38 x 97¼ x 42 in.
(96.5 x 247 x 106.7 cm)
Whitney Museum of American Art, New York; Gift of Mrs. Lillian Kiesler 89.8

environments and installations by such assemblagists as Wallace Berman, George Herms, Bruce Conner, and Edward Kienholz. These experimental venues—often the same ones that sponsored Beat poetry readings and independent-film screenings—played a critical role in supporting the expanding American avant-garde. Their vision is all the more astonishing given the noncommercial and ephemeral nature of environments.

Jim Dine's *The House* and Claes Oldenburg's *The Street* (fig. 143) were three-dimensional environments shown at the Judson Gallery in 1960. Both were

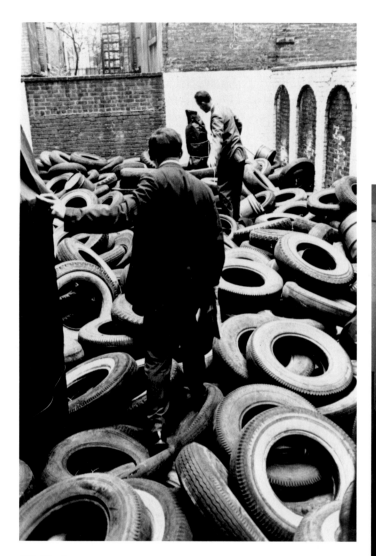

141. **Allan Kaprow**
Yard, 1961
Environment in the
backyard of the Martha
Jackson Gallery, New York
The Getty Research
Institute, Research
Library, Allan Kaprow
Archives, Los Angeles;
Courtesy of Wolfgang
Feelisch, Remscheid,
Germany
Photograph © Robert R.
McElroy/Licensed by
VAGA, New York, NY

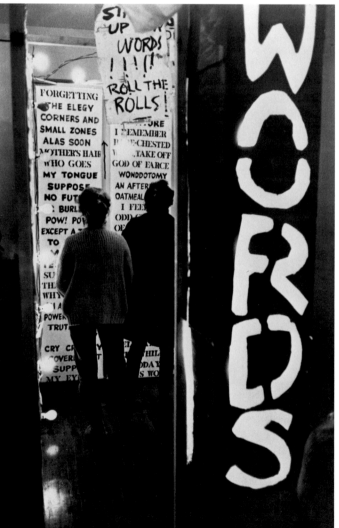

142. **Allan Kaprow**
Words, 1962
Environment at the
Smolin Gallery, New York
The Getty Research
Institute, Research
Library, Allan Kaprow
Archives, Los Angeles
Photograph © Robert R.
McElroy/Licensed by
VAGA, New York, NY

143. **Claes Oldenburg**
The Street, 1960
Performance at the Judson
Gallery, Judson Memorial
Church, New York,
photograph by Martha
Holmes

essentially assemblage spaces heavily encrusted with accumulations of found objects. *The House* used scavenged things such as bedsprings and newspapers, while *The Street*, an epic construction of paint on cardboard and newspaper, included drawings of standing, lying, and running figures, signs, marquees, and metamorphosed objects: cigar butts, houses, towers, and cars (fig. 143). Dine and Oldenburg both used urban cast-offs such as rags, cardboard, crates, string, and newspaper to achieve a crude, textural richness and a new palette of browns, blacks, and grays that some viewed as a continuation of the realism of the earlier twentieth-century Ashcan School. In an ecstatic list reminiscent of Jack Kerouac's description of Robert Frank's photographs, Oldenburg described the contrasts, excitement, and rhythms of the street, the tide of life that would be embodied in his installation:

144. **Edward Kienholz**
The Beanery, 1965
Mixed-media environment,
84 x 72 x 22 in. (213.4 x
182.9 x 55.9 cm)
Stedelijk Museum,
Amsterdam

> There will be men and women and heroes and bums and children and drunks and cripples and streetchicks and boxers and walkers and sitters and spitters and trucks and cars and bikes and manholes and stoplights and shadows and cats and doggys and bright light and darkness; fires and collisions and cockroaches and mornings and evenings and guns and newspapers and pissers and cops and mamagangers and a lot more etc.[66]

For Oldenburg and other artists, the street was a microcosm of the world and the cycle of life—a place of impermanence and excitation. Like the work of the Beats before him, Oldenburg's art was one of a brutally honest realism:

> I am for an art that imitates the human, that is comic, if necessary, or violent, or whatever is necessary. I am for an art that takes its form from the lines of life itself, that twists and extends and accumulates and spits and drips, and is heavy and coarse and blunt and sweet and stupid as life itself.[67]

Edward Kienholz shared Oldenburg's taste for an honest view of all sides of human nature. In his room-scale tableaux of the early sixties, the sordid nature of humanity is conveyed through the searing graphic detail of a freak show. Kienholz was the most important West Coast assemblage artist to extend his work into environments that engaged the body and mind. In *Roxy's*, a re-creation of an Idaho whorehouse, the madam has a boar skull for a head and is surrounded by other chilling hybrid figures, among them Five Dollar Billy with the word "fuck" carved on his base. Kienholz's work is a theater of cruelty suffused with social satire, commenting on capital punishment, illegal abortions, bigotry, and other forms of human degradation. In *The Beanery*, he re-created a West Hollywood bar and café out of junk (fig. 144). This walk-through work features patrons with clocks in place of faces. Time is frozen at 10:10. The palpable presence of death is accompanied by an audiotape of music, clinking glasses, and laughter.

145. **Allan Kaprow**
Environment for *18 Happenings in 6 Parts*, 1959
Happening at the Reuben Gallery, New York
The Getty Research Institute, Research Library, Allan Kaprow Archives, Los Angeles

The elaborate and spontaneous tableaux of Claes Oldenburg, Jim Dine, Robert Whitman, Allan Kaprow, and Red Grooms (fig. 151) soon became a stage for public events that led to the emergence of a new art form called Happenings. Happenings, in which the event itself was dominant, grew out of Action Painting and junk environments in combination with John Cage's aesthetic philosophy.

Kaprow, one of Cage's students, had early on seen the potential for literalizing

145. **Allan Kaprow**
Environment for *18 Happenings in 6 Parts*, 1959
Happening at the Reuben Gallery, New York
The Getty Research Institute, Research Library, Allan Kaprow Archives, Los Angeles

Action Painting—by extending the performative aspect of Abstract Expressionism into both three-dimensional environments and live-performance events for an audience. He envisioned Jackson Pollock's expansive movements carried forward through "total art" in "entirely unheard of happenings and events, found in garbage cans, police files, hotel lobbies, seen in store windows and on the streets, and sensed in dreams and horrible accidents."[68]

The first self-described Happening was Kaprow's *18 Happenings in 6 Parts*, presented for the opening of the Reuben Gallery in 1959 (fig. 145). Translucent

146. **Claes Oldenburg**
Snapshots from the City, from *Ray Gun Spex*, 1960
Performances at the Judson Gallery, Judson Memorial Church, New York, photograph by Martha Holmes

147. **Claes Oldenburg**
World's Fair II, from *Ray Gun Theater*, 1962
Series of ten performances at 107 East 2nd Street, New York
Photograph © Robert R. McElroy/Licensed by VAGA, New York, NY

New
Frontiers
1960–1967

The 1960s opened with the inauguration of President John F. Kennedy in January 1961—at forty-three, the nation's youngest president. His youth, energy, and charisma inspired confidence and enthusiasm at a time of increasing political and economic influence for the United States. Kennedy's tenure in office was marked by several events that reinforced America's sense of self-assurance in the international sphere. In 1962, when it was discovered that the Soviet Union had installed missiles in Cuba, the president forced the Russians to remove them in a tense encounter that Kennedy won through diplomacy, dialogue, and restraint. The following year, the Soviet Union and the United States signed the Nuclear Test Ban Treaty, an important, if short-lived, relaxation of Cold War tensions. And nothing symbolizes the spirit of the time more than Kennedy's enthusiastic support for the space program, including his ambitious goal of landing Americans on the moon before the end of the decade.

Kennedy also initiated two important pieces of domestic legislation: a tax-cut bill, which stimulated the economy and put money back into the hands of the middle class and corporate America; and the more important civil rights bills, which were ultimately pushed through Congress by his successor, Lyndon B. Johnson. Kennedy had won 70 percent of the black vote in the election, but moved cautiously at first on civil rights reforms, believing that black America should develop

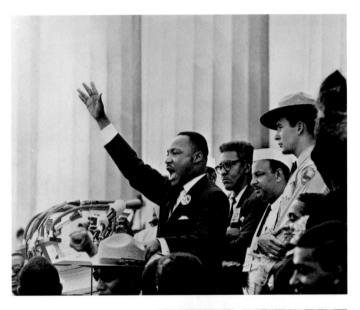

161. *Martin Luther King, Jr., Delivering His "I Have A Dream" Speech on the Steps of the Lincoln Memorial, Washington, D.C.*, 1963, photograph by Bob Adelman

162. *John F. Kennedy's Funeral Procession*, 1963

political power through the polls. Only after riots broke out in Birmingham, Alabama, did Kennedy consider serious civil rights legislation. The 1963 march on Washington, D.C., at which Martin Luther King, Jr., delivered his famous "I Have a Dream" speech (fig. 161), galvanized support for civil rights reforms.

John F. Kennedy is also recognized as the first president to fully understand and exploit the power of television. During the election campaign, he debated with the Republican candidate Richard Nixon on live television, and his striking physical presence helped win him votes (fig. 163). In 1962, Jackie Kennedy gave a televised tour of the newly redecorated White House, bringing the domestic milieu of the First Family into the homes of every American. The Camelot years, as they have come to be known, formed a media event in which the entire nation participated—as it did during the tragic days of November 1963, after Kennedy was assassinated, when tens of millions of people watched clips of the shooting over and over again, and attended the solemn funeral through broadcast television (fig. 162).

As Kennedy understood, the power and the influence of the media was here to stay. The media fed the consumer culture through advertising and the promotion of a lifestyle that encouraged spending on both necessities and luxuries. By 1960, the acquisition of manufactured goods was becoming a national pastime.

Television sets and cars joined apple pie and the flag as quintessential symbols of America.

The culture of consumption had begun to transform America drastically in the fifties. McDonald's was founded in 1955, and the Disneyland Park opened the same year (fig. 164). Standardization and mass production reinforced the status quo, while allowing higher-quality goods to reach ever-larger audiences at home and abroad. Everyone could enjoy a hamburger or a Coke, and, as Andy Warhol said, they tasted the same to the queen of England and the man on the street.

Cognizant of the fierce competition to reach this burgeoning consumer culture, companies employed brilliant designers such as Charles Eames and Donald Deskey to distinguish their products (fig. 166). Many of the era's classic products (the Bertoia chair, Eames lounge chair, Saarinen pedestal table) and packaging designs (Crest, Tide [fig. 165], Brillo, Heinz Catsup, Coca-Cola) are still in production and on the shelves with only slight updatings forty years later.

Promotion, advertising, and market research became billion-dollar industries designed to persuade consumers to buy, even if it meant using sublimated messages and unrealistic promises. A new shampoo could bring you romance, a new laundry detergent a happier home, and a brand of cigarettes greater virility. Motivational analysts were called on to find ways to sell by manipulating subconscious fears, desires, guilt feelings, and anxieties.[72] The imagery of advertising had become so pervasive—and invasive—that it was an essential feature of American life and identity.

163. *Televised Debate Between Vice President Richard M. Nixon and Senator John F. Kennedy*, 1960
UPI/Corbis-Bettman

164. *McDonald's Restaurant, Des Plaines, Illinois*, c. 1955–56

165. *Tide Box*, 1958
Procter & Gamble
Archives, Cincinnati

166. *Donald Deskey with Packaging Designs for Procter & Gamble*, 1950s
Procter & Gamble
Archives, Cincinnati

THE 1964 WORLD'S FAIR

The look and atmosphere of the 1964 World's Fair in Flushing Meadows, New York (fig. 167), reflected the new consumer landscape. The 1939 World's Fair, held on the same grounds, had been seen as a beacon of light out of the Depression. The 1964 Fair, by contrast, celebrated the success and monopoly of big business. Robert Moses, president of the Fair, fostered free-market competition. Most of the pavilions were devoted to corporate giants such as General Electric, IBM, Ford, General Motors (GM), Goodyear, and DuPont. Images of consumption in the design of the pavilions were as evident as in Pop art: the Goodyear Ferris wheel in the shape of a tire; the IBM building (designed by Eero Saarinen and Charles Eames) resembling the new Selectric typewriter ball; the GM building's cantilevered, curving wall that inclined away from its base to look like an automobile tail fin. These buildings were blatant advertisements—architecture as signs, in keeping with the developing roadside architecture of the commercial strip or the crazy, fanciful commercial imagery of Las Vegas architecture, which would soon be mined by Pop architects such as Robert Venturi.

167. **Gilmore D. Clarke** and **Peter Muller-Munk Associates**
Unisphere, from the 1964 World's Fair, New York
World's Fair Archives, The Queens Museum of Art, New York

The published themes for the Fair were "achievements in an expanding universe," "peace through understanding," and "it's a small world," all reinforcing the old credo that progress through science and technology would unite the world, that new technologies and broadening communications would foster greater understanding and peace and turn the world into a global village.

Another infatuation of the World's Fair was the new phenomenon of space exploration, following Alan Shepard's foray into space in 1961. Numerous displays, exhibits, and simulated rides into space dominated the Fair. New technologies and communications tools were also featured as the information age dawned: satellites, lasers, undersea cables, computers, photocopying machines, and nuclear power. The Fair also became an occasion to introduce innovative products such as recycling machines, synthetic heart valves, synthetic polymers for clothing, and plastics.

The environmental implications and potential disasters lurking behind these new technologies were not yet comprehended by the public, which accepted the inventions as evidence of progress. It was not until the disasters of Vietnam, the energy crisis, Three Mile Island, Love Canal, acid rain, the hole in the ozone layer, the Star Wars weapons program, Bhopal, Chernobyl, and the explosion of the space shuttle *Challenger* that Americans began to question their naive and idealistic views about the wonders of technology and started to seriously weigh the risks.

Unlike the 1939 World's Fair, the 1964 version was architecturally undistinguished, even banal. Robert Moses had rejected several visionary proposals by Walter Dorwin Teague and Paul Rudolph, and was not particularly interested in incorporating fine art within the Fair, as had been done in 1939 under his stewardship. His lack of enthusiasm may have resulted from frustrated efforts to persuade Joseph Hirshhorn to place his collection in a pavilion that would become a permanent museum in Queens. (Hirshhorn's collection later went to the Smithsonian Institution in Washington, D.C., as the Hirshhorn Museum and Sculpture Garden.) Moses did however negotiate with the Vatican to bring some of their treasures to the Fair—including Michelangelo's *Pietà*, which drew record crowds who passed by the sculpture on a moving platform. In addition, the Spanish Pavilion, featuring masterpieces by Goya, Velázquez, Picasso, and Miró, was a very popular attraction. The general public was clearly growing interested in art, especially art it could recognize as great.

The architect Philip Johnson, who designed the New York State Pavilion, took some initiative in the direction of contemporary art by inviting several Pop artists to contribute murals and sculptures to the circular facade of the theater: Andy Warhol, Roy Lichtenstein (fig. 168), James Rosenquist, Robert Indiana, Robert Rauschenberg, and John Chamberlain. Warhol's contribution, a mural entitled *Thirteen Most Wanted Men* (fig. 169), was painted over within a few days for political reasons (New York's Governor Nelson Rockefeller feared lawsuits because many of the depicted were reputed Mafiosi, some of whom had been vindicated by the courts). The mural also stood as a reminder of unpleasant social problems nowhere else in evidence at the Fair. —L. P.

Pop Culture Reigns

Pop art, building on the explorations of Johns, Rauschenberg, and the assemblagists, originated as yet another effort to bring art and life into intimate proximity. But rather than reject the materialism that had come to pervade American culture, Pop embraced it by taking consumer packaging and products as well as media icons as source material for a cool, mechanical art. This practice set Pop apart from earlier vanguard movements, which for most of the century had explored various forms of abstraction. Pop was the first representational movement that looked revolutionary rather than reactionary since Stuart Davis and Charles Demuth had celebrated the American vernacular and commercial culture in the 1920s and 1930s.

The Pop artists—Claes Oldenburg, Jim Dine, George Segal, Roy Lichtenstein, Tom Wesselmann, James Rosenquist, Robert Indiana, Richard Artschwager (fig. 183), Marisol (fig. 174), Ed Ruscha, and Andy Warhol—used unprivileged, common images from mass culture and from the man-made environment to create a distinctly American art form. They were responding to the new American visual landscape, a vista of advertising, billboards, commercial products, automobiles, strip malls, fast food, television, and comic strips (figs. 176, 178). They therefore took print, film, and television images from media-based reality and transformed them into art, often through various mechanical means. Their pictures were often images of images, copies of copies, a twice-removed effect that echoed the techniques of mass production, the media, and marketing.

170. **Andy Warhol**
Dick Tracy, 1960
Acrylic on canvas, 79 x
45 in. (200.7 x 114.3 cm)
Collection of David Geffen

Given their commercial-based techniques and imagery, it is not surprising to find that many of the Pop artists, including Warhol, Lichtenstein, Rosenquist, and Ruscha, had worked as commercial artists, doing advertising illustrations, layout designs, or painting billboards. Rauschenberg and Johns (under the joint pseudonym Matson Jones), Warhol, and Rosenquist all designed window displays for Bonwit Teller and Tiffany's (figs. 177, 179). From this firsthand experience, they understood not only the techniques of display but the importance of presentation. To them, art was another product in the consumer landscape.

The mechanical, impersonal style of imagery associated with Pop masks its history. In fact, the earliest manifestations of Pop art (1958–62) show a connection

171. **Robert Rauschenberg**
Retroactive I, 1964
Oil on canvas, 84 x 60 in.
(213.4 x 152.4 cm)
Wadsworth Atheneum,
Hartford; Gift of Susan
Morse Hilles
© Robert Rauschenberg/
Licensed by VAGA, New
York, NY

178. **Ed Ruscha**
Standard, Amarillo, Texas
(printed 1989), from the
portfolio *Twenty-six Gasoline
Stations*, 1962
Gelatin silver print, 10¼ x
10¾ in. (26 x 27.3 cm)
Collection of Emily Fisher
Landau

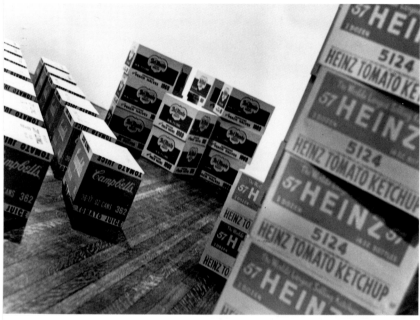

176. **Andy Warhol**
Installation view of
Campbell's Soup Cans,
Del Monte, and *Heinz 57
Boxes* at the Stable
Gallery, New York, 1964,
photograph by Billy Name

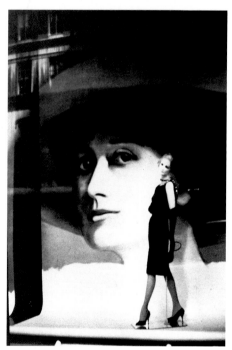

177. **James Rosenquist**
*Window Display for Bonwit
Teller, New York*, 1959
© James Rosenquist/
Licensed by VAGA, New
York, NY

179. **Andy Warhol**
*Window Display for Bonwit
Teller, New York*, 1961

to Abstract Expressionism in their relatively loose, hand-painted, often gestural character. Andy Warhol painted his early images of dance step diagrams, comic strips, and advertisements by hand (figs. 170, 184). Handwork was also evident in Oldenburg's and Dine's gestural style, beginning with their environments and Happenings and continuing into the early sixties with Oldenburg's painted plaster sculpture and Dine's monochromatic paintings with objects attached (fig. 173). Roy Lichtenstein, too, used expressionist gestures in his early cartoon drawings. They were all strongly influenced by Rauschenberg and Johns, who had in the fifties incorporated familiar popular icons such as the American flag and the Coca-Cola bottle into their work, transformed by smears, drools, and the alchemy of paint. Even earlier, the master of Action Painting himself, Willem de Kooning, not impervious to the power of mass culture and advertising, had collaged a woman's mouth

from a Camel cigarette ad onto one of his earliest studies for the Woman series (figs. 180, 181).

In 1962, the connection to Abstract Expressionist rituals of painting was severed when both Warhol and Rauschenberg introduced their photo-silkscreen paintings. This technique enabled them to transfer photographic images directly onto the surface of the canvas. There has been some confusion about where the silkscreen transfer idea originated, since Warhol both credited himself with the invention and admitted having gotten the idea from Rauschenberg. As early as 1958, Rauschenberg had begun to transfer photographic images from newspapers and magazines onto paper by using

180. *Camel Cigarette Advertisement*, 1949 (detail)
General Research Division, The New York Public Library, Astor, Lenox and Tilden Foundations

181. **Willem de Kooning** *Woman*, 1950
Oil, enamel, and pasted paper on paper, 14¾ x 11⅝ in. (37.5 x 29.5 cm)
Collection of Thomas B. Hess, jointly owned by The Metropolitan Museum of Art, New York, and the heirs of Thomas B. Hess

lighter fluid as a solvent to absorb the image and then rubbing the reverse side to transfer it. These "photo transfers" are the clear precedent for what the photo-silkscreens in 1962 accomplished on a much larger scale. The canvas became a surface onto which data was entered. Colliding and abundant fragments of visual information from magazines, movie stills, and tabloids were not attached and glued to the canvas as collage elements, but were appropriated as ready-made images and mechanically transferred onto the surface.

Rauschenberg's canvases were loaded with image shards, incorporating the sensory world in an inclusive Walt Whitmanesque spirit of democracy. His scrapyard of images produced a buzz—a kind of visual interference on the pictorial surface that alluded to the space of a billboard, television, or projection screen (fig. 171). These products of the technological age replaced the mirror and the window as models of pictorial space. The surface of the painting now received a kaleidoscope of information, a process that created what the art historian Leo Steinberg called a "flatbed picture plane." He further observed that this flatbed picture plane was a metaphor for the contemporary mind itself—a "running transformer of the external world, constantly ingesting incoming unprocessed data to be mapped in an overcharged field."[73]

If Rauschenberg's flatbed picture plane stood for the contemporary mind, then Warhol's silkscreen paintings implied the merging of mind and machine. Warhol's use of the photosilkscreen introduced a whole new ethic, dramatized by one of his

182. **Claes Oldenburg**
Bedroom Ensemble,
Replica I, 1969
Mixed-media environment,
303 x 512 x 648 in.
(769.6 x 1300.5 x
1645.9 cm)
Museum für Moderne
Kunst, Frankfurt am Main

183. **Richard Artschwager**
Le Frak City, 1962
Acrylic, celotex, and
Formica, 44½ x 97½ in.
(113 x 247.7 cm)
Collection of Irma and
Norman Braman

184. **Andy Warhol**
Icebox, 1961
Oil, ink, and graphite on
canvas, 67 x 53⅛ in.
(170.2 x 134.9 cm)
The Menil Collection,
Houston

characteristically blunt statements: "Paintings are too hard. The things I want to show are mechanical. Machines have less problems. I'd like to be a machine, wouldn't you?"[74] Instead of a collage-style agglomeration of images, Warhol selected a single image—Marilyn Monroe, a Campbell's soup can, a Coke bottle—and either presented it alone as an icon or repeated it in a gridlike formation, like a proof sheet from a high-speed press (figs. 185, 187, 188). Warhol also made endless variations of the same image, as if he were thinking in terms of print multiples on canvas. He also applied the technique to wallpaper (fig. 186). And he profoundly rejected the idea of individual creativity by employing assistants. Since the means of production were mechanical, these assistants often had as much of a "hand" in the final work as he did—a far cry from the Abstract Expressionist myth of the artist laboring alone in his studio, expressing existential angst through gestures on

185. **Andy Warhol**
Installation view of
Campbell's Soup Cans at
the Ferus Gallery, Los
Angeles, 1962

187. **Andy Warhol**
*Twenty-five Colored
Marilyns*, 1962
Acrylic on canvas, 82¼ x
66¾ x 1⅜ in. (208.9 x
169.5 x 3.5 cm)
Modern Art Museum of Fort
Worth, Texas; Purchase,
The Benjamin J. Tillar
Memorial Trust, acquired
from the Collection of
Vernon Nikkel, Clovis, New
Mexico

186. **Andy Warhol**
Installation view of *Cow
Wallpaper* at the Leo
Castelli Gallery, New York,
1966

188. **Andy Warhol**
Green Coca-Cola Bottles,
1962
Oil on canvas, 82½ x 57
in. (209.6 x 144.8 cm)
Whitney Museum of
American Art, New York;
Purchase, with funds from
the Friends of the Whitney
Museum of American Art
68.25

189. *Andy Warhol at the Factory*, 1966
PaceWildensteinMacGill, New York
© Stephen Shore

WARHOL'S FACTORY: THE MANUFACTURE OF ART AND IMAGE

In late 1963, Andy Warhol moved his studio to the top floor of a former hat factory at 231 East 47th Street, New York. Leaving the 4,000-square-foot floor open, partitioned only by mirrors and screens, he engaged a twenty-one-year-old hairdresser and lighting man named Billy Linich (later known as Billy Name) to cover the pipes, windows, ceiling, and crumbling brick walls with silver foil. Whatever could not be covered by foil—floor, cabinets, and a pay phone—was painted silver. Reflective surfaces extended to the bathroom, where even the toilet bowl was silver. A multifaceted ballroom globe hanging from the ceiling revolved slowly, throwing light irregularly throughout the darkened space. Warhol commented on his unusual choice of color: "It must have been the amphetamine but it was the perfect time to think silver. Silver was the future, it was spacey—the astronauts. . . . And silver was also the past—the Silver Screen. . . . And maybe more than anything else, silver was narcissism—mirrors were backed with silver" (fig. 189).

190. *Andy Warhol and Gerard Malanga Screenprinting Campbell's Soup Can Paintings*, c. 1964–65

Making reference to its previous function, Warhol's coterie dubbed this insular, self-reflexive environment the silver Factory, or simply the Factory. With an appellation connoting the efficiency and conformity advocated by corporate America, and an ambience redolent of drug use and self-indulgent behavior, the Factory provided a paradoxical new model of the artist's studio that consciously subverted those of the preceding decade. Warhol produced some of his best-known series here, including the Brillo Box sculptures, the Jackie paintings, and the Flower paintings, all images drawn from the worlds of advertising and media. In keeping with their site of production, they were made with the help of his assistant, a poet named Gerard Malanga, among others (fig. 190).

During his four years at the 47th Street Factory, Warhol also directed and produced over fifty films, including *Empire*, *Henry Geldzahler*, *Poor Little Rich Girl*, *The Velvet Underground and Nico*, *The Chelsea Girls*, and *24 Hour Movie*. It was an intensely social place, populated by a cross section of downtown bohemians and uptown socialites—

canvas. Together, Warhol and a succession of assistants cranked out paintings—sometimes as many as eighty a day—in assembly-line fashion in his East 47th Street studio, a workplace appropriately called the Factory.

In the fall of 1962, just as Rauschenberg and Warhol were completing their first silkscreen paintings, Pop art entered public consciousness with a bang through the "New Realists" exhibition at the Sidney Janis Gallery, New York (fig. 192). The artists' blatant, unapologetic reference to mass and consumer culture "hit the New York art world with the force of an earthquake."[75] Janis had previously shown and represented many of the leaders of Abstract Expressionism, but when this show opened, all of them left the gallery in protest, with the exception of de Kooning.[76]

The "New Realists" exhibition introduced the American Pop artists Andy Warhol, Roy Lichtenstein, James Rosenquist, Tom Wesselmann, Jim Dine, Claes Oldenburg, Robert Indiana, George Segal, and Wayne Thiebaud alongside European Nouveaux Réalistes—Arman, Jean Tinguely, Daniel Spoerri, Yves Klein, Martial Rayasse, and Raymond Hains—in an effort to put the Americans in a broader international context. But it was nonetheless clear that a fresh, new American art had arrived, one that was democratic in spirit and validated commercial art and consumer life as high art. Most of the work by Americans in the show featured domestic scenes and common household appliances such as Lichtenstein's *Refrigerator* (fig. 193), Oldenburg's plaster sculpture *The Stove*, Jim Dine's assemblage *Four Soap Dishes*, Segal's plaster and wood tableaux *The Dinner Table*, and Thiebaud's painting *Salad, Sandwiches, and Desserts*. These subjects, drawn from a much larger repertoire of consumer products, were presented in a cool, deadpan style, often using methods drawn from commercial printing (Lichtenstein's Benday dots), billboards (Rosenquist's oversize details and fragments of everyday life [figs. 195–97]), or signage (Indiana's crisp, vibrant graphics, fig. 220). Even Dine and Oldenburg had cleaned up their earlier messy, expressionistic style into a hard-edge, hygienic presentation.

both groups marginal from a mainstream perspective—as well as rock musicians such as Mick Jagger, Lou Reed, and Jim Morrison (fig. 191). From this varied mix of local talent, Warhol selected actors and actresses to star in his largely improvisational films. He was as interested in manufacturing celebrity as in producing the films themselves. Naomi Levine, Baby Jane Holzer, Edie Sedgwick, Brigid Polk, and Viva are some of the best-known underground celebrities—superstars who enjoyed their fifteen minutes of fame.

Early in 1968, Warhol moved the Factory to 33 Union Square West. Six months later, he was shot by Valerie Solanas, a Factory habitué who wanted to be in his films. Although Warhol recovered and continued to direct the new Factory, it never fully recaptured the distinctive energy and vitality of its former years. —E. T.

191. *The Velvet Underground and Nico in Hollywood*, 1966, photograph by Gerard Malanga

192. Installation view of "The New Realists" at the Sidney Janis Gallery, New York, 1962

193. **Roy Lichtenstein**
The Refrigerator, 1962
Oil on canvas, 68 x 56 in.
(172.7 x 142.2 cm)
© Estate of Roy
Lichtenstein

194. **Wayne Thiebaud**
Desserts, 1961
Oil on canvas, 24⅛ x
30⅛ in. (61.3 x 76.5 cm)
PaineWebber Group Inc.,
New York

195. **Tom Wesselmann**
*Great American Nude
#57*, 1964
Synthetic polymer paint
on board, 48 x 65 in.
(121.9 x 165.1 cm)
Whitney Museum of
American Art, New York;
Purchase, with funds from
the Friends of the Whitney
Museum of American Art
65.10
© Tom Wesselmann/
Licensed by VAGA, New
York, NY

196. **Tom Wesselmann**
Still Life Number 36, 1964
Oil and collage on canvas,
four panels, 120 x 192¼ in.
(304.8 x 488.3 cm) overall
Whitney Museum of
American Art, New York;
Gift of the artist 69.151
© Tom Wesselmann/
Licensed by VAGA, New
York, NY

197. James Rosenquist
President Elect, 1960
Oil on masonite, three
panels, 84 x 144 in. (213.4
x 365.8 cm) overall
Musée national d'art
moderne, Centre Georges
Pompidou, Paris
© James Rosenquist/
Licensed by VAGA, New
York, NY

With this exhibition, the Pop artists were thrust into the spotlight and were quickly embraced by dealers, collectors, institutions, and the media. Glossy magazines covered this new phenomenon, nouveau riche collectors clamored for it, and people who didn't know much about art responded to it because it depicted something familiar, something they knew. But one group that did not jump on the bandwagon was the art critics. First of all, Pop was an affront to all those who had supported the humanistic values of Abstract Expressionism. Many thought that the Pop artists' uncritical embrace of consumer culture was tantamount to saying, "If you can't beat it, join it." The British scholar and critic Herbert Read wrote that they were "sacrificing formal rigor" and represented "novelty as distinct from originality."[77] He lamented the lack of a heroic and mythic dimension. Pop was an avant-garde movement that did not follow the modernist prescriptions for aesthetic and utopian monumentality. Most important, it seemed to glorify rather than to critique consumerism, conflating forms of high and mass culture that significantly "served the latter's commodity production as a virtual laboratory of new forms and fashions."[78] The conservative editor of *Arts Magazine*, Hilton Kramer, felt Pop's "social effect is simply to reconcile us to a world of commodities, banalities and vulgarities—which is to say, an effect indistinguishable from advertising art."[79] Another major objection to Pop art was that it did not seem to transform the imagery it appropriated—a deficiency, critics felt, that reduced Pop to something inauthentic, to mere copying. Art historian Dore Ashton exclaimed, "The attitude of the pop artist is diffident. He doesn't aspire to interpret or re-present, but only to present."[80]

Critics saw Pop as decadent, immoral, anti-humanistic, and even nihilistic. They could not abide its apparent transgression of good taste. Some also puzzled at the public's acceptance of Pop, which they took as a signal that "the nature of art collecting, which for centuries meant the gathering together of rare and beautiful objects, has changed in recent years."[81]

These diatribes notwithstanding, Pop continued to captivate audiences in America and abroad, dealing a serious blow to the credibility of the critical establishment. Of course, the artists did have their adherents and champions, including the British critic and Guggenheim Museum curator Lawrence Alloway. It was Alloway, in fact, who first used the term "Pop art" in print, in 1958, in reference to the British Independents Group, whose London exhibition "This Is Tomorrow" had demonstrated early Pop tendencies and the use of images from the mass media. Other Pop advocates included Henry Geldzahler, the young associate curator at The Metropolitan Museum of Art, and Alan Solomon, curator at The Jewish Museum. They acknowledged Pop's underlying ambivalence between celebration and irony—and considered this ambivalence a key to its strength.

Pop art's success in the market was fostered by a new generation of dealers (Allan Stone, Martha Jackson, Richard Bellamy, Sidney Janis, Eleanor Ward, Ivan Karp, Irving Blum, and Leo Castelli) and self-made collectors (Robert Scull, Frederick Weisman, and Ben Heller), who saw collecting as a means to social status. The support of curators, collectors, and dealers more than compensated for the lack of critical affirmation. The new breed of dealers, with Leo Castelli leading the pack, understood the virtues of clever marketing, promotion, and salesmanship. Their sometimes brash approach was as much at odds with the past as the art itself was. Jasper Johns' famous sculpture of Ballantine Ale cans (fig. 198) was a response to de Kooning's quip about Castelli: "That son-of-a-bitch; you could give him two

198. **Jasper Johns**
Painted Bronze (Ale Cans), 1960
Oil on bronze, 5½ x 8 x 4¾ in. (14 x 20.3 x 12.1 cm)
Museum Ludwig, Cologne
© Jasper Johns/Licensed by VAGA, New York, NY

199. **Andy Warhol**
Ethel Scull 36 Times,
1963
Synthetic polymer
paint silkscreened on
canvas,
79¾ x 143¼ in.
(202.6 x 363.9 cm)
Whitney Museum of
American Art, New
York; Gift of Ethel
Redner Scull
86.61a–jj

beer cans and he could sell them."[82] Castelli used his European connections to promote Pop art abroad—particularly through the Paris gallery of his ex-wife, Ileana
Sonnabend. He developed a network of satellite gallery affiliates throughout the
world, ensuring his artists maximum exposure.[83]

But the artists also understood the benefits of promotion, and as they became
increasingly visible public figures, they learned how to capitalize on the power of
the media. They courted public attention, giving numerous interviews in mass-
circulation magazines, which preempted the negative response of the critics. These
artists could speak directly to their public, without the mediation of professional
interpreters—a phenomenon that dramatically changed the way artists perceived
themselves in society.

Of all the Pop artists, Andy Warhol was the one who most brilliantly exploited
and transformed the culture industry by perfecting the art of publicity. He understood the cult of persona and mined it by celebrating celebrity in his portraits of
"superstars" (a term he coined), such as Elizabeth Taylor, Marilyn Monroe, Elvis
Presley, and Marlon Brando, as well as prominent social figures and friends (fig.
199). He also cultivated his own persona. He was a unique character—cool, pallid,
passive, asexual, with signature eccentric habits such as sporting a silver wig and
speaking in monosyllables. Warhol's ultimate product was himself. He even took
to sending out a double to lecture for him on college campuses. With his entourage
of handsome boys, artists, drag queens, and rock stars (fig. 191), he never failed to
infuse a charge into any social gathering. It was inevitable that, with such a keen
understanding of celebrity, Warhol would soon move directly into the mass media,
directing films such as *The Chelsea Girls* (figs. 200, 201), the first commercially
successful underground film, and in the fall of 1969 publishing his own magazine,
Interview, to give people what he called their "fifteen minutes" of fame (fig. 203).

Regarding his entrepreneurial spirit, Warhol later confessed, "Business art is
the step that comes after Art. I started as a commercial artist, and I want to finish
as a business artist. . . .Being good in business is the most fascinating kind of art."[84]
He was a genius at tapping into the zeitgeist, soliciting suggestions, and putting
other people's ideas into practice. Critics found this particularly galling. It appeared
that he lacked not only technical skills but ideas as well. Over time, it has become

200. **Andy Warhol**
Nico in *Nico Crying*, from
The Chelsea Girls, 1966
© 1967, The Andy Warhol
Museum, Pittsburgh,
A Museum of Carnegie
Institute

201. **Andy Warhol**
Ondine in *The Pope
Ondine Story*, from *The
Chelsea Girls*, 1966
© 1967, The Andy Warhol
Museum, Pittsburgh,
A Museum of Carnegie
Institute

202. *Banner for an Andy
Warhol Event, New York*,
1966
Photograph copyright ©
Fred W. McDarrah

203. The first issue of
Interview magazine, 1969

clear that Warhol lacked neither. Rather, he was a brilliant and complex individual who permanently altered the relationship between art and society through his brazen love of money, famous people, and superstar status. He reflected something at work in the culture at large—the notion that celebrity had replaced genius as the new authority.

Pop art also signaled a change in the economic structure of the art world: for the first time, an avant-garde art movement was both the height of "chic" and embraced by upper-middle class urban sophisticates, who flocked to super-charged openings in droves. Sales of works—such as Rosenquist's *F-III* (fig. 218) to Robert Scull for $60,000—were covered on the front page of *The New York Times* and in *Time* magazine.[85] Contemporary art became big business, hard currency, a profitable investment, and a speculative growth stock during the boom years of the sixties. The "art public" was no longer a select, small group, as Allan Kaprow observed,

> upon whom an artist can depend for a stock response, favorable or otherwise. It is now a large, diffused mass, soon to be called "the public-in-general." This expanding audience [is] comprised of readers of the weeklies, viewers of T.V., visitors to Worlds Fairs here and abroad, members of "culture" clubs and subscribers to mail-order art lessons, charitable organizations, civic-improvement committees, political campaigners, schools and universities—

AMERICAN UNDERGROUND CINEMA: 1960–1968

The exuberant, carnivalesque atmosphere of the early 1960s produced a rich mixture of new alternative practices and an unprecedented crossover between different artistic media, out of which emerged the avant-garde genre that came to be known as underground film. Centered in New York, it began in 1959 with Robert Frank and Alfred Leslie's Beat film *Pull My Daisy* (fig. 90) and soon gained notoriety for its sexually explicit imagery. By the end of the 1960s, with the loosening of censorship laws, the movement petered out. Underground film developed alongside, and was influenced by, Performance art, Happenings, Pop, Fluxus, alternative theater, rock music, and dance, as well as by the new civil rights movement and hallucinogenic drugs, forming a key strand in early sixties counterculture. Filmmaking became an improvisational activity, a performance. Between 1962 and 1966, a group of artists, poets, musicians, writers, and scientists—including Nam June Paik, Yoko Ono, Paul Sharits, George Brecht, George Maciunas, Robert Watts, and Mieko (Chieko) Shiomi—made forty short Fluxfilms, experimental conceptual pieces often focused on a single performative action.

In 1962, Jonas Mekas, Stan Brakhage, Shirley Clarke, and others established the Film-makers' Cooperative, which replaced Amos Vogel's Cinema 16 and was unique in its practice of accepting and distributing all submitted films. As performance and Happenings took place in alternative spaces, so Mekas screened underground film in various small cinemas around New York.

The counterculture of the early sixties challenged middle-class taste and standards by celebrating, among other things, the "grotesque" body and the sexual body as sources of power and symbols of liberation. Many of the films screened by Mekas—Jack Smith's *Flaming Creatures* (fig. 204), Andy Warhol's early films *Kiss* (1963) and *Blow Job* (1964), Kenneth Anger's *Scorpio Rising* (fig. 206) and *Inauguration of the Pleasure Dome* (1966), and Barbara Rubin's *Christmas on Earth* (1963)—epitomized this blatantly transgressive, homoerotic mode. Mainstream Hollywood cinema was referenced ironically in camp tableaux, meshing taboo with fantasy.

In Smith's *Flaming Creatures*, a flamboyant mélange of androgenous naked bodies and transvestites indulge in unashamed erotic and, in places, sadistic theater. The sexual explicitness of the film led to Mekas' arrest when he showed it in 1964 at the New Bowery Theater in New York. As the censorship of underground film continued through that year, Mekas and the movement were cast in a besieged role, battling against the establishment. Ken Jacobs' *Blonde Cobra* (1959–63), made with Bob Fleischner and featuring Smith in vignettes of childish despair, sexual longing, and camp, was so anarchic and unstructured that it appeared to reject the very existence of cinematic structure.

A less direct attack on mainstream cinema was made by the Kuchar brothers, George and Michael. In George Kuchar's *Hold Me While I'm Naked* (1966), a parody of

204. **Jack Smith**
Flaming Creatures, 1962
16 mm film, sound,
black-and-white; 45 min.
Anthology Film Archives,
New York

a Hollywood B movie, Kuchar appears as both director and actor. Anger's classic *Scorpio Rising* adopts a similarly ambivalent attitude toward Hollywood cinema, simultaneously rebelling against it and interacting with it. Fantasy images of the hero Scorpio and of homosexual motorbike subculture are intercut with found footage of James Dean and a religious gathering, set to pop music.

The films of Andy Warhol came to epitomize the sensibility of American underground filmmaking in the sixties. Warhol embraced Hollywood's power as a mass medium and used it in his films, just as he had incorporated celebrities and advertising into his paintings. He saw many of Mekas' screenings and was strongly influenced by the work of Jack Smith. Warhol's filmmaking was a logical extension of his painting. His early films, including *Kiss*, *Empire* (8 hours long, with Mekas as cameraman), *Sleep* (6 hours), *Eat*, *Haircut*, and *Blow Job*, all made in 1963–64, recorded a single, simple action over a long period of time. Each film was black-and-white, silent, unedited, shot in a fixed frame, and screened at 16 frames-per-second, a slower speed than the normal 24 frames-per-second. The films' minimal content and focus on a single subject evoked both Warhol's portrait paintings and the spareness of Minimalist art. They also anticipated the conceptual framework of Structuralist film, which emerged in the late sixties, in their investigation of the medium of cinema and in their emphasis on temporal duration.

Some of Warhol's early films included sound, script, and camera movement as well. At the beginning of 1965, he bought a sound camera, and the focus of his production shifted to feature-length sound films, including *Poor Little Rich Girl*, *Vinyl*, *Camp*, and *My Hustler* (all 1965). Warhol revived and parodied the classic Hollywood star system. His film activity at the Factory attracted drag queens, hustlers, friends, would-be actors, the outcast, and the eccentric, all of whom he cast into the same glamorous limelight. Edie Sedgwick, Ronald Tavel, Gerard Malanga, Taylor Mead, Baby Jane Holzer, Ondine, and others all became Warhol "stars." The low-budget, deadpan format of the porn movie that Warhol adopted in *Couch* (1964), *Blow Job*, *Kiss*, and later, most explicitly, *Blue Movie* (1968), similarly subverted the structure and expectations of mainstream cinema.

In 1965 and 1966, Warhol experimented with double-screen projection and multi-screen environments, which culminated in a series of performances with the Velvet Underground in 1966. One of these, *The Exploding Plastic Inevitable*, combined slide and film projections, light shows, and live rock music. Following his first commercial success, the double-screen film *The Chelsea Girls* (figs. 200, 201), Warhol's films became more professionally structured. Color features such as *Flesh* (1968), *Trash* (1970), and *Heat* (1972) were directed by Paul Morrissey, and Warhol distanced himself from the social circle that had generated his earlier films. —C. I.

205. **Jordan Belson**
Samadhi, 1966–67
16 mm film, sound, color;
6 min.
Anthology Film Archives,
New York

206. **Kenneth Anger**
Scorpio Rising, 1963
16 mm film, sound, color;
29 min.
Anthology Film Archives,
New York

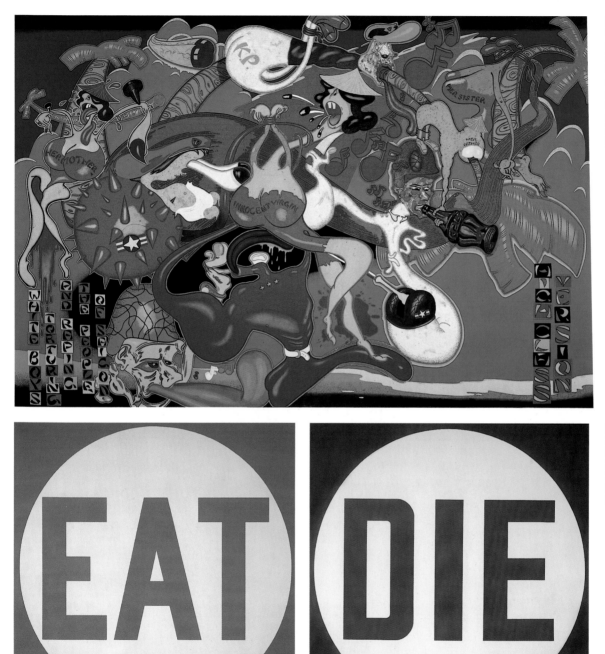

219. **Peter Saul**
Saigon, 1967
Oil on canvas, 92¾ x
142 in. (253.6 x
360.7 cm)
Whitney Museum of
American Art, New York;
Purchase, with funds from
the Friends of the Whitney
Museum of American Art
69.103

220. **Robert Indiana**
Eat/Die, 1962
Oil on canvas, two panels,
72 x 60 in. (182.9 x
152.4 cm) each
Private collection; cour-
tesy Simon Salama-Caro

223. **Andy Warhol**
Big Electric Chair, 1967
Synthetic polymer and
silkscreen ink on canvas,
54 x 73⅛ in. (137.2 x
185.7 cm)
The Menil Collection,
Houston

224. **Andy Warhol**
16 Jackies, 1964
Acrylic and enamel on
canvas, 80⅜ x 64⅜ in.
(204.2 x 163.5 cm)
Walker Art Center,
Minneapolis; Art Center
Acquisition Fund

225. **Andy Warhol**
Red Race Riot, 1963
Synthetic polymer and
silkscreen ink on canvas,
137 x 82½ in. (348 x
209.6 cm)
Museum Ludwig, Cologne

SPACE INTO ENVIRONMENT: NEW FORMS OF CRITIQUE

In 1961, Jane Jacobs, a popular journalist and outsider to architecture, wrote a scathing critique of the architectural profession and of modernism in general in her best-selling book *The Death and Life of Great American Cities*. Attacking the technocratic regime of city planners and social engineers, Jacobs' book registered a growing anxiety about the dehumanization of American urban life. Enormous housing blocks, such as the Pruitt-Igoe complex in St. Louis built by Minoru Yamasaki in the 1950s (fig. 226)—torn down in 1972 in belated agreement with Jacobs' critique—urban renewal and slum-clearing schemes, and monumental master planning for city centers were singled out as especially destructive to the quality of everyday life. Jacobs was not alone in her increasingly environmental concerns, although the forms this populism took differed widely. For some architects, such as Charles Moore, the solution to the perceived formalism of high modernism and the alienation it was believed to have caused was a return to local building styles, familiar materials, and informal, picturesque planning. Moore's Sea Ranch, California, complex of 1963 marks an important moment in the evolution of American neopopulist architecture. For other architects, social activism and grassroots community development became the means of combating the impersonal impositions of government planning authorities. Neighborhood watches, studies of how design could control urban crime, and local design review boards and historic-preservation groups grew out of this form of critique.

Still another response, which had perhaps the greatest influence on the subsequent development of architecture as a discipline—precisely the authority Jacobs sought to undermine—paralleled the acerbic social critique of Pop art and was spearheaded by the work of Robert Venturi and Denise Scott Brown. Venturi had already begun his version of what would become known as postmodernism, when he published his "gentle manifesto" against modernist formalism, *Complexity and Contradiction in Architecture* (1966). With his now famous dictum "less is a bore," Venturi sought to undermine the singular and heroic logic of modernism, particularly that promulgated by Ludwig Mies van der Rohe, with more historically complex and apparently socially inclusive architectural forms. Venturi had recently completed a housing complex for elderly Quakers in Philadelphia, the Guild House (fig. 227), which combined the simple red bricks and double-hung windows typical of innumerable anonymous residential buildings with the massing, proportions, and formal ironies of sixteenth-century Italian Mannerism. All this was to have been crowned by a massive aluminum television antenna. While the latter offended local community sensibilities, the formal modesty of the building itself

226. *Demolition of Pruitt-Igoe Public Housing Complex, St. Louis*, 1972
UPI/Corbis-Bettmann

227. **Venturi, Scott Brown, and Associates**
Guild House, Philadelphia, 1960–63

229. **Ellsworth Kelly**
Green, Blue, Red, 1964
Oil on canvas, 73 x 100 in.
(185.4 x 254 cm)
Whitney Museum of
American Art, New York;
Purchase, with funds from
the Friends of the Whitney
Museum of American Art
66.80

230. **Robert
Mangold**
*1/2 Manila
Curved Area*, 1967
Oil on board, 72 x 144
in. (182.9 x 365.8 cm)
Whitney Museum of
American Art, New York;
Purchase, with funds from
the Friends of the Whitney
Museum of American Art
68.14

231. **Frank Stella**
Die Fahne Hoch, 1959
Enamel on canvas,
121½ x 73 in.
(308.6 x 185.4 cm)
Whitney Museum of
American Art, New York;
Gift of Mr. and Mrs.
Eugene M. Schwartz and
purchase, with funds from
the John I. H. Baur
Purchase Fund; the
Charles and Anita Blatt
Fund; Peter M. Brant;
B. H. Friedman; the
Gilman Foundation, Inc.;
Susan Morse Hilles; The
Lauder Foundation;
Frances and Sydney
Lewis; the Albert A. List
Fund; Philip Morris
Incorporated; Sandra
Payson; Mr. and Mrs.
Albrecht Saalfield; Mrs.
Percy Uris; Warner
Communications Inc. and
the National Endowment
for the Arts 75.22

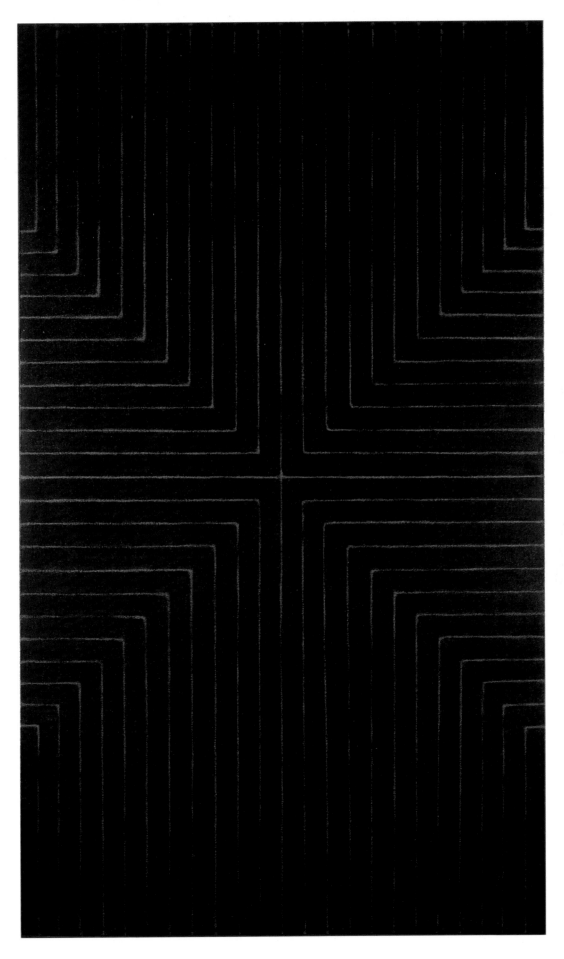

232. **Jo Baer**
Untitled, 1962
Oil on canvas, 72 x 72 in.
(182.9 x 182.9 cm)
Whitney Museum of
American Art, New York;
Gift of Arthur Fleischer, Jr.
95.217

233. **Ad Reinhardt**
Installation view of "Ad
Reinhardt" at the Whitney
Museum of American Art,
New York, 1998
Left to right: *Abstract
Painting*, 1960–66,
Abstract Painting,
1960–66, and *Abstract
Painting*, 1960–63

236. **Sol LeWitt**
Installation view of
Incomplete Open Cubes,
1974
122 painted wood struc-
tures on a painted wood
base and 122 framed
photographs and drawings
on paper, 8 x 8 x 8 in.
(20.3 x 20.3 x 20.3 cm)
each structure

THE SOUNDS OF SILENCE: SERIOUS MUSIC SURVIVES

Over the past fifty years, abstract music has developed and thrived on the margins of the pop music industry. Perhaps the most influential figure in this regard is an eccentric French composer named Erik Satie, who worked at the turn of the century, was much admired by modern artists, and made his living playing popular tunes on the piano in bohemian nightclubs. Satie developed what he called "furniture" music, which involved the use of boredom and repetition to change the sense of how music is used and enjoyed in modern society.

A brilliant American composer, John Cage, turned Satie's ideas into the foundation of serious music in the latter half of the twentieth century. Cage began by imitating the haunting tone poetry of Satie's *Gymnopédies* in solo piano pieces he called "Imaginary Landscapes." He soon moved beyond imitation, however, to develop Satie's concept of ambient sound as a kind of aural sense of negative space. He became notorious for a piece named *4' 33"*, which is literally four minutes and thirty-three seconds of silence—the point being, of course, that there is no such thing as silence and that people should be more aware of the sounds that surround their daily lives. Cage also developed compositional techniques, inspired by Marcel Duchamp, based on chance and the mixing of traditional performance with "found" sounds accessed through live radio broadcasts and records played

237. La Monte Young and Marian Zazeela performing *Map of 49's Dream the Two Systems of Eleven Sets of Galactic Intervals Ornamental Lightyears Tracery* in the Dream House, 1970

on a turntable. One of the most famous of these pieces, *Credo in US*, inspired not only a generation of academically trained composers but also the most famous pop group of our time, the Beatles. By 1967, John Lennon had come under the influence of Yoko Ono, a Fluxus artist who was a student of Cage's. On the Beatles' so-called *White Album* (1968), Lennon included a direct homage to Cage's work, "Revolution Number 9," the first piece of pop music constructed entirely from preexisting sounds.

But Cage's most significant disciple in the pop arena was a British keyboard player, Brian Eno, who got his start in the glitter rock band Roxy Music. By the late 1970s, Eno began to develop what he called ambient music, a close relative to the furniture music created by Satie. However, Eno started to apply the concept to the recording process itself rather than to performance. Many musicians at that time were experimenting with electronic synthesizers, which allowed entirely new sounds to be made. But Eno was among the first to understand that the synthesizer was more than a novel instrument: it signaled, rather, a fundamental shift in the way music could be made and disseminated.

In the field of what used to be called classical music, the composer La Monte Young adapted Cage's conceptual ideas to a compositional style that has come to be known as Minimalism (fig. 237). Young's radical approach was to think of music as a system of vibrations registered as frequencies that could be set into deliberate formal permutations. By the mid-seventies, a new generation of composers was creating remarkably complex and pleasurable pieces based on the ideas of sonic abstraction and modal repetition first explored in the work of Satie, Cage, and Young.

Steve Reich's *Music for 18 Musicians*, created between 1974 and 1976, added a new dimension of rich harmonic and structural innovation to his signature style of creating compositions from a steady repetitive pulse and rhythm (fig. 238). The piece was directly inspired by the Balinese gamelan tradition, which, like much tribal music, is based upon interlocking performances by large groups in which the sound is governed by the natural limits of breath and physical stamina rather than by a conductor and score. The overall effect of these organic layers is a shimmering pulse that overshadows any individual performance. On another level, the use of tribal forms in Reich's work exemplifies a significant feature of most important music of the late twentieth century—that it is the product of a clash between European and non-Western principles. This is not limited to classical music. In the genres of jazz and funk, Miles Davis and James Brown, respectively, were doing something quite similar by reducing rhythms to minimal repetitive patterns and then changing them over time to add a sense of form and structure.

Contemporaneously with Reich, Philip Glass emerged from the downtown New York art scene to create stunningly modern music based on the repetition of seemingly minimal forms (fig. 239). This approach reached its apex in the opera *Einstein on the Beach* (1976), created in collaboration with Robert Wilson. It is an artistic meditation on the relativity of time, using music, choreography, lighting and stage design to transport the audience into another dimension, where the hidden nature of things becomes apparent (fig. 410).

Over the past fifty years the distinction between serious and popular music has become so blurred that it no longer makes much sense. We are left to judge music from a variety of expected and unexpected sources in terms of its intrinsic value rather than its adherence to any particular form or tradition. This is in large part due to the tendency in the arts of our century to break down conventional barriers between and within genres. But it is also attributable to the growing sophistication of audio recording, which allows musical performances to be as highly manipulated and constructed as compositions were during the golden age of Western classical music. —J. C.

238. Steve Reich in spread from *Anti-Illusion: Procedures/Materials* New York: Whitney Museum of American Art, 1969

239. *Philip Glass in Rehearsal at the Peppermint Lounge, New York*, 1980, photograph by Paula Court

Dan Flavin used an available standard fluorescent tube—first a single white one placed at a 45-degree angle on the wall, then others in various configurations and color combinations (figs. 240, 241). Like his colleague Carl Andre, Flavin was indebted to the geometric idealism of the Russian Constructivists—one of his 1969 light pieces pays homage to Vladimir Tatlin's famous *Monument to the Third International* of 1919–20.[92] Andre, who started out in the fifties creating totemic wood sculptures (fig. 244), made an abrupt changeover in the next decade to standardized industrial materials—first using bricks lined or stacked on the floor, then working with metal plates spread out on the floor in a line or grid (figs. 242, 243). For Andre and other Minimalists, the sculptural act lay not in creating the forms but in selecting and placing them. To emphasize a lack of preciousness and more closely involve the audience in the "experience" of the sculpture, viewers were permitted to walk on Andre's work, which, like a rug, ran along the plane of the floor.

240. **Dan Flavin**
Installation view of "Dan Flavin" at the Green Gallery, New York, 1964

241. **Dan Flavin**
"Monument" for V. Tatlin, 1969
Fluorescent lights, 119 x 23 x 4 in. (302.3 x 58.4 x 10.2 cm)
Courtesy Leo Castelli Gallery, New York

242. **Carl Andre**
144 Zinc Square, 1967
Zinc, 144 x 144 in.
(365.8 x 365.8 cm)
Milwaukee Art Museum;
Purchase, National
Endowment for the Arts
Matching Funds
© Carl Andre/Licensed by
VAGA, New York, NY

On wall:
Robert Morris
Untitled, 1970 (detail)
Felt, 10 x 25 ft.
(3 x 7.6 m)
Milwaukee Art Museum;
Gift of Friends of Art

243. **Carl Andre**
Lever, 1966
137 firebricks, 4½ x 8⅞ x
348 in. (11.4 x 22.5 x
883.9 cm)
National Gallery of
Canada, Ottawa;
Purchased 1969
© Carl Andre/Licensed by
VAGA, New York, NY

244. **Carl Andre**
Last Ladder, 1959
Wood, 84¼ x 6⅛ x 6⅛ in.
(214 x 15.6 x 15.6 cm)
Tate Gallery, London
© Carl Andre/Licensed by
VAGA, New York, NY

The artist who most epitomized the philosophical rigor of Minimalism was the sculptor Donald Judd. A master of exacting forms, technique, and incisive prose, he made his living as an art critic between 1959 and 1965, writing some of the first reviews of his peers, including Frank Stella, Dan Flavin, and John Chamberlain. Though he had studied painting, he began to make painted reliefs around 1961–62 (fig. 245) and then quickly moved into three-dimensional forms—most of them variations on the hollow box (fig. 246). He made horizontal progressions on the wall, and stacks of evenly placed units from floor to ceiling (fig. 248). Judd's emphasis was on space as opposed to mass, and the resulting hollowness appealed to his belief that nothing should be hidden.

In 1965, Judd wrote an essay entitled "Specific Objects," in which he espoused "actual space" as the means of defeating illusionism. He accepted internal compositional motifs only if they had an explicit connection to overall shape and structure, echoing the frame edge, for instance, as Stella's Black paintings had.[93] Judd agreed with Clement Greenberg's prescription that the pure plastic qualities of art should be emphasized, which required eliminating spatial illusionism. Greenberg, however, did not care for Minimalism and considered it an idea that remained an idea, "something deduced instead of felt and discovered."[94]

Judd was uncompromising and authoritarian. His desire for total control over the presentation of his work (and perhaps his life) ultimately led him in 1971 to create a massive complex in Marfa, Texas (fig. 247). He virtually transformed this dusty town (where the 1950s movie classic *Giant* had been filmed) into a public environmental installation of his art and a monument to his philosophy. Many of the town's residents became his employees, painstakingly restoring buildings (most

245. **Donald Judd**
Untitled, 1963
Oil on wood with galvanized iron and aluminum, 76 x 96 x 11¾ in. (193 x 243.8 x 29.8 cm)
Collection of Robert A. M. Stern
© Donald Judd/Licensed by VAGA, New York, NY

246. **Donald Judd**
Untitled, 1965
Brown enamel on aluminum and galvanized iron, 30 x 150 x 30 in. (76.2 x 381 x 76.2 cm)
PaceWildenstein, New York
© Donald Judd/Licensed by VAGA, New York, NY

of them army Quonset huts) and maintaining the proper conditions for the sculpture. Everything in this complex was carefully designed by Judd—from the installation of his work both indoors and out, to the architectural details, right down to the furniture and barbecue. Only the environmental projects of Frank Lloyd Wright, such as Taliesin West in Phoenix, Arizona, begun in 1938, or the Shaker Village, a utopian community founded in 1787 in upstate New York on standards of simplicity and harmony, can approach the total environment of Marfa.

The sculpture of Judd, LeWitt, Andre, Flavin, and Morris was a far cry from both the emotional, open-welded sculpture of the fifties and improvisational junk

247. **Donald Judd**
Untitled, 1982
Concrete and steel, three
units, 98⅞₆ x 196⅞₆ x
98⅞₆ in. (250 x 499 x
250 cm) each
The Chinati Foundation,
Marfa, Texas
© Donald Judd/Licensed
by VAGA, New York, NY

248. **Donald Judd**
Untitled, 1969
Brass and colored
fluorescent plexiglass on
steel brackets,
116½ x 27 x 24 in.
(295.9 x 68.6 x 61 cm)
Hirshhorn Museum and
Sculpture Garden,
Smithsonian Institution,
Washington, D.C.; Gift of
Joseph H. Hirshhorn,
1972
© Donald Judd/Licensed
by VAGA, New York, NY

249. **David Smith**
Cubi I, 1963
Stainless steel,
124 x 34½ x 33½ in.
(315 x 87.6 x 85.1 cm)
The Detroit Institute of Arts
© David Smith/Licensed by
VAGA, New York, NY

sculpture. It was closer to the American Precisionist aesthetic of the 1920s or the earlier Arts and Crafts ethic of "truth to materials." In fact, Minimalist sculpture seemed to have more in common with architecture—with the International Style's "less is more" and its clear, sober geometries, or with new Brutalist works such as Marcel Breuer's Whitney Museum of American Art, completed in 1966, which was ideally suited to exhibit Minimalism (fig. 250).

250. **Marcel Breuer**
Whitney Museum of American Art, New York,
1966

Tony Smith, an architect by training, was an older artist who had anticipated the developments of Minimalism, though his work was exhibited contemporaneously. As an architect, he had been attracted to the modular systems of Frank Lloyd Wright and the structural simplicity of the tatami mats around which Japanese houses were designed, as well as the structural regularity and unilateral symmetry of the International Style. In his early paintings, he had experimented with geometric modules and gone on to use modular structures in his sculptures. Though he had already been at work

251. Installation view of "Primary Structures" at The Jewish Museum, New York, 1966
Left to right: Donald Judd, *Untitled*, 1966, and *Untitled*, 1966; Robert Morris, *Untitled (2 L-Beams)*, 1965; Robert Grosvenor, *Transoxiana*, 1965

252. **Tony Smith**
Die, 1962
Steel, 72⅜ x 72⅜ x 72⅜ in.
(183.8 x 183.8 x
183.8 cm)
Whitney Museum of
American Art, New York;
Purchase, with funds from
the Louis and Bessie Adler
Foundation, Inc., James
Block, the Sondra and
Charles Gilman, Jr.,
Foundation, Inc., Penny
and Mike Winton, and the
Painting and Sculpture
Committee 89.6

for twenty years, it was not until 1963 that his sculpture was publicly shown, at
Hartford's Wadsworth Atheneum, followed in 1966 by his inclusion in the seminal
"Primary Structures" exhibition at The Jewish Museum, New York, the first time
Minimalist sculpture received institutional recognition (fig. 251). A generation
older than the other emerging Minimalists, he had been well known as a teacher
(Robert Morris was among his students). Some of Smith's works were simple, like
Die (fig. 252); others explored more complex aggregates of tetrahedral forms in
works that shifted dynamically as the viewer moved around them (fig. 253). In a
work such as *Die*, the title as well as the roughly human height of the simple cube
conjure up not only industrial but emotional associations. Through this junction
of affect and industry, Smith served as a bridge figure between the Abstract
Expressionists and the Minimalists.

The Minimalist aesthetic of functionalism, repetition, and serial forms echoed
through other media at the time—in the dance of the Judson Dance Theater, in the
serial music of La Monte Young, Terry Riley, Steve Reich, and Philip Glass, and
in the structuralist films of Paul Sharits, Michael Snow, and Hollis Frampton.

The Judson Dance Theater was founded in 1962 by disciples of Merce
Cunningham in New York and Anna Halprin in San Francisco. The Judson
dancers were intent on breaking free from the conventions of dance—from
structure, rules, and techniques. They emphasized the body, freed dance from its
dependence on music, used untrained dancers, and often produced dances from
written scores specifying repetitive actions and commonplace tasks such as sleeping, walking, and eating that each individual dancer would interpret (fig. 258). The
dancers sometimes performed nude, stripped down, as it were, to "bare" essentials.

There was a literal connection between visual arts and performance in the
Judson Dance Theater as well. Robert Morris, a member of the Theater who
had studied under Anna Halprin in San Francisco, was making sculpture at the
same time he was performing. Some of his early works were performing objects,

253. Tony Smith
Installation view of *Smoke* at The Corcoran Gallery of Art, Washington, D.C., 1967 (no longer exists)
Plywood mock-up, 24 x 48 x 31 ft. (7.3 x 14.6 x 9.4 m)

America
at the
Crossroads
1964–1976

As the 1960s progressed, more and more Americans began to question institutional authority. The rebellion initiated in the fifties by the Beats, on the one hand, and civil rights activism, on the other, exploded into a full-fledged counterculture by 1968. This counterculture gained momentum alongside reforms legislated by the government. Lyndon B. Johnson, who became president after John F. Kennedy was assassinated in November 1963 (fig. 275), was responsible for enacting the most extensive array of social reforms since President Franklin D. Roosevelt's New Deal in the 1930s. Johnson's domestic agenda was designed to create what he called the "Great Society," and included welfare reforms, Medicare, and a "War on Poverty."

275. *Vice President Lyndon B. Johnson, with His Wife and Jacqueline Kennedy, Taking the Presidential Oath of Office on* Air Force One *Immediately After President John F. Kennedy's Assassination,* 1963
UPI/Corbis-Bettmann

From 1964 to 1968, more than fourteen million Americans saw their incomes rise above poverty levels, which dropped from 22 percent to 11 percent of the population. Johnson offered something for all: tax cuts for big business, additions to the National Parks, air and water pollution standards, mass transit, and truth-in-packaging for consumers.

But one of the most significant accomplishments of Johnson's presidency was the passage of the 1964 Civil Rights Act, initiated a year earlier by John F. Kennedy. The most sweeping civil rights legislation since the Reconstruction years following the Civil War, this act outlawed segregation in schools and public facilities and spaces, provided for fairness in housing and employment, and banned discrimination in business and education. Though the "separate but equal" Jim Crow laws had been defeated in the 1954 *Brown* v. *Board of Education* Supreme Court ruling, four Southern states had failed as late as 1960 to integrate any of their public schools. The 1964 Civil Rights Act sent a clear

276. *Robert F. Kennedy Lying Wounded on the Floor of the Ambassador Hotel, Having Been Shot Shortly After His Victory Speech in the California Primary Election,* 1968
Photograph © Ron Bennett
UPI/Corbis-Bettmann

signal that pervasive racial discrimination would no longer be officially tolerated. The following year, protests in Alabama against racial discrimination in voter registration rules prompted the passage of the 1965 Voting Rights Act.

For some black leaders, however, change was too slow in coming. Frustrated by the inconsistencies between America's egalitarian ideals and the inequality of legal, social, and economic conditions, they preached separatism in the form of black nationalism. Others advocated violence or promoted the Black Power movement, which was reinforced by the Student Organization for Black Unity and the Black Panther party—the latter a radical group founded in Oakland, California, in 1966. Race riots broke out across America—in Los Angeles in 1965; in Chicago, New York, Cleveland, and Baltimore in 1966; and, in 1967, in Detroit, Newark, New Jersey, Rochester, New York, Birmingham, Alabama, and New Britain, Connecticut.

In these same years, other newly empowered voices began to be heard. Native Americans and feminists joined the growing ranks of students and blacks who were becoming increasingly disillusioned with the social and political status quo. Groups such as the Students for a Democratic Society and the National

277. *National Guardsmen with Bayonets Block Beale Street in Memphis, Tennessee, as Protesters Wear Signs That Read, "I AM A MAN,"* 1968 UPI/Corbis-Bettmann

278. *Anti-Vietnam War Demonstrator Shot by National Guardsmen at Kent State University, Ohio,* 1970, photograph by John Filo

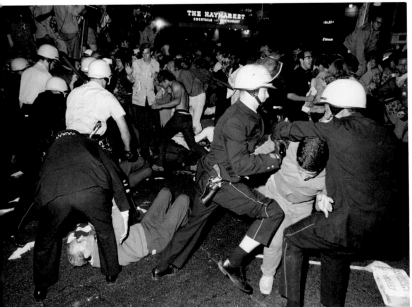

279. *Police and Antiwar Demonstrators Clashing on Michigan Avenue During the 1968 Democratic National Convention in Chicago* UPI/Corbis-Bettmann

280. *Anti-Vietnam War Peace March, Washington, D.C.,* 1967

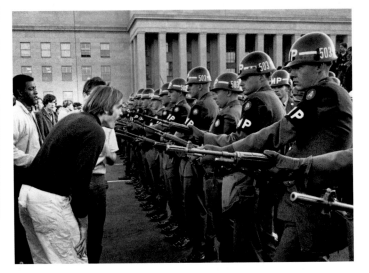

281. *A Peace Demonstrator Taunts Military Police in Front of the Pentagon During an Anti-Vietnam War Protest, Washington, D.C.,* 1967 UPI/Corbis-Bettmann

Organization for Women gained political power by organizing and challenging assumptions about technological progress, war, sexual mores, and gender and racial stereotypes. This mounting insurgency culminated in the global revolutionary events of 1968, as students rioted in Paris, at Columbia University in New York, and at the University of California at Berkeley.

Nationwide violence put an end to the mood of optimism and idealism that had opened the decade. In the wake of Kennedy's assassination came a wave of political assassinations that stunned the nation and further shook America's self-confidence. The black nationalist leader Malcolm X was shot at a rally in New York in 1965; in 1968, Martin Luther King, Jr., and Robert F. Kennedy were both slain by assassins' bullets (fig. 276). Public figures were moving targets, even in the art world: the day before Robert Kennedy's murder, an attempt had been made on Andy Warhol's life. All these events, along with America's involvement in Vietnam, initiated a dark period in America, a period of cynicism, fear, and anger. Many began to wonder what was wrong with the country.

Americans responded to the growing undercurrent of violence in different ways: some retreated to pre-industrial forms of life—like the hippies living in self-sufficient communes, preaching peace, love, and "flower power" (fig. 286). Along with a dreamy narcissism, more than a few opted for "dropping out" through drugs. Others, as we have seen, engaged in radical politics and protest, through both nonviolent means and violent confrontations that had links to student revolutions and liberation movements around the globe (fig. 277). Young people's anguished self-examination led to an oedipal hostility toward the older generation and establishment institutions such as the government and police (fig. 279).

Consensus culture in America, which had been disintegrating around civil rights issues, unraveled in the late 1960s over U.S. involvement in Vietnam. After the French withdrew from Vietnam in 1954, the country was divided, with a pro-Communist regime taking control of the North. President Eisenhower sent military advisers to

THEATER IN THE VIETNAM ERA

The American theater experienced one of its most radically experimental and political phases between 1965 and 1979. In the mid-1960s, it was sharply divided between the staid aesthetic and commercial tendencies of Broadway and most of Off-Broadway, on the one hand, and the bohemian experimentalism of Off-Off-Broadway, on the other. There were nevertheless glimmers of social consciousness on Broadway: Howard Sackler's Pulitzer Prize-winning *The Great White Hope* (1968) addressed race relations, while the musical *Hair* (fig. 282), originally produced Off-Broadway in 1967, was the Great White Way's highly successful representation of the hippie counterculture. Far more typical were comedies such as Neil Simon's *The Odd Couple* (1965) and Woody Allen's *Play It Again, Sam* (1969). Good examples of a popular Broadway genre, they reflect the commercial theater's obliviousness to the social upheavals surrounding the civil rights and antiwar movements.

The American theatrical avant-garde had earlier in the decade come to regard Off-Broadway theater as overly commercial and had shifted its base of operations to Off-Off-Broadway. Partly because of licensing regulations, many Off-Off-Broadway "theaters" were not theaters at all, but coffeehouses or clubs. A few, like La Mama Experimental Theater Club, founded in 1963 by Ellen Stewart, evolved into important theatrical institutions. Among the major American playwrights who began their careers Off-Off-Broadway were Sam Shepard, Lanford Wilson, Terrence McNally, and John Guare.

Off-Off-Broadway offered a vast range of sensibilities and subjects—and not all of them were focused on literary values. By 1964–65, the highly influential Living Theater was moving away from its earlier commitment to a poetic theater and toward a performance style based on physical improvisation and anarchist politics. The Living Theater inspired the formation of many aesthetically, politically, and socially radical troupes Off-Off-Broadway, among them the Open Theater, the Bread and Puppet Theater, the Manhattan Project, and the Performance Group. Unlike Broadway companies, they directly addressed social issues, particularly the Vietnam War. Like the antiwar movement itself, the radical theater was national in scope: by the late 1960s, almost every medium- to large-sized American city had at least one experimental theater company. —P. A.

282. Paul Jabara, Steve Gamet, Leata Galloway, and Suzannah Norstrand in the stage production of *Hair*, 1968
UPI/Corbis-Bettmann

train the anti-Communist South Vietnamese. During Kennedy's term of office, the number of advisers rose from 2,000 to 15,000. In 1964, the war escalated when Johnson ordered retaliatory air strikes against a North Vietnamese offensive. By 1968, some 525,000 American soldiers were fighting in a small Southeast Asian country that most Americans had never heard of, let alone could find on a map. The war in Vietnam bitterly divided the nation (figs. 280, 281). There was increasing suspicion that America was driven by anti-Communist paranoia, or by the economic greed of the military-industrial complex, or by racist attitudes. But most Americans were pragmatists: American troops and high-tech weaponry seemed unable to defeat the North Vietnamese and their guerrilla warfare tactics, and the cost in American lives was becoming too high. Marches on Washington to protest the war began in 1965. Over the next three years, such protests spread around the country and some of them were violent; police and protesters clashed and thousands were arrested. When National Guardsmen shot and killed four demonstrating students at Kent State University in Ohio in 1970, the country appeared to be on the verge of a civil war (fig. 278).

ANTI-ESTABLISHMENT AND DISESTABLISHMENT IN THE FILM INDUSTRY

Although the decrease in moviegoing and the apparent demise of the studios were thought to be fatal stakes through the heart of Hollywood, the creature did not die. Instead, its vitals were transplanted to pump life into massive conglomerates that one by one acquired the major studios during the 1960s and 1970s and collectively created a new beast called the entertainment industry. This period of corporate upheaval in the studios coincided with an epoch of political and social upheaval bracketed by the assassination of John F. Kennedy in 1963 and the resignation of Richard Nixon in 1974.

In 1968, the Motion Picture Production Code of 1934, which had barred all but discreet depictions of sex and violence, was replaced with a ratings system that permitted graphic content. And as institutions everywhere from Washington to Hollywood collapsed, a cultural gap emerged that divided America much as did the undeclared war in Vietnam. Certain filmmakers revered the stability of the old order, while others celebrated a dizzying new disorder. On one side of this divide was a grizzled John Wayne as the law-abiding marshal Rooster Cogburn in *True Grit* (1969, Henry Hathaway) aiming his six-guns toward the other side—at outlaw heroes such as Faye Dunaway and Warren Beatty in *Bonnie and Clyde* (fig. 283). Ideologically and cinematically, these two films illustrate an emerging generation gap, the formidable Wayne reinforcing traditional values and storytelling techniques, the ambivalent Beatty challenging both in a film startling for its amorality and jump cuts.

Institutional authority was the constant and beleaguered target of the era, in musicals (*Camelot*, 1967, Joshua Logan), in comedies (*The Graduate*, 1967, Mike Nichols), and in police thrillers (*In the Heat of the Night*, fig. 284). Whether it was Lancelot (Franco Nero) betraying King Arthur, the collegian Benjamin Braddock (Dustin Hoffman) kidnapping his girlfriend during her wedding to another fellow, or Mr. Tibbs (Sidney Poitier) provoking a redneck sheriff, the authority of monarch, church, and state was decisively challenged.

Poitier, as Tibbs and as the black scientist engaged to the daughter of white liberals in *Guess Who's Coming to Dinner* (1967, Stanley Kramer), represented the intellectually and morally superior black man whom Hollywood endorsed as inspirational to white Americans. Only independently made films, such as *Nothing But a Man* (1964, Michael Roemer), showed blacks enduring extraordinary prejudice while trying to lead ordinary lives.

The cultural ambivalence toward authority is the stuff of high satire in *Dr.*

283. Faye Dunaway and Warren Beatty in *Bonnie and Clyde*, directed by Arthur Penn, 1967 Courtesy Warner Bros.

284. Rod Steiger and Sidney Poitier in *In the Heat of the Night*, directed by Norman Jewison, 1967 Courtesy United Artists

Questioning the Canon

The convulsive social and political events of the sixties were reflected everywhere in the arts of the time. From the radical sounds of electronic rock by such musicians as the The Doors and Jimi Hendrix to countercultural films like *Easy Rider* and *Midnight Cowboy* and the political activism of the Bread and Puppet Theater, a shake-up of the old social order was evident. In the visual arts, there was intense questioning of the modernist "canon," and a simultaneous redefinition of boundaries. It was a revolutionary period in American art that, in the years between 1966 and 1972, produced such fecund new forms and overlapping movements as Postminimalism, Earthworks, Conceptual art, Body art, Performance art, and video. The climate of questioning and experimentation in the visual arts was intensified by new federal subsidies for the arts through the National Endowment for the Arts (NEA) and the National Endowment for the Humanities (NEH). These agencies, created in 1965 as part of President Johnson's Great Society, provided indispensable support for vanguard artists, new art forms, and new venues, and they raised public consciousness about art. For the next twenty years, the NEA's policy of unrestricted grants to

Strangelove (1964, Stanley Kubrick), in which U.S. generals (Sterling Hayden and George C. Scott), fearful of a Communist doomsday device, launch nuclear warheads toward Moscow. Ambivalence is the stuff of high tragedy in *Patton* (1970, Franklin Schaffner), also starring Scott, a portrait of the World War II antihero General George S. Patton as a maniacal and self-destructive genius.

The common theme of movies as diverse as *Dr. Strangelove*, *Patton*, *The Wild Bunch* (1969, Sam Peckinpah), and *Easy Rider* (fig. 285) was America, land of random violence. Although Peckinpah's elegy to the American West was set in pistol-packing 1914 and Hopper's mod odyssey in pot-smoking 1969, the landscape of suspicion that turns American pilgrims into mercenary outlaws is interchangeable. Even the serio-comedy *Butch Cassidy and the Sundance Kid* (1969, George Roy Hill), starring Paul Newman and Robert Redford, cheers the outlaw heroes who outwit the sheriff's posse.

Stanley Kubrick's *Dr. Strangelove* and *2001: A Space Odyssey* (1968) were visual trendsetters. Moreover, the chrome-and-neon decors of the one and the machine aesthetic of the other mirrored the methods and the materials of Minimalist art. Both movies express a simultaneous love and fear of man-made devices (the bomb, the computer), making their mixed messages something akin to Technology equals Liberation equals Death.

In this valley of ambivalence, the laughs came from the stampede of stand-up comics—among them Woody Allen and Mel Brooks—armed with irreverence. Allen's *Take the Money and Run* (1969), which he wrote, directed, and starred in, profiled a compulsively funny compulsive thief. Similarly, Brooks' *The Producers* (1968) starred Zero Mostel and Gene Wilder as Broadway hustlers who sell 25,000 percent of a surefire flop—an upbeat musical about Hitler—that turns out to be a runaway hit.

No film was more irreverent than Robert Altman's *M*A*S*H* (1970), a black comedy set in an army hospital during the Korean War that potently linked war, gore, and absurdism. Compare this with *The Love Bug* (1969, Robert Stevenson), a family-friendly Disney affair about a temperamental Volkswagen, and you have the most extreme example of the era's yin and yang. —C. R.

285. Dennis Hopper, Peter Fonda, and Jack Nicholson in *Easy Rider*, directed by Dennis Hopper, 1969
Courtesy Columbia Pictures

individual artists was crucial to the development of avant-garde art in America.

Like much else in the late 1960s, the art world was in a state of instability, uncertainty, and discovery. Although artists reacted in different ways, the new art of this period shared certain general characteristics: an emphasis on disorientation, dislocation, dematerialization, and debris—qualities that paralleled the dismantling of institutional structures in the larger social sphere (fig. 287). Whether the artist unloaded a pile of rocks on the floor of a gallery, drew a chalk line on the desert ground, or removed chunks of a building, political attitudes infiltrated form. In another sense, however, these practices can be seen as part of a countertradition that had been developing since the fifties, when traditional genres and categories were fractured and the prosaic materials and imagery of the real world were welcomed into art.

286. *Hog Farm Commune, New York City*, 1969

287. **Robert Morris**
Untitled, 1968
Thread, mirrors, asphalt, aluminum, lead, felt, copper, and steel, dimensions variable
Leo Castelli Gallery, New York

Hippie culture, rock music, and drugs were also important influences on the visual arts as the sixties went on, as was the new global culture connected through enhanced communications technologies, such as improvements in international telephone service and jet travel, which made possible ever faster transmission of information. It was an era whose art works were more interrogative than declarative and repudiated absolutes, mirroring the tendency of society at large.

Artists continued to ask "What is an object?" but in contrast to Donald Judd, who in 1965 drew the blunt conclusion that clear unitary forms best expressed the "thingness" of art, many artists now preferred to ask "How do we know or experience an object?" The stern formalism of the Minimalists and their absolute certainties had come to seem both utopian and puritanical—and uninvolved with the world. Some younger artists conceived of objects as mutable—as things in process—and therefore unstable, irregular, and disorderly. To emphasize the process of art making and its effect on materials, they often relocated the work to an expanded field that could include outdoor and architectural contexts. Other artists stressed the thought process over form, declaring the conception of the work to be the end product. One critic described these two tendencies, the process-oriented and the conceptual, as "the tidal pull between epistemological and ontological concerns."[99]

288. *Bob Dylan*, n. d.
© Fotex-Drechsler/
Shooting Star

POP APOTHEOSIS: ROCK MUSIC RULES

As the 1960s began, the quality of popular music hit an all-time low. However, it was a great time for jazz music, particularly the emergence of John Coltrane from the Miles Davis Quintet. Coltrane's transformation from leading soloist to legendary artist culminated in one of the greatest artistic achievements of our time, the thirty-five-minute masterpiece *A Love Supreme*, recorded in 1964.

While Coltrane and contemporaries such as Ornette Coleman freed jazz to attain new levels of expression, other indigenous genres of music (blues, folk, and country) were being swept aside by the explosion of rock and pop. In England, however, young kids crazed for traditional American music seemed better able to enjoy and emulate the black musicians who had been replaced by bland white versions in the U.S. marketplace. This so-called British invasion was led by two childhood friends from Liverpool, John Lennon and Paul McCartney. Their band, the Beatles, started out as one of many covering rhythm and blues hits from the United States. They were soon joined by many other groups, most of which faded into obscurity after a hit or two. The Beatles, however, along with the Rolling Stones and, later, Eric Clapton, the Who, and Led Zeppelin, began to write and record original material that expanded on their blues roots, developed the idea of records as an album of related material, and established the basic format of a rock 'n' roll band. Lennon, in particular, experimented with song structures, unusual instrumentation, and wordplay, in a way that illuminated a new path for everyone around him.

At roughly the same moment in the mid-sixties, Bob Dylan began performing in New York (fig. 288), adopting the guise of an old folk musician in direct imitation of Woody Guthrie. But Dylan, like the Beatles, quickly moved beyond his roots to write complex lyrical songs that ranged from powerful social commentary to symbolic tales with profound poetic imagery. In 1966, he stunned his fans by recasting his music with an electric rock 'n' roll band whose raw power amplified his increasingly caustic and inventive lyrics. The Beatles and the Stones grew equally more inspired by mid-decade, lacing their work with unexpected sounds and using the studio itself as an instrument, manipulating tape to create unheard-of effects and ever more complex compositions. In fact, the Beatles' music grew so dependent upon studio effects that by the time their albums *Revolver* (1966) and *Sgt. Pepper's Lonely Hearts Club Band* (1967) were released, they could no longer re-create the music live and stopped giving concert performances altogether.

While British bands revitalized rock, American music continued to break new

289. *The Supremes on* The Ed Sullivan Show, 1966

314. **Alan Saret**
True Jungle, 1968
Wire, dimensions variable
Whitney Museum of
American Art, New York;
Gift of the Howard and
Jean Lipman Foundation,
Inc. 69.7

315. **Bruce Nauman**
Untitled, 1965–66
Latex on burlap, 14 x
49 x 35 in. (35.6 x
124.5 x 88.9 cm)
Whitney Museum of
American Art, New York;
Gift of Mr. and Mrs. Peter
M. Brant 76.43

316. **Lynda Benglis**
For Carl Andre, 1970
Acrylic foam, 56¼ x 53½ x
46⅜ in. (142.9 x 135.9 x
117.3 cm)
Modern Art Museum, Fort
Worth, Texas; Museum
Purchase, The Benjamin J.
Tillar Memorial Trust
© Lynda Benglis/Licensed
by VAGA, New York, NY

317. **Robert Smithson**
Eight Part Piece (Cayuga Salt Mine Project), 1969
Rock salt and mirrors,
11 x 360 x 30 in.
(27.9 x 914.4 x 76.2 cm)
Estate of the artist
© Estate of Robert Smithson/Licensed by VAGA, New York, NY

318. **Robert Morris**
Felt, 1967–68
Felt, dimensions variable
Whitney Museum of American Art, New York; Purchase, with funds from the Howard and Jean Lipman Foundation, Inc. 69.23

319. **Eva Hesse**
Sans II, 1968
Fiberglass, 38 x 170¾ x
6⅛ in. (96.5 x 433.7 x
15.6 cm) overall
Whitney Museum of
American Art, New York;
Purchase, with funds from
Ethelyn and Lester J.
Honig and the Albert A.
List Family 69.105
© The Estate of Eva
Hesse

320. **Eva Hesse**
Accession II, 1969
Galvanized steel and
plastic tubing, 30¾ x
30¾ x 30¾ in. (78.1 x
78.1 x 78.1 cm)
The Detroit Institute of
Arts; Founders Society
Purchase, Friend of
Modern Art Fund and
Miscellaneous Gifts Fund
© The Estate of Eva
Hesse

321. **Eva Hesse**
Untitled, or Not Yet, 1966
Nine dyed fishnet bags
with clear polyethylene,
paper, sand, and cotton
string, 71 x 15½ x 8¼ in.
(180.3 x 39.4 x 21 cm)
overall
San Francisco Museum of
Modern Art; Purchase
through Gift of Mrs. Paul
L. Wattis
© The Estate of Eva Hesse

322. Eva Hesse
Untitled (Rope Piece), 1970
Latex over rope, string,
and wire, two strands,
dimensions variable
Whitney Museum of American
Art, New York; Purchase, with
funds from Eli and Edythe L.
Broad, the Percy Uris
Purchase Fund, and the
Painting and Sculpture
Committee 88.17a–b
© The Estate of Eva Hesse

connections between their work and the outside world, a consideration of context became paramount. The forms were often dictated by their site—the surrounding architecture, such as industrial lofts, or landscape. This sculpture in an expanded field focused on the phenomenological experience—our experience of the work in space and time.[106] Duration or temporality was what the formalist critic Michael Fried had so strenuously objected to in his influential polemic "Art and Objecthood," when he reproached the Minimalists for the theatrical character of their work—for expecting the viewer to be in motion to experience it.[107]

The Postminimalists, with their emphasis on site and phenomenology, pushed the idea of spectator participation even further. By 1968, theatricality and the active role of the viewer in space and time had become central to the reformulation of sculpture. The importance of site to the experience of sculpture had been envisioned in the

THE NEW NONFICTION NOVEL

The new nonfiction novel of the 1960s—developed by Tom Wolfe, Truman Capote, Norman Mailer, Joan Didion, and Hunter S. Thompson—was a revolutionary conception with a retrospective touch, antagonistic to the rules that governed postwar fiction and journalism, but respectful of the tradition of literary realism embodied in the novels of Daniel Defoe in the eighteenth century and in those of Charles Dickens in the nineteenth. In part, the new nonfiction writers saw themselves rebelling against the exaltation of modernist experimentation during the 1950s and 1960s, which was to be leading talented authors toward introversion just when the country was filled to bursting with peerless subject matter: "No novelist," Wolfe claimed with characteristic audacity, "will be remembered as the novelist who captured the Sixties in America."

Although these writers saw themselves as filling that gap, they were also assaulting the conventions of journalism—particularly, the idea of "objective distance." Often, they began their careers laboring on the fringes of the journalistic establishment. Tom Wolfe, for example, wrote features for the Sunday supplement of the *New York Herald Tribune*. By the late 1960s, in books such as Wolfe's *Electric Kool-Aid Acid Test* (fig. 323), an astonishing chronicle of the burgeoning LSD culture, Manhattan reporters were displaying a new confidence that meshed with the growing regard for the creative nonfiction of novelists like Capote, who called *In Cold Blood* (1965), his account of a mass murder in Kansas, the "first nonfiction novel," and Mailer, whose *Armies of the Night* (fig. 324) read like a memoir of the antiwar movement co-written by Edward R. Murrow and W. C. Fields. Didion and Thompson (whose writing was dubbed "gonzo journalism") catalyzed a growing California literary scene that balanced East Coast excess with West Coast excess. And dispatches from Vietnam correspondents such as Michael Herr and John Sack matched Herr's claim that "conventional journalism could no more reveal this war than conventional firepower could win it."

If what these authors composed was "realistic," it was not gray or sedate but shared the party-colored politics and skepticism toward authority that marked much of 1960s culture. What stood out about the new nonfiction writers, more often than not, was how rarely they sounded the transparent, neutral voice that had been the trademark of postwar reporting since George Orwell: there was no precedent for Wolfe's freewheeling sentence structure ("Barreling across America with the microphones picking it all up, the whole roar, and microphone up top gets eerie in a great rush and then *skakkkkkkkkkkkkkk* it is ripping and roaring"), Thompson's weaving between reality and

323. *The Electric Kool-Aid Acid Test*, by Tom Wolfe
New York: Farrar, Straus, and Giroux, 1968
Berg Collection of English and American Literature, The New York Public Library, Astor, Lenox and Tilden Foundations

324. *The Armies of the Night*, by Norman Mailer
New York: New American Library, 1968
Harry Ransom Humanities Research Center at The University of Texas at Austin

early 1950s by the sculptor Tony Smith. One evening, he took a group of students to the then unfinished New Jersey Turnpike.

> It was a dark night and there were no lights or shoulder markers, lines, railing, or anything at all except the dark pavement moving through the landscape of the flats, rimmed by hills in the distance, but punctuated by stacks, towers, fumes, and colored lights. This drive was a revealing experience. The road and much of the landscape was artificial, and yet it couldn't be called a work of art. On the other hand, it did something for me that art had never done. At first I didn't know what it was, but its effect was to liberate me from many of the views I had had about art. . . . There is no way you can frame it, you just have to experience it.[108]

Although Michael Fried explicitly attacked Smith's ruminations in "Art and Objecthood," Robert Smithson defended the sculptor in a letter to the editor, praising Smith's recognition of the industrial landscape as suitable, experiential territory for art.

That same year, 1967, Smithson published an article that was also an art work: "The Monuments of Passaic." In this text, accompanied by photographs, Smithson identified as "monuments" pontoons and pumping derricks in the Passaic River, pipes spewing water into the river, and concrete abutments supporting the shoulders of a new highway under construction (fig. 327).[109] He referred to them as postindustrial ruins—ruins in reverse—things that became ruins *before* they were built rather than *after*. Smithson was preoccupied with "penumbral zones"— areas not thought of as picturesque, such as urban fringe developments, the

hallucination ("The rest of that day blurs into madness. The rest of that night too. And all the next day and night"), or even Didion's gorgeous deadpan ("This is the California where it is possible to live and die without ever eating an artichoke"). Readers also tended to notice (and traditional journalists to criticize) how often the new nonfiction writers set themselves up as the third-person omniscient narrator to describe the inner thoughts of their subjects. In their defense, the new nonfiction writers argued, "We had to gather all the materials the conventional journalist was after—and then keep going" (Wolfe). In fact, the new nonfictionists sometimes seemed more like performance artists than writers. George Plimpton's best-selling *Paper Lion* (1966), for instance, followed its half-terrified, half-elated narrator through a pro-football training camp and into the game huddle. But even Plimpton's experiences seemed cautious when compared with Thompson's *Hell's Angels: A Strange and Terrible Saga* (1967), which culminates with the gang members' beating the author into visionary unconsciousness.

The New Journalists and nonfiction novelists were brash, sometimes too brash: amid their stylistic pyrotechnics, a *New York Times* reviewer wondered, "could a reader. . . tell the truth?" At the same time, they seemed to understand better than anyone that the sixties were great theater, an experimental time that did not necessarily require experimental writers, but writers who were willing to do a reporter's legwork. And while many works of new nonfiction lost their sense of timeliness as the decade passed, the movement's influence has endured. *In Cold Blood* helped revive the "true crime" genre, and the influence of writers like Didion can be felt in the newfound respect paid to the memoir and the personal essay. And whereas university courses such as John McPhee's legendary "Literature of Fact" at Princeton were once rare, they now enjoy unprecedented popularity, proof that the new nonfiction has become an established part of American letters. —A. L.

effluvia of industrialization, and other entropic landscapes. Entropy, the inevitable disintegration of matter, was the ultimate destiny of the universe, according to Smithson.[110] (Could he have foreseen that the Passaic River would later be found to contain the country's highest levels of dioxin, an environmental poison, caused by a factory producing Agent Orange?)

"The Monuments of Passaic," which identified the industrial wasteland as a paradigm for art and life, illuminated the direction Smithson's sculpture was taking. By 1967, he was moving away from quasi-Minimalist forms and geometric progressions and beginning to work in the landscape. This enterprise started with a series of "non-sites," as he called them—archaeological samples of rocks from sites in New Jersey such as the Pine Barrens, Franklin Mineral Dumps, and the Palisades in Edgewater (fig. 328). He brought the rocks indoors, placed them in geometric metal bins, added photographs, maps, and written descriptions of the site to create an indoor-outdoor dialectic about industrial archaeology.

329. *Unveiling of Pablo Picasso's Chicago Civic Center Sculpture*, 1967

ART REENTERS THE AMERICAN CITY

On Wednesday, July 26, 1967, a *New York Times* headline screamed, "TROOPS BATTLE DETROIT SNIPERS, FIRING MACHINE GUNS FROM TANKS. DETROIT TOLL IS 31." Three weeks later, on August 15, 1967, the *Chicago Tribune* declared, "READY OR NOT, CHICAGO ENTERS ITS PICASSO ERA IN CIVIC CENTER. 50-FOOT SCULPTURE UNVEILED BY MAYOR." These two headlines are intimately related.

After World War II, many cities in the United States went into an economic decline. The new American dream for returning veterans was a suburban home with a yard and a car. As the white middle class fled to the suburbs, followed by corporate offices and factories, the drain on the cities was immense. Meanwhile, African Americans, moving north to avoid Jim Crow laws that limited their horizons in the South, were systematically excluded from the suburbs. Inner cities were becoming largely poor and African American, but the police forces remained mainly white. Tensions grew, and by the mid-1960s riots were a frequent occurrence—twenty-one major riots in 1966, eighty-three the following year. To this grim picture, add the chaos of the public sector: subway strikes, urban mismanagement, the threat of municipal bankruptcy.

Urban planners, architects, and public officials were looking for ways to revitalize and renew American cities. Artists were enlisted in the effort to attract people back to downtown areas. The national move toward public art came in the 1970s, just after the nadir of urban despair. In general, the local public art ordinances passed during this period required that 1 percent of the construction budgets of public buildings be set aside for permanently installed art works. The federal government got involved as well. In 1967, the National Endowment for the Arts had created its Art in Public Places Program; the first work commissioned was Alexander Calder's *La Grande Vitesse*, installed in Grand Rapids, Michigan, in 1969. In these early years, public art was synonymous with internationally recognized artists—Calder, Pablo Picasso, and Henry Moore—who were called upon to create symbols of a new urban identity. Indeed, in an oft-cited success, an image of *La Grande Vitesse* ended up on the Grand Rapids city stationery and graces civic garbage trucks even to this day.

Perhaps the most highly publicized monument installed in an American city during this period was the so-called Chicago Picasso (fig. 329), commissioned for the Civic Center Plaza. Although people on the streets in Chicago had their reservations about it, the rhetoric from public officials was optimistic, and it was very nice to be optimistic about *something* in an American city during the long, hot summer of 1967. Tens of thousands of citizens showed up for the unveiling, and the *Chicago Tribune* hailed the sculpture as Chicago's Eiffel Tower or Statue of Liberty. In describing his sources for the Civic Center Plaza, the architect from Skidmore, Owings & Merrill invoked St. Paul's Cathedral in London and St. Peter's in Rome. The initial impetus was conservative—a nostalgia for the grand public spaces of Europe that routinely integrated art and architecture.

If the social upheaval in American cities led to a new beginning for official public art programs on the national and local level, it also led to the birth of an activist public art, which often took the form of performance or temporary installations. As *La Grande Vitesse* was being installed in 1969, Mierle Laderman Ukeles was writing her *Maintenance Art Manifesto*, in which she formulated a unity between her everyday maintenance activities and her art. This resulted in a series of "Maintenance Art" performances, from cleaning museums to ballets for garbage barges on rivers to processions for maintenance vehicles. That same year, Vito Acconci traced routes through New York City by following unsuspecting strangers in his performance/action *Following Piece* (fig. 330). In the late 1960s, the difference between Ukeles' and Acconci's participatory actions and the official works of Calder and Picasso made the umbrella term "public art" inadequate. Today, however, the term has greater relevance. Ukeles and Acconci, along with many other artists, have managed to translate their urban art into a practice that includes permanent public works. These newer forms of public art combine the lessons of participation with the economics and technical necessities of permanent public display. Whether it is a permanent installation in a public landfill by Ukeles, or Acconci's flexible series of benches and conversation nooks woven through a community center in Arvada, Colorado, this new public art seeks to create social and physical space for public dialogue. An image of *La Grande Vitesse* may be painted on a garbage truck in Grand Rapids, but Ukeles has made a long-term commitment to working in collaboration with the people who drive the trucks. —T. F.

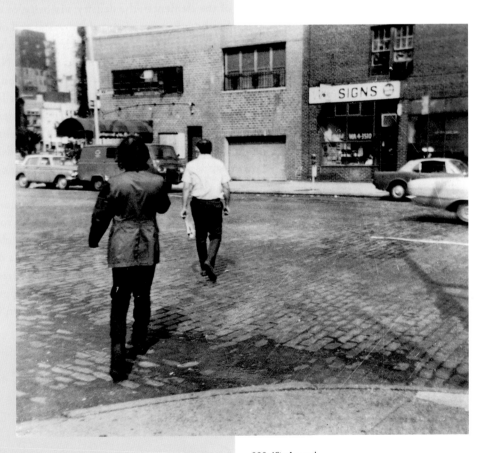

330. **Vito Acconci**
Following Piece, from the series *Street Works IV*, 1969
Performance/action, New York
Sponsored by the Architectural League of New York

333. **Walter de Maria**
The New York Earth Room, 1977
Earth, 250 yd.³ (197 m³)
Dia Center for the Arts,
New York

forces of entropy that fascinated Smithson. In time, nature reclaimed the jetty—the red lake waters rose, covering the work, then receded to reveal white salt crystals, and then rose again, so that the work was invisible for a number of years. Recently, the waters have receded again and the outlines of the jetty can be seen once more.

Some of the best surviving examples of Earth art, in addition to Smithson's *Spiral Jetty*, are Walter de Maria's *Lightning Field*, a rectangular grid of polished stainless steel poles, which sometimes attract lightning, in the remote desert of New Mexico (fig. 339), and Michael Heizer's *Double Negative* (fig. 335)—two cuts in the earth, 30 feet wide and 50 feet deep, straddling opposite sides of a ravine.

It is hardly surprising that the arrival of Earthworks coincided with the "back to the earth" movement and environmental awareness. Renewed attention was being focused on the earth, the exhaustible resources of nature, and the threat technology posed to nature's delicate equilibrium. *Spiral Jetty* was started in 1969, the year U.S. astronauts landed on the moon and inspired a new awareness of geological and galactic time, time measured in millennia. Earthworks brought these associations together: the vastness of the cosmos and ancient structures such as the mounds of America, Mayan ruins, and Stonehenge. They can also be seen as a continuation of America's fascination with the frontier and the country's sublime expanses, which had been explored by nineteenth-century artists and resonated in the 1950s in the paintings of Mark Rothko, Clyfford Still, and Barnett Newman. The solitude, immensity, and silence of the sites chosen for Earthworks represent a contemporary expression of the sublime. As de Maria put it, "Isolation is the essence of Land art."[III]

334. **Walter de Maria**
Mile-Long Drawing, 1968
(destroyed)
Two parallel chalk lines,
4 in. (10.2 cm) width,
144 in. (365.8 cm) apart,
1 mile (1.6 km) length
Mohave Desert, California

Earth artists, like the Postminimalists, were also concerned with the viewer's experience of the work in space and time. It takes a great effort to get to these Earthworks, most of which are in the remote areas of the desert Southwest. They are pilgrimage sites, sometimes accessible only by a dirt road, and visitor accommodations are primitive or nonexistent. Once there, the spectator faces further demands: hiking, skirting rattlesnakes, and enduring extremes of heat or cold. The experience of our bodies—the physical passage through space and time—is an underlying subject of all these works. They require time to be experienced, and they must be physically entered and moved through.

But most of us know Earthworks only through photographs, films, or videotapes (fig. 341). Photography became an essential corollary to Earth art, as well as to other ephemeral actions, documenting what could not be visited or could no longer be seen. Although the photographs of Earthwork sites were usually not considered art, but rather evidence of a work's existence, they are prized today for their independent aesthetic value.

335. **Michael Heizer**
Double Negative, 1969
240,000-ton displace-
ment of earth from
Mormon Mesa, Nevada,
500 x 50 x 30 ft.
(152.4 x 15.2 x 9.1 m)
The Museum of
Contemporary Art, Los
Angeles

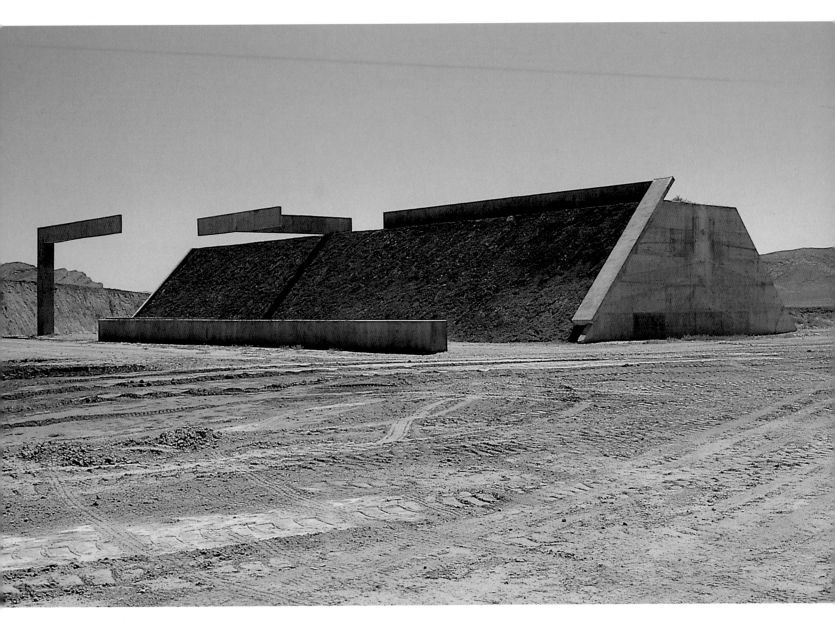

336. **Michael Heizer**
Complex One, 1972
Concrete, steel, and earth
from central eastern
Nevada, 282 x 1680 x
1320 in. (716.3 x
4267.2 x 3352.8 cm)
Dia Center for the Arts,
New York

337. Nancy Holt
Sun Tunnels, 1973–76
Concrete, four tunnels,
86 ft. (26.2 m) total
length
Great Basin Desert, Utah
© Nancy Holt/Licensed by
VAGA, New York, NY

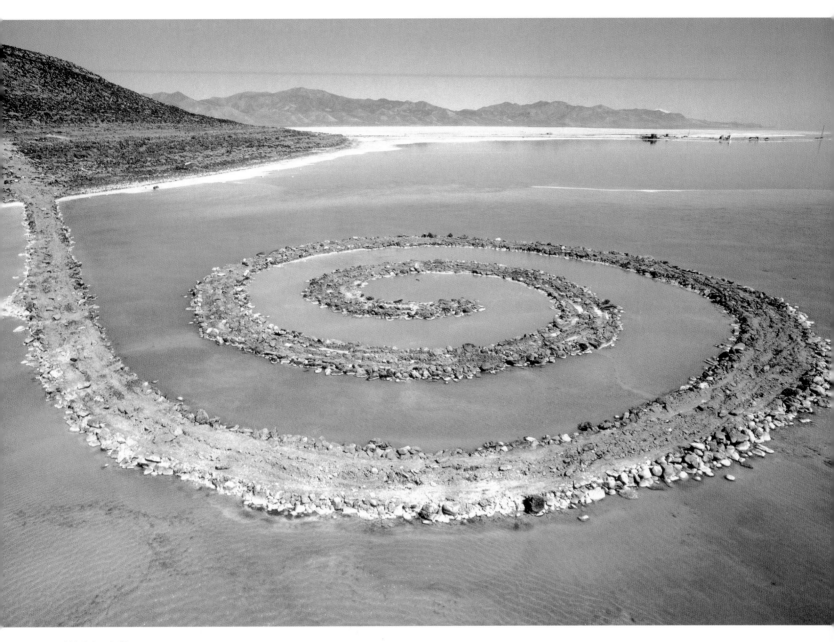

338. Robert Smithson
Spiral Jetty, 1970
Rock, salt crystals, earth,
and water with algae,
1500 ft. (457.2 m)
length, approximately
15 ft. (4.6 m) width
Great Salt Lake, Utah
© Estate of Robert
Smithson/Licensed by
VAGA, New York, NY
Photograph © Gianfranco
Gorgoni

When Earthworks were conceived, they had a noncommercial orientation: they could never be shown in a museum or collector's home. But producing this art required big, expensive machinery (240,000 tons of dirt had to moved for *Double Negative*) and therefore substantial financial support. Though the artists wanted to defy the market, private patronage was critical. Artists became dependent on generous and visionary patrons, among them Virginia Dwan, Heiner Friedrich, the Dia Art Foundation, Robert Scull, Horace Solomon, John de Menil, Bruno Bischofsberger, and Count Panza di Biumo. Some of these patrons were indefatigable collectors who would not be deterred by the monumental and site-specific nature of the works. Robert Scull, for example, purchased Earthworks *in situ*, as did a number of museums and foundations.

The urban counterpart to Earthworks was Anarchitecture. Fusing anarchy with architecture, the anarchitects, which included the artists Suzanne Harris, Jene Highstein, Jeffrey Lew, and Laurie Anderson, revolved around the young and charismatic Gordon Matta-Clark, son of the Surrealist painter Matta (Echaurren). Matta-Clark and his cohorts were mobilized by the revolutionary events of 1968 that called for the radical critique of social structures and, by extension, of culture. Their extemporaneous, ad hoc activities in public spaces, which sometimes broke the law, represented their version of anarchy. In addition, their dismantling of architecture corresponded to the breakdown of social structure.

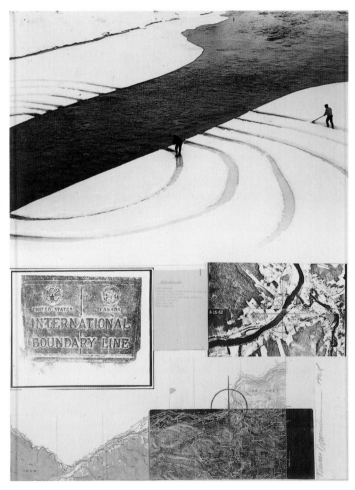

341. **Dennis Oppenheim**
Annual Rings, 1968
Gelatin silver prints,
maps, and text, 40 x 30
in. (101.6 x 76.2 cm)
John Weber Gallery,
New York

Matta-Clark became acquainted with Earthworks while studying architecture at Cornell University, where he assisted Dennis Oppenheim with a piece for an Earthworks exhibition. After moving to New York City, he began to work with neglected structures such as abandoned buildings and piers slated for demolition. He was interested in revealing both the formal and the contextual character of the architecture through carefully planned "cuts," as he called them. Using a chain saw, he would slice through a structure or cut up building elements to expose the historical aspects of vernacular architecture or visual vestiges of urban subculture, such as graffiti.

In his seminal work, *Splitting*, Matta-Clark made two parallel cuts straight down the center of a two-story clapboard house in Englewood, New Jersey (fig. 343). He drove a wedge through the middle of this middle-class American home and then cut out the four corners on the second floor—exposing the layers of shingles, plywood, beams, lathing, and sheetrock (fig. 342). By removing and excising pieces, Matta-Clark created form from *absence*, as Michael Heizer had done in *Double Negative*.

342. Gordon Matta-Clark
Installation view of
Splitting: Four Corners,
1974
Four building fragments,
approximately 57 x
42 x 42 in. (144.8 x
106.7 x 106.7 cm) each
Estate of the artist;
courtesy Holly Solomon
Gallery, New York

343. Gordon Matta-Clark
Splitting, 1974
Silver dye bleach print
(Cibachrome), 30 x 40 in.
(76.2 x 101.6 cm)
Estate of the artist;
courtesy Holly Solomon
Gallery, New York

Like Smithson, Matta-Clark was a catalyzing, charismatic presence. But the two artists belonged to social groups with pronounced differences: Smithson's was a vehemently opinionated, argumentative, male-dominated international clique that showed at the Dwan Gallery and came out of Minimalism. Matta-Clark was part of a more free-spirited group that was preoccupied with the breakdown of form, actively opposed to materialist aspirations—and included many strong women artists, such as Anderson and Harris. The group set up provisional exhibition spaces in SoHo, notably, a dilapidated street-front loft at 112 Greene Street, founded by the artist Jeffrey Lew, and the similarly scrappy 98 Greene Street, operated by Horace and Holly Solomon and built by Matta-Clark. They also congregated in the SoHo restaurant Food, which Matta-Clark had opened in 1971 as a way to employ artists.

Smithson and Matta-Clark were both aesthetic visionaries and loomed large in the seventies despite—or perhaps partly because of—their untimely deaths: Smithson in a plane crash in 1973, at the age of thirty-five, and Matta-Clark from cancer in 1978 at the same age.

THE NEW YORK "SIX" AND THE CALIFORNIA ONE

In the midst of, or perhaps because of, a prevailing populism and demand for communal responsibility in the late 1960s, architecture found itself at risk of being transformed from a form of cultural experimentation and critique into a service industry to be evaluated in only the most mundane of economic terms. In response to this threat, real or perceived, a group of architects, collectively known as the New York Five—Peter Eisenman, John Hejduk, Richard Meier, Michael Graves, and Charles Gwathmey—invented and immersed themselves in what Eisenman, the primary theorist of the group, termed a world of "autonomous" architecture. In this realm, only other architecture had either meaningful or instrumental value. It was this internal reconfiguration that engendered new alternatives.

The primary historical figure whose work was redeployed in this context was Le Corbusier (Charles-Édouard Jeanneret), particularly his villas of the 1920s. Each of the New York Five, in fact, had built or designed a significant Neo-Corbusian house by the late 1960s, such as Meier's Smith House (1965–67), Eisenman's House I (fig. 344), and Graves' Hanselman House (1970). Despite differences among individual architects, they all employed elements of high modernism to produce buildings beyond modernism. If Le Corbusier used platonic geometry to create clarity, Meier used overlapping geometries to produce complexity; where Le Corbusier used white to convey purity, Eisenman used multiple shades of white to suggest ambiguity; Le Corbusier relied on painterly forms for harmony, while Graves used them for collage.

An important aspect of the profound influence of the New York Five was their sense of institutional affiliation and intellectual allegiance. Their work was powerfully shaped by the writings and teaching of Colin Rowe, who wrote the introduction to the publication from which the group's name derives, *Five Architects* (1972). Rowe's writing on Le Corbusier introduced to the New York Five the rigorous formalism of critics such as Clement Greenberg and the generative possibilities of decontextualized comparative analysis. In such analysis, the work of Le Corbusier in the twentieth century and Palladio in the sixteenth, for example, could be seen to perform similar architectural operations, despite historical and cultural disconnection.

The Five remained involved in teaching—Hejduk at Cooper Union, Graves at Princeton, and Eisenman at several universities and, most important, at the Institute for Architecture and Urban Studies, which he founded in New York in 1967. Indeed, it was perhaps the very ambition to elevate architecture to the status of an institution, combined with the rich cultural capital of New York, that led to a bizarre incident and produced what might be regarded as the repressed sixth member of the New York Five.

In 1976, having been invited to participate in an exhibition at the Institute for Architecture and Urban Studies, Gordon Matta-Clark instead came in the middle of

344. **Peter Eisenman**
*Peter Eisenman House I,
Princeton, New Jersey,
1967–68*

pre-opening night and shot out the windows of the exhibition space with a BB gun. Although Matta-Clark had studied architecture at Cornell, was deeply involved with the New York art world, and founded several of its more important institutions, he rigorously rejected the New York Five's formal autonomy. He engaged in a more socially activist practice of Happenings, performances, and "cuts"—chain-saw slices through architectural structures, often focusing not on pristine Corbusian villas but on abandoned warehouses and run-down brownstones. The irony of what Matta-Clark called an "anarchitectural enterprise" is that, particularly in the cuttings and their photographic documentation, it produced spatial effects of Piranesian complexity that rival, within a different ethos, the phenomenological ambiguities sought by the New York Five.

Perhaps the first architect able to discern the underlying link between Matta-Clark and the New York Five and to develop elements of both strategies was Frank Gehry. In his early career, working far outside the New York power structures in the looser world of the Los Angeles art scene, Gehry had a divided practice: half of his work was devoted to socially engaged city planning, urban renewal, and public housing, while the rest—his Danziger Studio of 1964, for example—explored the formal implications of Minimalism for architecture. The explosive struggle to join these apparently disparate concerns finally erupted with the construction of Gehry's own house in 1978 (fig. 345). This pink shingled bungalow wrapped in a concatenation of chain-link and corrugated sheet metal combined the formal density and rigor of the New York Five with the social critique and underground culture of the New York Sixth. Gehry's multiple aspirations continue to drive what has become one of the most successful American architectural practices of the postwar era. —S. L.

345. **Frank Gehry**
Frank Gehry House, Santa Monica, California, 1977–78
Photograph © Tim Street-Porter/Esto. All Rights Reserved

346. **Frank Gehry**
Wiggle Side Chair, 1971
Corrugated cardboard and pressed fiber, 33½ x 16½ x 21½ in. (85.1 x 41.9 x 54.6 cm)

CONCEPTUAL ART

Given all the unorthodox art forms developed in the late 1960s, confused spectators and critics—like those who viewed Duchamp's readymades early in the century—wondered whether art could be art just because the artist said it was. With the growing use of non-art materials—cloth, plastic, dirt, organic matter—and the increasing impermanence and unpredictability of these works, a renewed debate arose about the meaning of art. As the Conceptual artist Joseph Kosuth wrote in 1968, "A work of art is a tautology in that it is a presentation of the artist's intention, that is, he is saying that a particular work of art *is* art, which means, is a *definition* of art. Thus, that it is art is true *a priori*."[112]

In the summer 1967 issue of *Artforum*, Sol LeWitt contributed a seminal essay, "Paragraphs on Conceptual art," in which he proposed a new art form—one where "the idea becomes a machine that makes the art."[113] This art was no longer about morphological characteristics but about an inquiry into what art means. Conceptual art had a long lineage, beginning with Marcel Duchamp, whose unassisted readymades changed the focus from the form of the work, from "appearance" to "conception." Other proto-Conceptual statements had been made in Europe by Yves Klein and Piero Manzoni, who canned his feces and sold them for their weight in gold; by the American correspondence artist Ray Johnson (fig. 76); and by On Kawara, who obsessively created small paintings with nothing but the date of each day's work painted across the surface.

With Conceptual art's renewed emphasis on the meaning of art, it is not surprising that text and language assumed a more prominent role: as criticism, as writings by the artists, and as texts incorporated into their work. "At its most strict and radical extreme the art I call conceptual is such because it is based on. . .the understanding of the linguistic nature of all art propositions, be they past or present, and regardless of the elements used in their construction," wrote Kosuth in "Art as Idea as Idea."[114] At that time, Kosuth was producing his Definition works, in which an enlarged dictionary definition would stand on its own or next to a photograph of an object, accompanied by the real object itself (figs. 349, 350).

347. **Bruce Nauman**
The True Artist Helps the World by Revealing Mystic Truths (Window or Wall Sign), 1967
Neon with glass tubing suspension frame, 59 x 55 x 2 in. (149.9 x 139.7 x 5.1 cm)
Private collection

The emergence of language as a medium for advanced art—as in the work of artists such as Kosuth, Lawrence Weiner (fig. 348), and Douglas Huebler—was a radical assault against late modernism and formalist methodologies. But it did allow for a closer relation between art and philosophy, theory, and criticism. Criticism became increasingly important as the divide between the formalists and anti-formalists widened and new aesthetic languages were hotly contested. Theory

surfaced as a powerful force in the growing opposition to the hegemony of modernism. Many strong critical voices emerged during this period, among them those of Lucy Lippard, Rosalind Krauss, Annette Michelson, and Max Kozloff. Artists themselves were articulate defenders of the new art, and many of them wrote powerful polemical essays in journals such as *Artforum*. After moving from Los Angeles to New York in 1967, *Artforum* established itself, under the editorial leadership of Philip Leider and John Coplans, as the most important ideological battleground in the arts (a position it held for at least a decade).

The eruption of language into the aesthetic field was first felt in the art criticism and writing of Robert Smithson, Donald Judd, Dan Flavin, Robert Morris, Sol LeWitt, Carl Andre, Yvonne Rainer, and Mel Bochner (fig. 351). Their writings signaled a shift from the visual to the verbal field as an arena of expression. The same 1967 issue of *Artforum* that contained LeWitt's article on Conceptual art, for example, also included Michael Fried's "Art and Objecthood" and Robert Morris' "Notes on Sculpture."

The pages of art journals became not only important forums for debate but also "sites" for works of art. It could be argued that Smithson's essays, such as "The Monuments of Passaic," were works in themselves and perhaps his most important legacy. Other artists increasingly sought to use publishing as a means to disseminate their ideas, and these projects also became primary works. For instance, Joseph Kosuth, Dan Graham, and Adrian Piper purchased ad space in magazines and newspapers to *present*—not to *represent*—their art (figs. 352, 353). The Conceptual art promoter Seth Siegelaub reinvented the role of the art dealer by curating "alternate sites," among them publications, artists' books, tapes, and exhibition catalogs, which he believed could be the sole form in which an exhibition took place.[115] These avenues of communication and distribution enabled artists to speed past institutional and geographical boundaries. Books, the mail, advertisements, billboards, and magazines became principal expressive vehicles for the work. As the artist Douglas Huebler stated in 1969, "The world is full of objects, more or less interesting: I do not wish to add any more."[116]

Though Conceptual art was an extreme manifestation of art's dematerialization, it still took various forms—texts, processes, situations, and information—using language, mathematical and organizational systems (fig. 354), photography, publications, notational drawings, video, film, and performance to address the

351. **Mel Bochner**
Study for Theory of Painting (Parts One and Four), 1969
Graphite, ink, and colored pencil on paper, 8½ x 11 in. (21.6 x 27.9 cm) each
Collection of Sarah-Ann and Werner H. Kramarsky

352. **Dan Graham**
Homes for America, from
Arts magazine, 1966

353. **Dan Graham**
Figurative, from *Harper's
Bazaar*, 1965

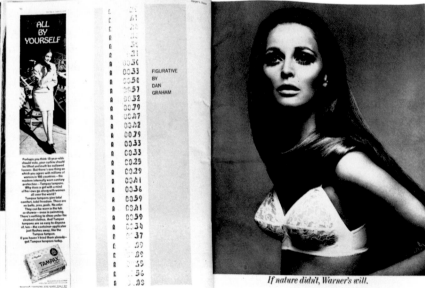

physical, social, and institutional context of the art object. As a product of the political ferment of the time, some Conceptual art also exposed sociopolitical inequities. The self-referentiality of modernism had shifted to an examination of how art functions as part of a social system.

Hans Haacke took on the Guggenheim Museum board of trustees and corporate art patrons such as the Chase Manhattan Bank, Philip Morris, Mobil, and PaineWebber in a series of phototext pieces that mimic corporate ad campaigns.

Through these works, he meticulously revealed how key institutional and corporate leaders were affiliated with Third World exploitation, right-wing groups, and the CIA (fig. 357). Support for art, his work tells us, often comes from tarnished dollars. Haacke's distinctive form of muckraking unveiled the politically charged relationships among art, society, and institutions of power.

Most Conceptual artists, exploring the social underpinnings or meaning of a work of art, took an aggressive, anti-style position. John Baldessari went so far as to give up painting in 1966—and destroy all the works that remained in his possession. After 1967, he made photographically based work on canvas with simple, deadpan lines of text executed by a sign painter—"Everything is purged from this painting but art, no ideas have entered this work" or "This is not to be looked at" (fig. 355). Commenting on the ontology of a work of art, he was attempting to make art that did not emanate art signals. In 1970, he made a Conceptual work about

354. **Mel Bochner**
Ten to 10, 1972
Stone, 120 in. (304.8 cm) diameter
Whitney Museum of American Art, New York; Purchase, with funds from the Gilman Foundation, Inc. 77.28

the destruction of his early paintings in the form of a newspaper announcement that read, "Notice is hereby given that all works of art done by the undersigned between May, 1953, and March, 1966, in his possession as of July 24, 1970, were cremated on July 24, 1970, in San Diego, California."[117]

Many artists believed that the traditional object of art was irrelevant, unnecessary, and dead. They also extended the "post-studio" movement (Carl Andre's term), where artists had works fabricated, worked on site, or simply made instructions for others to execute. To Conceptual artists, the studio had become more of a thinking space, a study space, or a writing space.[118] Photography, often in combination with text, was an important component of the post-studio Conceptual practice (figs. 355, 356, 358, 359). Just as Earth artists used photography as a documentary record, Conceptual artists valued the photograph as a source of pure, factual information and technical data. Its impersonality, mechanical quality, and supposed objectivity served well the development of an anti-style.

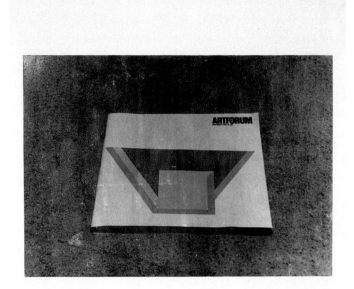

THIS IS NOT TO BE LOOKED AT.

AN ARTIST IS NOT MERELY THE SLAVISH
ANNOUNCER OF A SERIES OF FACTS.
WHICH IN THIS CASE THE CAMERA HAS
HAD TO ACCEPT AND MECHANICALLY
RECORD.

355. **John Baldessari**
*This Is Not to Be Looked
At*, 1966–68
Acrylic and photoemulsion
on canvas, 59 x 45 in.
(149.9 x 114.3 cm)
Collection of Joel Wachs

356. **John Baldessari**
*An Artist Is Not Merely the
Slavish Announcer. . .*,
1967–68
Photoemulsion, varnish,
and gesso on canvas,
59⅛ x 45⅛ in. (150.2 x
114.6 cm)
Whitney Museum of
American Art, New York;
Purchase, with funds from
the Painting and Sculpture
Committee 83.8a–m

357. **Hans Haacke**
Shapolsky et al. Manhattan Real Estate Holdings—A Real Time Social System, As of May 1, 1971, 1971
Six photographic enlargements with typewritten sheets, 20 x 48 in. (50.8 x 121.9 cm) overall
Wadsworth Atheneum, Hartford, Connecticut

358. **Douglas Huebler**
Duration Piece #4, 1968
(detail)
Nine gelatin silver prints with text panel,
7½ x 6 in. (19.1 x 15.2 cm) each print
Estate of the artist

Duration Piece #4
Bradford, Massachusetts

Photographs of two children playing "jump-rope" were made in the following order:

I.   Three photographs were made at 10 second intervals.

II.   Three photographs were made at 20 second intervals.

III. Three photographs were made at 30 second intervals.

The nine photographs have been scrambled out of sequence and join with this statement to constitute the form of this piece.

September, 1968   Douglas Huebler

Despite the anti-style and anti-commercial nature of much Conceptual art, it has today taken its place in the art-historical pantheon. Anti-style became a style, rebellion and dissent were historicized, and works that were casual, mass-produced, and ephemeral are now paradoxically considered precious. Even at its inception, Conceptual art was taken up by museums in some of the most daring exhibitions of the day—notably "Live in Your Head: When Attitudes Become Form," at the Kunsthalle Bern (1969), and "Information," at The Museum of Modern Art, New York (1970). Both exhibitions featured Conceptual art, together with process-oriented Postminimalism and Earth art, demonstrating that the boundaries among the three were fuzzy and that the communities overlapped. The international characters of the shows, moreover, signaled that the world was fast turning into a global village. Finally, each exhibition was accompanied by a catalog conceived as a Conceptual publication: in *Information*, the artists designed their own pages, while *Attitudes* was designed in the form of an address book.

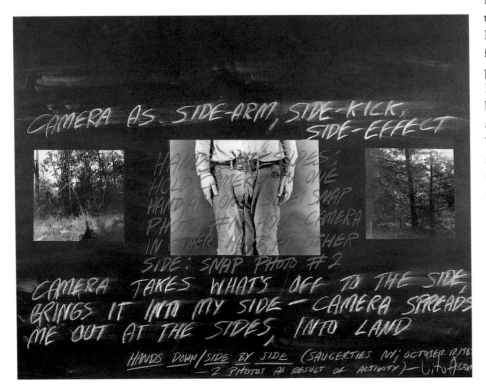

359. **Vito Acconci**
Hands Down/Side by Side,
1969
Gelatin silver prints and
chalk on paperboard,
29⅞ x 39¹⁵⁄₁₆ in.
(75.9 x 101.4 cm)
Whitney Museum of
American Art, New York;
Purchase, with funds from
the Photography
Committee 92.12

Conceptual art provoked the ire of many mainstream critics, prompting Robert Hughes, for one, to announce "The Decline and Fall of the Avant-Garde" in a 1972 article in *Time*:

"Advanced" art—whether conceptual art, process art, video, body art, or any of their proliferating hybrids—avoids the object like the plague. The public has retreated, in turn, from it. This is a worldwide phenomenon, and what now exists is not simply a recession of interest (and talent) but a general weariness—a reluctance to believe in the avant-garde as principle. . . . The inherent purposelessness of anti-object art becomes a real liability in one area: conceptualism. The basic claim of conceptual art is that making objects is irrelevant. . . . And so a thicket of verbiage protects, and supports, the most banal propositions.[119]

What Hughes derided was, for Conceptual artists and advocates, fundamental to their enterprise: the belief that art, indeed vision itself, is determined by language. The sense of sight is not a neutral biological function. What we see is the product of the words we have read and heard—of the language we bring to the act of vision. By extension, the social and cultural structures that control our actions and attitudes are also determined by language. Language, text-based Conceptual artists declared, is central to an understanding of art, culture, and identity. This proposition mapped out the route along which artists, and many critics, would travel for the next thirty years as the old canons of art were finally overturned by a host of new voices.

The Ascendance of Alternatives

Liberation movements—Black Power, feminism, gay rights—that began in the 1960s at the margins of society soon permeated the mainstream and irrevocably altered American life. As often happens, the root causes of these changes can be found in the social and political climate. In March 1968, President Johnson, unable to resolve the war in Vietnam, announced that he would not run for reelection. That November, the Republican candidate, Richard M. Nixon, was elected president on a promise to make peace in Vietnam. Initially, he seemed to succeed, finalizing the Paris peace talks begun during Johnson's administration. Troop withdrawals started in 1969, but the peace was short-lived. The following year, Nixon extended the war to Laos and Cambodia, and it was not until 1973, in the face of continuing U.S. losses, that American troops withdrew from Vietnam.

On other fronts, however, Nixon's foreign policy was a record of triumphs: in 1972, he made an unprecedented visit to Communist China, reopening relations with it for the first time in more than twenty years; in November 1973, he oversaw a U.S.-sponsored peace accord between Egypt and Israel, ending the war that had broken out the month before; and he relaxed tensions with the Soviet Union through, among

THEATER IN THE 1970S

Both the literary and the radical manifestations of Off-Off-Broadway had lost momentum by 1975—part of the general waning of the counterculture after the Nixon years. Most of the radical troupes disbanded, and Off-Off-Broadway became a training ground for actors, directors, and playwrights who aspired to success in the commercial theater.

Throughout the nation, the avant-garde theater of the 1970s largely turned away from social engagement, in favor of introspection and self-examination. The work of the Performance Group in this period shifted from physical, ritualistic performance to the staging of literary dramas, though in highly unconventional ways. (In 1975, the Performance Group became the Wooster Group, fig. 360.) In 1974, two members of the group, Elizabeth LeCompte and Spalding Gray, formed a workshop to produce more overtly aestheticizing, abstract, and formalistic works derived from Gray's life. *Sakonnet Point* (1975) was a virtually silent, wholly abstract meditation on childhood, while the powerful *Rumstick Road* (1977) dealt with the suicide of Gray's mother. Tendencies toward formalism, abstraction, and autobiography were apparent in the work of other experimental groups of the 1970s, including Michael Kirby's Structuralist Workshop and Mabou Mines. Richard Foreman's productions with his Ontological Hysterical Theater set out to explore consciousness itself by re-creating on stage the processes by which the mind builds an idea of the world outside itself. Robert Wilson's "theater of visions" staged the flow of visual images emanating from his own imagination, making no necessary reference to any external reality.

Yet the activism that had infused the radical theater of the 1960s did not disappear altogether in the 1970s. David Rabe, a Vietnam veteran, wrote a series of powerful plays that forced audiences to confront the legacy of the Vietnam War (*The Basic Training of Pavlo Hummel*, 1971; *Sticks and Bones*, 1971; and *Streamers*, 1976), using the physical and psychological effects of the war as metaphors for problems endemic to American society. But unlike the Off-Off-Broadway playwrights of the 1960s, Rabe was skeptical that social change could be effected: his characters seem trapped, unable to transcend their social circumstances.

The 1970s also saw the emergence of work that addressed not humanity in general but the concerns of particular social and political groups, including African Americans, Asian Americans, Hispanic Americans, feminists, and gays and lesbians. Originating in the avant-garde theater of the late 1960s, this theater moved more toward the

360. **The Wooster Group**
Nayatt School, directed by Elizabeth Lecompte, 1977–78, photograph by Clem Fior

other things, a U.S.-Soviet summit in May 1972 and the first round of the Strategic Arms Limitation Talks. But these accomplishments were eclipsed by the Watergate scandal. In the election year of 1972, five men were arrested while attempting to bug Democratic National Committee headquarters, located in the Watergate apartment complex in Washington, D.C. Nixon at first denied knowledge of their activities, but a few months later evidence of his involvement began to leak out. In August 1974, after the House Judiciary Committee adopted three articles of impeachment, Nixon resigned, and his vice president, Gerald Ford, was sworn in (fig. 361).

mainstream in the course of the next decade. Whereas African American theater of the 1960s had been galvanized by the Black Power movement, by the 1970s African American actors and writers, many of whom had begun their careers in the avant-garde, were gaining visibility in the establishment. The distinguished Negro Ensemble Company, a relatively traditional Off-Broadway theater founded in 1969, consolidated the gains made by its more radical predecessors.

Just as African American actors and playwrights wanted their own theaters, some women performers left radical troupes that did not specifically address their interests. By the end of the 1970s, well over one hundred self-consciously feminist theaters were active in the United States, including some dealing specifically with the lesbian experience. A generation of more mainstream women playwrights, including Beth Henley, Marsha Norman, and Wendy Wasserstein, also emerged in the 1970s. The extravagantly campy productions of the Theater of the Ridiculous pioneered a gay male sensibility in theater from the late 1960s through the 1970s. Sadly, this community was destined to find its strongest theatrical voice with the advent of the AIDS crisis in the 1980s.
—P. A.

Nixon's duplicity and abuse of authority compounded the sense of disillusionment with the power structure that had begun with America's misadventures in Vietnam. At the same time, Americans became uncomfortably aware of their dependence on the resources of other countries, as when Saudi Arabia and other Arab countries placed an embargo on oil shipments to the United States in 1973 in retaliation for America's support of Israel and Israeli victory in the Yom Kippur War. The embargo caused a steep rise in the prices of heating oil and gasoline, commodities whose relative cheapness Americans had long taken for granted. A deep recession ensued, and the American economy stagnated. In another arena, alarming environmental concerns erupted in the seventies after the discovery of toxic-waste dumping in such areas as the Love Canal in upstate New York; and the dangers posed by nuclear power plants were graphically demonstrated by the malfunction of the Three Mile Island plant in Pennsylvania, which allowed lethal radiation to escape into the surrounding area (fig. 362).

Political betrayals, economic uncertainties, and fears of ecological disaster made many Americans mistrustful, cynical, and critical of official institutions of power and their public statements.

The cynicism of the era, the breakdown of confidence in government, found expression in the anarchism of Punk rock and in dark film dramas such as *Taxi Driver* (1976, Martin Scorsese) and *Apocalypse Now* (1979, Francis Ford Coppola). Some artists retreated into themselves—a new

361. *President Richard M. Nixon Resigns, Washington, D.C.*, 1974

362. *Nuclear Power Plant at Three Mile Island, Pennsylvania*, 1979, photograph by Fred S. Prousor/ Liaison Agency Inc.

concern for autobiography and an exploration of consciousness, for example, are evident in the performing arts during the seventies. For many Americans, retreat meant turning away from social and political problems to focus on personal achievements and pleasures—which led the author Tom Wolfe to characterize the seventies as "the me decade."

But, as in the fifties and sixties, there were always social and political activists who made it their responsibility to effect change. A vast underground that included radical political organizations, gay rights activists, and feminists helped fuel a transformation in American life by demanding status for special-interest groups.

THE "MOVIE BRATS" RECONFIGURE HOLLYWOOD

In a country where young men were called upon to fight an unpopular war in Vietnam, the possession and corruption of American youth was a recurring theme of the films of the 1970s. First sounded in Francis Ford Coppola's Mafia opera *The Godfather* (fig. 363), it echoed through William Friedkin's portrait of demonic possession in *The Exorcist* (1973), Martin Scorsese's altar boy-meets-mob story *Mean Streets* (fig. 364), and Brian De Palma's supernatural melodrama *Carrie* (1976). Significantly, Coppola, Scorsese, and De Palma—along with Steven Spielberg and George Lucas—were young filmmakers, the first generation to come out of the film schools proliferating across the country. Because of their youth and encyclopedic knowledge of Hollywood, they were dubbed "the movie brats."

The brats likewise mythologized the other defining event of the era: the break-in of Democratic Party headquarters at the Watergate complex in 1972, which was sanctioned by President Nixon and which led to his resignation in 1974. Films as diverse as Spielberg's *Jaws* (1975) and *Close Encounters of the Third Kind* (1977), Lucas' *Star Wars* (fig. 365), and Hal Ashby's *Shampoo* (1975) had Watergate references and resonances. In *Jaws*, the political establishment in a beach town tries to suppress the news of a shark attack. Set on the eve of Nixon's 1968 election, *Shampoo* depicts the Los Angeles establishment suppressing political and sexual hypocrisy. Coppola's *The Conversation* (1974) eerily presaged Watergate in its depiction of a surveillance expert (Gene Hackman) who invades the privacy of citizens and gets destroyed. Then there was *All the President's Men* (1976, Alan J. Pakula), with Robert Redford and Dustin Hoffman as the investigative reporters who blew the lid off Watergate.

These films represent one extreme of the decade—a cinema that unblinkingly confronted contemporary disillusion and discord. At the other extreme were misty-eyed paeans to "the way we were," to borrow the title of the 1973 Sydney Pollack movie about the 1940s romance between an idealist (Barbra Streisand) and a pragmatist (Robert Redford). Redford was the decade's posterboy of nostalgia for lost illusions, trying to win Mia Farrow in *The Great Gatsby* (1974, Jack Clayton, screenplay by Coppola) and win money with Paul Newman in *The Sting* (1973, George Roy Hill). These movies about glamorous con artists in vintage duds seemed to say that amorality has always been around, but that it looks better worn with a fedora.

The difference between nostalgic excursions such as *Gatsby* and *The Sting* and serious period trips such as *The Godfather* I and II, and *Chinatown* (1974, Roman Polanski) is that the latter movies, which trace the rise and fall of the Corleone crime

363. Al Pacino and Marlon Brando in *The Godfather*, directed by Francis Ford Coppola, 1972
Courtesy Paramount Pictures

364. Robert DeNiro in *Mean Streets*, directed by Martin Scorsese, 1973
Courtesy Taplin-Perry-Scorsese

377. Nancy Spero
Codex Artaud XVII, 1972
Type and painted collage
on paper, 45 x 18 in.
(114.3 x 45.7 cm)
Collection of the artist

378. Miriam Schapiro,
with **Sherry Brody**
The Doll House, from
Womanhouse, 1972
Mixed media, 84 x 40 x
41 in. (213.4 x 101.6 x
104.1 cm)
National Museum of
American Art, Smithsonian
Institution, Washington,
D.C.; Museum purchase
through the Gene Davis
Memorial Fund

379. **Judy Chicago**
The Dinner Party, 1974–79
Painted porcelain and
needlework, 576 x 576 x
36 in. (1463 x 1463 x
91.4 cm)
Collection of the artist
© 1979 Judy Chicago

PATTERN AND DECORATION

The introduction of craft by women nourished one of the primary art trends of the 1970s, a movement known as P+D, or Pattern and Decoration, which drew directly on various craft traditions and favored painterly, flat, floral, abstract decoration. Miriam Schapiro, among early practitioners of this style, used fabrics, wallpaper, and flower designs that honored the female domestic sphere. Like Minimalism, Pattern painting was based on the repetition of a motif in an all-over composition and often relied on the structure of overlapping grids. But the motifs employed, far from being reductive and geometric, were arabesque in conception.

Pattern painters—both male and female—defied the elitist and puritanical viewpoint epitomized by the critic Clement Greenberg's early admonishment: only when painting "becomes mere decoration does abstract art proceed in a void and really turn into 'dehumanized' art."[126] Rejecting such dogma, Pattern painting, by embracing the decorative and ornamental, opened up art to a host of non-Western and nonmainstream traditions, from Far Eastern to Celtic, Native American to Islamic. Artists such as Ree Morton, Robert Kushner, Kim MacConnel, and Joyce Kozloff challenged male-dominated Western high art with multicultural sources, nonhierarchical imagery, visceral, narrative, and personal content (figs. 380, 381). The old hierarchy dividing art and craft was upset by artists such as Thomas Lanigan-Schmidt, who raided ethnic neighborhoods such as New York's Chinatown for his sculptures of foil, glitter, and brightly colored plastic, or Robert Kushner, who exhibited fabric fashion creations as "paintings" (figs. 382, 383).

The repetition and patterning in folk and outsider art found favor with the Chicago artist Roger Brown, who subjected his figurative imagery to an overall mesmerizing patterning (fig. 384). Chicago had long been a bastion of a regional imagist tradition, going back to the Monster Roster of the 1950s. In the late sixties and early seventies, this tradition was still flowering, albeit in a different guise, and in 1974 came to national attention through the traveling survey exhibition "Made in Chicago." This work, by Ed Paschke, Roger Brown, Jim Nutt, Karl Wirsum, and Gladys Nilsson, among others, drew on sources in primitive, untutored outsider art, street art, and comic books to create a unique, defiantly nonmainstream art. The Chicago Imagists, as they were called, often used shocking color combinations, black humor, and crude, distorted, or sadistic subject matter (figs. 385, 386), making a local contribution to the "cult of the ugly" or "bad painting" that was developing elsewhere in the seventies. The recognition of regional styles and cultures exemplified by these Chicago artists was part of the pluralism of the decade.

Even Frank Stella, known for his Minimalist geometric abstractions in the 1960s, made an abrupt shift in the 1970s to exuberant embellishment. In his Exotic

380. **Ree Morton**
The Plant That Heals May Also Poison, 1974
Celastic, glitter, and paint on wood, 46 x 64 x 4 in. (116.8 x 162.6 x 10.2 cm)
Private collection; courtesy Alexander and Bonin, New York

381. **Kim MacConnel**
Formidable, 1981
Synthetic polymer on
cotton, 97¼ x 129¼ in.
(247 x 328.3 cm)
Whitney Museum of
American Art, New York;
Purchase, with funds from
the Louis and Bessie Adler
Foundation, Inc., Seymour
M. Klein, President 82.8

382. **Robert Kushner**
Biarritz, from *The Persian
Line: Part II*, 1976
Acrylic on cotton, synthetic
brocade, and fringe, 74 x
86³⁄₁₆ in. (188 x 219 cm)
Courtesy the artist and DC
Moore Gallery, New York

383. **Thomas Lanigan-Schmidt**
Panis Angelicus, 1970–87
Mixed-media installation with monstrance, candlesticks, and altar cloth, 7 x 6 x 3½ ft. (2.1 x 1.8 x 1.1 m)
Groninger Museum, The Netherlands

384. **Roger Brown**
The Entry of Christ into Chicago in 1976, 1976
Oil on canvas, 72 x 120 in. (182.9 x 304.8 cm)
Whitney Museum of American Art, New York; Purchase, with funds from Mr. and Mrs. Edwin A. Bergman and the National Endowment for the Arts, and Joel and Anne Ehrenkranz, by exchange 77.56

385. **Jim Nutt**
Running Wild, 1970
Acrylic on plexiglass and
enamel on wood frame,
46 x 43½ in.
(116.8 x 110.5 cm)
Collection of Lawrence
and Evelyn Aronson; cour-
tesy Phyllis Kind Gallery,
New York

386. **Ed Paschke**
Fumar, 1979
Oil on canvas, 60 x 46 in.
(152.4 x 116.8 cm)
Collection of Ellen and
Richard Sandor

Bird series, inspired by a trip to India, curvilinear cut-metal reliefs are covered with glitter and bright, brushy paint strokes (fig. 387). Jasper Johns turned to patterned "cross-hatch" paintings in the seventies (fig. 388), and Lucas Samaras produced elaborate fabric quilt works hung on the wall like paintings. Although all three artists had previously engaged patterning as an element in their work, the events of the decade encouraged them to give it a new, extravagant focus. Sol LeWitt, who had moved from Minimalism to Conceptualism in the late sixties, turned his attention to large wall drawings that transformed architectural interiors (figs. 389, 390). Based on simple instructions that could be executed by trained assistants, such as "line to point to plane," the wall drawings were visually mesmerizing and often flamboyant and colorful. Pattern painting and Patterning reverberated in related disciplines as well. The architect Robert Venturi proclaimed, "Less is a bore," and advocated an architecture of vernacular exuberance.[127] He regarded the International Style as insensitive and tyrannical, not adequate to the complexity and contradiction of contemporary life.

387. **Frank Stella**
Bonin Night Heron,
1976–77
Mixed media on aluminum,
99 x 125⅜ in.
(251.5 x 318.5 cm)
Albright-Knox Art Gallery,
Buffalo; Gift of Seymour H.
Knox

388. **Jasper Johns**
Corpse and Mirror, 1974
Oil, encaustic, newsprint,
paper fragments, and
crayon on canvas, 50 x
68⅛ in. (127 x 173 cm)
Private collection
© Jasper Johns/Licensed
by VAGA, New York, NY

389. **Sol LeWitt**
Cover design for *Music in
Twelve Parts, Parts 1 & 2*,
by Philip Glass, 1974

390. **Sol LeWitt**
Installation view of
"Sol LeWitt" at The
Museum of Modern Art,
New York, 1978

Center wall:
Wall Drawing #289, 1976
(detail)
Crayon and graphite,
dimensions variable
Whitney Museum of
American Art, New York;
Purchase, with funds from
the Gilman Foundation,
Inc. 78.1.1–4

Left and right walls:
Wall Drawing #308, 1978
Crayon, dimensions
variable
Private collection

395. **Ana Mendieta**
Untitled, from the *Silueta*
series, 1976
Performance on beach
with red pigment
Private collection

396. Ana Mendieta
Anima (Alma/Soul), 1976
Performance with bamboo
armature and fireworks
Private collection

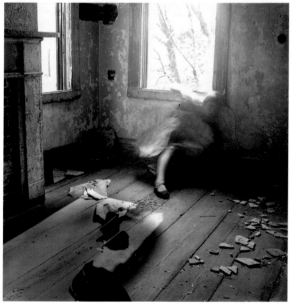

397. Francesca Woodman
House 3, Providence,
1975–76
Gelatin silver print, 8 x 10
in. (20.3 x 25.4 cm)
Collection of George and
Betty Woodman

402. **Meredith Monk**
Education of the Girlchild,
1973, photograph by
Beatriz Schiller

of large-scale collaborations among choreographers, composers, and visual artists.
Both *Einstein* and *Dance* foreshadowed
new directions for dance in the 1980s.

Although the improvisational group
Grand Union (1970-76), which grew out
of Yvonne Rainer's work and included
Rainer, Trisha Brown, Steve Paxton, David
Gordon, and Douglas Dunn, was more theatrical than the Minimalist dances several
of its individual members made on their own (anything, from rock music to verbal play
to outrageous costumes, was fair game for the group), it nevertheless belongs to the
category of analytic postmodern dance, because it was so often engaged in revealing
conditions of performance. So, too, does Contact Improvisation, a duet form devised by
Steve Paxton (done either in an informal "jam" situation or in a theatrical setting) that
is based on aikido, sports, and social dancing and has spread as a community-based
practice to become an international network.

Analytic postmodern dance dominated the avant-garde dance scene, but another
strand of postmodern dance developed in the 1970s. Related to analytic postmodern
dance in its simplicity and austerity, metaphoric and metaphysical postmodern dance
drew on non-Western forms of dance, martial arts, and meditation and on countercultural interest in communal rituals and spiritual expression. Metaphoric postmodern
dance, like analytic postmodern dance, used techniques of radical juxtaposition, ordinary movements, and stillness and repetition—but often with a more theatrical presen-
tational style. Examples of metaphoric postmodern dance include Meredith Monk's
mythic "operas," such as *Education of the Girlchild* (fig. 402), about a mysterious
community of women, Kenneth King's dances that created metaphors for technological
information systems, and Laura Dean's spinning dances.

All this avant-garde activity took place on the crest of a dance boom in the 1970s
that saw an increase in audiences, funding, and training for all forms of dance. There
were regular—and longer—seasons by major ballet and modern dance companies (both
American and foreign) in New York, which in the 1970s became the dance capital of
the world. And, just as regional theater spread in the 1960s and 1970s, so the dance
boom of the 1970s expanded the regional ballet movement; small cities now often
boasted a ballet company as well as an opera and a symphony orchestra. A vigorous
black dance movement—whose practitioners included Alvin Ailey, Eleo Pomare, Rod
Rodgers, and Arthur Mitchell and the Dance Theater of Harlem—built audiences in
black communities and often explored political and social themes through techniques
that drew on traditional African American dance forms. Television, too, participated in
the dance boom, with regular broadcasting of dance documentaries and experiments in
the new genre of video dance. Both identity politics and the crossbreeding of dance and
mass media helped usher in a new phase of postmodern dance in the 1980s. —S. B.

Top, left and right:

403. **Vito Acconci**
Seedbed, 1972
Performance/installation
at Sonnabend Gallery,
New York
Wood ramp and loud-
speaker, 120 x 720 x
264 in. (304.8 x
1828.8 x 670.6 cm)
Courtesy Barbara
Gladstone Gallery,
New York
Photograph by Kathy
Dillon

404. **Scott Burton**
Group Behavior Tableau,
1972
Performance at the
Whitney Museum of
American Art, New York

405. **Chris Burden**
Through the Night Softly,
1973
Street performance,
Los Angeles
Collection of the artist

406. **Chris Burden**
Shoot, 1971, from *Chris Burden Deluxe Book: 1971–1973*, 1974
Loose-leaf binder with hand-painted cover containing fifty-three gelatin silver prints and text, 11½ x 11½ x 2 in. (29.2 x 29.2 x 5.1 cm) overall
Whitney Museum of American Art, New York; Purchase, with funds from Joanne Leonhardt Cassullo 92.70a–bbb

407. **Chris Burden**
Icarus, 1973
Performance, Venice, California
Collection of the artist

himself to a number of harrowing trials and tests of endurance and tolerance—such as locking himself in a 2 x 2 x 3-foot locker for five days, crawling through broken glass, or having a friend shoot him in the arm (figs. 405–07). These dangerous situations implicated the viewer as a witness and voyeur. At about the same time, the German artist Joseph Beuys performed *Coyote: I Like America and America Likes Me*, at the René Block Gallery in New York, where he lived with a wild coyote for a week (fig. 408). Performances such as these, played out in galleries before a small audience, were not widely known to the public. But the idea of performance itself was more influential and soon began to affect mainstream art forms, crossing over into film, theater, and opera.

PERFORMANCE ART: IN AND OUT OF THE MAINSTREAM

In the early seventies, performance art was the perfect antidote to Conceptual art, with its highly intellectual propositions and rarefied aesthetic of printed text and black-and-white photograph. Artists such as Joan Jonas, Vito Acconci, Scott Burton, and Dennis Oppenheim created performances which dealt directly with experience and perception, in real time and space, bringing to life the somewhat paradoxical concerns of Conceptual art. A few years later, by the mid-seventies, artists such as Adrian Piper, Julia Heyward, Michael Smith, and Laurie Anderson steeped in the Conceptual ethos of their mentors, added several new ingredients—autobiographical material, popular culture, and stylish execution—that would entirely change the direction of performance art. In eloquent multimedia monologues, street performances, and imitation TV soap operas, these artists shifted the focus of performance beyond the realm of art to the everyday. In doing so, they critiqued the impact of media on American life and triggered a discussion that would dominate the art of the eighties.

They also gravitated to New York, with its irresistible downtown art world made famous in the sixties by Andy Warhol's Factory and the Velvet Underground, and in the early seventies by artist-run alternative spaces such as 112 Greene Street, the Kitchen, and Franklin Furnace. The unique draw of downtown Manhattan was the availability of large inexpensive lofts in a compact urban neighborhood where artists, composers, choreographers, and filmmakers lived and worked side by side and generated a collective mood of invention. By the end of the seventies, the area was threaded through with new music venues as well. Crisscrossing the streets late at night, these artists moved easily from the art world to the punk music world of CBGB and the Mudd Club, the Ocean Club, or TR 3, with a sense that they were mixing a heady brew of high art and popular culture. Indeed, media-generation artists of the eighties viewed performance art as a means to shuttle between high and low. Laurie Anderson's historic crossing of the invisible divide, her opus *United States* (fig. 409) and her six-record contract with the industry giant Warner Brothers, showed that such a shift was possible. At the Brooklyn Academy of Music (BAM), on the same stage where Robert Wilson (fig. 410) had presented his groundbreaking, large-scale performance extravaganzas *Deafman Glance* (1971) and

408. **Joseph Beuys**
Coyote: I Like America and America Likes Me, 1974
Performance at the René Block Gallery, New York

409. **Laurie Anderson**
Let X = X, from *United States*, 1983
Performance at the Brooklyn Academy of Music, New York

414. **Nam June Paik**
TV Garden, 1974–78
Thirty color televisions,
one hundred plants, and
trees, dimensions variable
Collection of the artist
Photograph © The Estate
of Peter Moore/Licensed
by VAGA, New York, NY

415. **William Wegman**
*Man Ray
Contemplating a Bust
of Man Ray*, 1978
Gelatin silver print,
14 x 11 in. (35.6 x
27.9 cm)
Collection of the artist

416. **William Wegman**
Still from *Reel 4:
Wake Up*, 1973–74
Videotape, black-
and-white, sound;
21 min.
Collection of the artist

417. **Jud Yalkut** and **Nam June Paik**
Videotape Study No. 3, 1967–69
Videotape, black-and-white, sound; 4 min.
Electronic Arts Intermix, New York

VIDEO ART, FILM AND VIDEO INSTALLATION: 1965–1977

Video art was born out of three strands of 1960s American counter-culture: the utopian desire for an expanded perception through new technology, the anti-Vietnam War and civil rights movements, and a rebellion against the institutional authority of mainstream television. From its inception in the mid-sixties, video developed in three directions: psychedelically inflected image processing, politicized community activism, and performative art videotapes and installations. The first video image processing of the mid-sixties used audio synthesizers, echoing earlier experiments in electronic music by artists such as La Monte Young, Tony Conrad, and John Cage. Two of the key figures in early video art, Steina Vasulka and Nam June Paik, were both classically trained musicians. When Paik moved to New York from Germany in 1965, he bought one of the first Sony Portapak video recorders and began to collaborate with the filmmaker Jud Yalkut, who was shooting multimedia expanded cinema events and combining film with video. Together they made one of the first videotapes, *Videotape Study No. 3* (fig. 417). In the same year, Paik began his long collaboration with Charlotte Moorman, a classical cellist and the organizer of the New York Avant-Garde Festival, with whom he made numerous video performances (fig. 160).

In San Francisco, following the electronic experiments of the West Coast abstract filmmaker James Whitney in the early sixties, Bill Hearn, Eric Seigel, and Stephen Beck made the first video synthesizers in 1968–70. These devices enabled abstract images to be created on a TV screen without a camera, and black-and-white camera images to be artificially colorized. Seigel's videotape *Einstein* (1968), in which a photograph of Albert Einstein is psychedelically colorized by means of feedback, is one of the earliest examples of video image processing. Ed Emshwiller's early videotapes also used the early synthesizer techniques. Two major pioneers of video image processing, Steina and Woody Vasulka, made important early experiments, rescanning and manipulating the electronic image in works such as *Calligrams* (1970), whose didacticism evoked the materialist, reflexive inquiry of Structuralist film.

In 1969, Howard Wise presented the first exhibition in America devoted to video art at his gallery in New York; the show included Paik, Paul Ryan, Frank Gillette, Ira Schneider, Earl Reiback, and Aldo Tambellini. A proliferation of video exhibitions followed, first in alternative spaces and later in museums. After Wise closed his gallery in 1970, he formed the first artists' video distribution organization, Electronic Arts Intermix. Leo Castelli and Ileana Sonnabend followed, creating Castelli-Sonnabend Tapes and Films in 1972, and in 1976 Video Databank was founded in Chicago.

The technological optimism of the late 1960s also led to the founding of a number of collective groups, which sought to develop alternative systems of social relationships through video. Raindance, a collective founded in 1969, proposed radical theories of video as a new communications tool, influenced by Marshall McLuhan's and Buckminster Fuller's writings on technology. Antfarm, established in 1968 in San Francisco, made performances, alternative video events, and videotapes. Videofreex, founded in 1971, created an experimental alternative television center, Lanesville TV. Top Value Television

(TVTV), a collective that established the alternative video documentary movement, made a number of subversive documentaries,
such as *The Lord of the Universe* (1974), a scathing exposé of the
teenage guru Maharaj Ji.

From 1967 to the mid-seventies, several television stations
recognized the importance of the new creativity in video. WGBH
Boston, WNET in New York, and KQED TV in San Francisco
created residencies for artists with funds from the Rockefeller Foundation, and in 1969
WGBH broadcast *The Medium Is the Medium*, the first program of artists' video on television. Richard Serra's *Television Delivers People* (1973), produced with Carlotta
Schoolman, made a direct attack on the values of commercial television by scrolling
revealing statistical information about television consumers down the screen, backed by
a Muzak soundtrack.

By 1968, video was playing an important role in the new language of art making, reflecting the interdisciplinary experimentation with different media and artistic forms that characterized the
sixties and early seventies. The instant-feedback quality of video
aligned it with performance, Process art, and new dance, for which
it functioned as both document, mirror, and perceptual tool.
Artists such as Vito Acconci, Dennis Oppenheim, Peter Campus
(fig. 419), Keith Sonnier, Charlemagne Palestine, and William
Wegman on the East Coast, and Bruce Nauman, Terry Fox, John
Baldessari, Chris Burden, Howard Fried, Paul McCarthy, Doug
Hall, and Lynn Hershman on the West Coast, began a conceptual
examination of the physical and psychic self through video. Performative actions, made alone in the studio, sometimes over long
periods of time, were recorded by the fixed frame of the video
camera, which replaced a live audience. For Acconci, the video
camera functioned both as a documentation of his confrontational
performances and as a means of setting up a provocative dialogue
between himself and the viewer and, by extension, between public
and private space.

Video also became an important medium for a new generation
of women artists, for whom its democratic, time-based, art-historical properties offered
new possibilities for personal expression. Joan Jonas, Mary Lucier, Martha Rosler,
Adrian Piper, Beryl Korot, Shigeko Kubota, Dara Birnbaum, Hermine Freed, Nancy Holt,
Eleanor Antin, Lynda Benglis, Hannah Wilke, and Linda Montano, among others, made
videotapes and performances at the beginning of the seventies that questioned established perceptions of social, political, and erotic female identity. Jonas' *Vertical Roll*
(fig. 418) simultaneously deconstructed the female body and the technology of video by
filming sections of her body, both naked and costumed, and abstracting them within a
repeatedly shifting horizontal frame. Martha Rosler's *Semiotics of the Kitchen* (1975),
by contrast, parodied a cooking demonstration by using the utensils to express rage and

frustration. For male as well as female artists exploring new, radical forms, the time-based medium of video offered the potential for profound transformation, on personal, political, and formal levels, and remained a potent force for artists throughout the seventies.

From the mid-1960s onward, artists had also begun to use large-scale projected film, slide, and, later, video images to transform three-dimensional space into participatory environments. These early environments, which reflected the psychedelic sensibility of the decade, functioned as sensory, communal dream spaces, in which the audience became fully involved. By the end of the 1960s, artists had begun to experiment with other forms, using the newly emerging video technology, whose instant-feedback, real-time qualities enabled human behavior to be observed live. Live feedback became a central component of a new body of video installation work, shown mainly in alternative spaces and artists' studios, whose meaning was intimately connected with performance, Conceptual and Body art, and Minimalism's radical shift of meaning from the art object to the viewer's presence in space.

Frank Gillette and Ira Schneider's *Wipe Cycle* (1969) used several monitors and cameras, in time delay, to mix live shots of the viewer with a series of broadcast and taped television images, suggesting a new, participatory technological and televisual environment. Other conceptual video pieces in this mode include Beryl Korot's *Dachau* (1974), Mary Lucier's *Dawn Burn* (1975), and Nam June Paik's *TV Buddha* (1975). Bruce Nauman pushed video's perceptual inquiry to extremes in works such as the video installation *Live-Taped Video Corridor* (fig. 420). Nauman constructed each piece as a claustrophobic spatial environment, in which the viewer experienced physical restriction or disorientation. The close relation between video installation and performance was also demonstrated in the installation work of Vito Acconci and Dennis Oppenheim. Oppenheim produced a number of important performative films, videotapes, and film installations, including *Gingerbread Man* (1970–71), in which the body became the central subject.

The concept of mirroring was central to these and other psychological investigations of the artist's and viewer's presence in space. During the seventies, Peter Campus made a series of groundbreaking video installations, in which viewers encountered their often distorted reflection, recorded in real time by a hidden video camera. In Dan Graham's *Present Continuous Past(s)* (1974), time-delay video feedback created a fragmentation of the single spatial and temporal perceptual viewpoint. In a climate in which the concept of the autonomous self was breaking down, video installation became a primary site for the renegotiation of the boundaries between public and private space, the studio and the gallery, and between artist, art work, and viewer. —C. I.

420. **Bruce Nauman**
Live-Taped Video Corridor, 1969–70
Video installation, 384 x 144 x 20 in. (975.4 x 365.8 x 50.8 cm)
Solomon R. Guggenheim Museum, New York

428. **Jonathan Borofsky**
*Running Man at
2,550,116*, 1978
Acrylic on plywood,
89 x 110 in.
(226.1 x 279.4 cm)
The Patsy R. and
Raymond D. Nasher
Collection, Dallas

429. **Susan Rothenberg**
For the Light, 1978–79
Synthetic polymer and
vinyl paint on canvas,
105 x 87 in. (266.7 x
221 cm)
Whitney Museum of
American Art, New York;
Purchase, with funds from
Peggy and Richard
Danziger 79.23

430. Jennifer Bartlett
Installation view of
Rhapsody, 1976
987 steel plates, 12 x 12
in. (30.5 x 30.5 cm) each
The Edward R. Broida
Collection

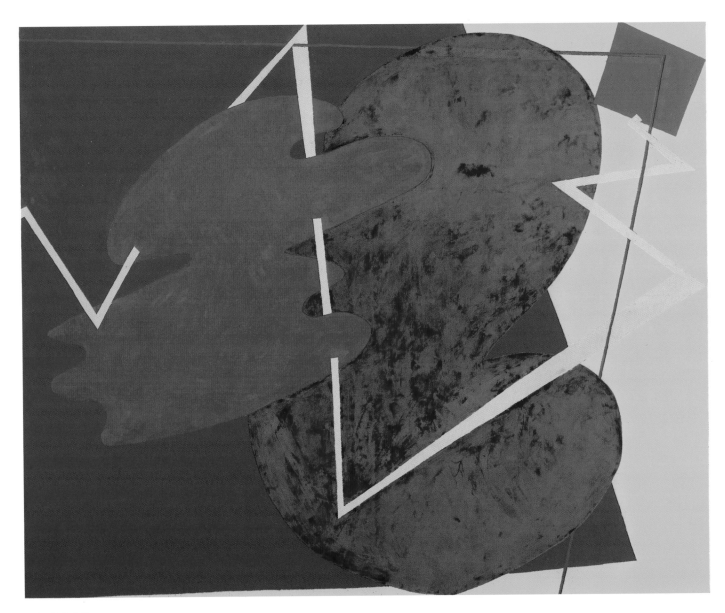

431. **Elizabeth Murray**
Children Meeting, 1978
Oil on canvas, 101 x 127
in. (256.5 x 322.6 cm)
Whitney Museum of
American Art, New York;
Purchase, with funds from
the Louis and Bessie
Adler Foundation, Inc.,
Seymour M. Klein,
President 78.34

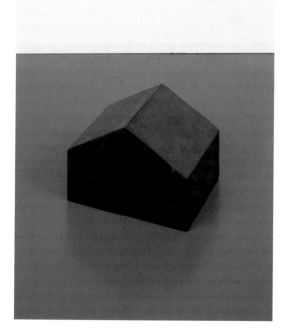

432. Joel Shapiro
Untitled, 1975
Cast iron, 7½ x 10¾ x 8½ in.
(19.1 x 27.3 x 21.6 cm)
The Museum of
Contemporary Art, Los
Angeles; The Barry Lowen
Collection

433. Bryan Hunt
*Empire State with
Hindenburg*, 1974
Silk, paper, plaster, and
wood, 100 x 66 x 29 in.
(254 x 167.6 x 73.7 cm)
overall
Whitney Museum of
American Art, New York;
Partial gift of Eli and
Edythe Broad 97.146

Restoration
and Reaction
1976–1990

In 1976, America celebrated its two hundredth birthday. The bicentennial was an occasion for renewing patriotic sentiments and looking back with pride at the history and achievements of the nation (though cynics viewed the festivities as a marketing bonanza—the "buy"centennial "sell"ebration). That same year, Jimmy Carter was elected president, following the short administration of Gerald Ford, who had taken office after Richard Nixon's resignation in 1974, and who had pardoned Nixon for his role in the Watergate scandal. Carter, the Democratic governor of Georgia, was a dark-horse candidate, but the country was eager for a new kind of leader—honest, compassionate, homegrown, and untainted by the political machinations that had characterized the Nixon years. Carter understood that Americans had lost confidence in their government, and he tried to heal the nation by identifying with the people and preaching a combination of idealism, common sense, and ethical values.

Under Carter's administration, a nuclear non-proliferation pact, curbing the spread of nuclear weapons, was signed in 1977 by fifteen countries, including the United States and the Soviet Union. The following year, Carter brokered a Middle East peace settlement between Egypt's President Anwar Sadat and Israel's Prime Minister Menachem Begin, and in 1979 he signed the SALT II arms-reduction agreement with Soviet President Leonid Brezhnev. Carter was especially sensitive to environmental issues—he created the Department of Energy, banned the dumping of raw sewage into the ocean, and established controls on strip mining. In view of the ongoing Arab oil embargo, he encouraged energy conservation and led by example, ordering the thermostat turned down in the White House.

In spite of these accomplishments, Carter's presidency was plagued by internal and external crises. Domestically, the oil embargo had contributed to a stagnant economy wracked by high inflation. On the international front, the Shah of Iran, long supported by the United States, was forced to abdicate in early 1979 and militant Islamic fundamentalists took power. In November, they seized the U.S. embassy in Tehran, taking more than sixty hostages. Despite constant efforts at negotiation, Carter was unable to arrange the release of the hostages. In late December, the Soviet Union invaded Afghanistan, unleashing world protests. Save for withdrawal from the 1980 Olympic Summer Games in Moscow, America seemed powerless.

If the administration was ultimately ineffectual, it was because Carter remained a Washington outsider whose lack of political connections in the capital and whose strong moral convictions made it difficult for him to succeed in the insider world of Washington politics. Ultimately, he was unable to build enough support in Congress to get many of his proposals passed.

The arts, however, thrived during Carter's administration, in no small part thanks to Joan Mondale, the vice president's wife, who was a vocal and visible advocate. One noticeable effect was an increased support for art at the community level, as artists themselves sought to forge meaningful connections with their communities and reach broader audiences.

The Mediated World: Art and Photography

In the late 1960s, a young man named Stewart Brand was sitting on his San Francisco rooftop, high on LSD, when he had an epiphany: that a photograph of earth from space would change the way everyone thought about our planet. He started a campaign, complete with buttons reading, "Why haven't we seen a photograph of the whole earth yet?" He sent some of these buttons to the National Aeronautics and Space Administration (NASA), and in 1967 *Lunar Orbiter 5* was outfitted to send back just such images. Brand put one of the black-and-white photographs of earth taken from space on the front and back covers of his *Whole Earth Catalog*, first published in 1968, and the ecology movement was born (fig. 435).

440. **Robert Adams**
*Along Interstate 25,
1968*, 1968
Gelatin silver print, 5⁹⁄₁₆ x
5¹³⁄₁₆ in. (14.1 x 14.8 cm)
Whitney Museum of
American Art, New York;
Purchase, with funds from
the Photography
Committee 96.10

441. **Richard Misrach**
Boojum Tree, 1976
Split toned silver print,
14 x 14 in.
(35.6 x 35.6 cm)
Robert Mann Gallery,
New York
© Richard Misrach

Right, top to bottom:

442–45. **Lewis Baltz**
*Element numbers 28, 29,
30,* and *31,* from *Park
City*, 1979
102 gelatin silver prints,
dimensions variable
Whitney Museum of
American Art, New York;
Partial and promised gift
of Michael R. Kaplan
P.14a–xxxx.97

America (figs. 440–45). Robert Adams, Lewis Baltz, Frank Gohlke, Richard Misrach, and the German team of Bernd and Hilla Becher cast a dispassionate eye on factory architecture, grain elevators, industrial parks, construction sites, and landfills, factually documenting the debris, deterioration, and contamination of the environment. The ecological sensibility of their work made conscious reference to nineteenth-century documentary photographs of a pristine American West, as they presented evidence of twentieth-century human intrusions on the environment.

While such manifestations of ecological awareness contributed to the popularity of straight photography in the seventies, the potential of the medium was being stretched in another direction. The appropriation of photographs in Pop and Conceptual art had opened

THE OFFICE PARK

During the 1970s, the American corporate headquarters, which at least since the completion of the Woolworth Building early in the century ideally had stood as an impressive office tower dominating an urban skyline, began to confront the material and conceptual implications of a new, suburban, car-driven society. Having left the city centers in the 1950s, white-collar workers now increasingly demanded to have offices as close to their single-family houses as the nearest freeway exit. Moreover, a post-1960s egalitarian and communal ethos made the manifest and vertical hierarchy of the corporate tower increasingly a thing of the past. A new model evolved instead, related to ideas first pursued by proponents of the German *Bürolandschaft*—a concept of "office landscape" developed in the 1960s—where an informal, horizontally organized office structure was meant to foster teamwork and collaboration. This interior-planning scheme depended on a flexible, open floor plan housed within a simple but unified exterior skin.

Skidmore, Owings & Merrill, Cesar Pelli, Kevin Roche, and many other architects contributed significantly to the refinement of this building type, which was perfectly suited to the Minimalist aesthetic of the era. Buildings such as Roche's 1968 Ford Foundation in New York (fig. 446) were meant to provide the image not only of an egalitarian work force but of a working community, by voiding the traditional center of the structure and providing instead an interior atrium and semiprivate landscape. Pelli's 1975 Pacific Design Center in Los Angeles (fig. 447), composed of large hangars of completely smooth yet brightly colored glass, paved the way for the soon-to-be ubiquitous mirrored office building, with which corporate culture attempted to minimize its bulk by integrating it into the surrounding environment. At the same time, however, the sites of these loftlike buildings with reflective surfaces and interior landscapes began to expand into extensive and perfectly manicured lawns. As these mirrored behemoths twinkled in their "golf course" settings, the office park occupied the landscape like an aristocratic country estate, while leisure and labor took on a new and peculiar relationship. —S. L.

446. **Kevin Roche**
Ford Foundation Building, New York, 1968, photograph by Ezra Stoller

447. **Cesar Pelli**
Pacific Design Center, West Hollywood, California, 1975, photograph by Marvin Rand

up new possibilities for a hybrid use of photography. Many kinds of hybrids proliferated in this decade—from the mural-scale collaged photographs of David Hockney to the hand-worked self-portraits in Lucas Samaras' series of *Autopolaroids*—images taken with a Polaroid camera, then manipulated during the development process to create dreamlike visions. Finally, the large-scale Cibachrome prints by Cindy Sherman, Sarah Charlesworth, or Andres Serrano, which came to prominence in the 1980s, rivaled painting and sculpture in size and in the spectacular saturated-color effects produced by the oil-based Cibachrome printing technique (figs. 454, 457, 551).

448. **Richard Estes**
The Candy Store, 1969
Oil and synthetic polymer on canvas, 47¾ x 68¾ in. (121.3 x 174.6 cm)
Whitney Museum of American Art, New York; Purchase, with funds from the Friends of the Whitney Museum of American Art 69.21
© Richard Estes/Licensed by VAGA, New York, NY

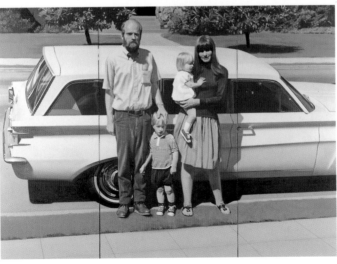

449. **Robert Bechtle**
'61 Pontiac, 1968–69
Oil on canvas, 59¾ x 84¼ in. (151.8 x 214 cm)
Whitney Museum of American Art, New York; Purchase, with funds from the Richard and Dorothy Rodgers Fund 70.16

Another manifestation of photography's growing reputation was the great popular success of Photorealism—a style of painting, based on photographs, that simulated photography's shiny, cold surfaces. Photorealism appealed to Americans' sense of literalness and took Pop's fascination with the consumer landscape to the level of superrealism. The painters Ralph Goings, Richard Estes, Robert Bechtle, and Robert Cottingham zeroed in on gleaming, reflective surfaces—the chrome and glass of shop windows, storefronts, car fenders, mirrors—to produce a somewhat dislocating, hyperreal landscape (figs. 448, 449). Their paintings communicated the seamless surface of the photograph and the mechanical nature of the camera's eye. Duane Hanson, a sculptor, similarly applied a photographic hyperverisimilitude to his polyester resin and polyvinyl three-dimensional replicas of ordinary people—a maid, a security guard, a tourist couple— who in a gallery setting are sometimes difficult to distinguish from the viewers (fig. 450).

Perhaps the most important contribution to photography in the 1970s, and into the 1980s, was made by artists engaged in a critical dialogue about the nature of photographic representation. Many of these artists (who did not even consider themselves photographers) felt that images rather than real experience had come to define the world. As the critic Douglas Crimp wrote in the exhibition catalog for "Pictures," the 1977 landmark exhibition at Artists Space that introduced some artists of this generation, "To an ever greater extent our experience is governed by pictures, pictures in newspapers and magazines, on television and in the cinema. Next to these pictures firsthand experience begins to retreat, to seem more and more trivial. While it once seemed that pictures had the function of interpreting reality, it now seems that they have usurped it."[132]

These artists, raised on television, understood the power of pictures. Yet, as witnesses to the Vietnam War and the Watergate scandal, they also evinced a healthy skepticism about the truth of received images and considered the issue of representation to be a crucial problem. "Representation," wrote the critic Craig Owens, "is not—nor can it be—neutral; it is an act—indeed the founding act—of power in our culture."[133] To artists and theorists alike, the photograph had lost its status as a paradigm of veracity.

This questioning of photographic representation constituted a rite of passage for a whole generation of artists—Barbara Kruger, Sherrie Levine, Cindy Sherman, Richard Prince, Robert Longo, David Salle, Sarah Charlesworth, Allan McCollum, and Laurie Simmons. These artists were media literate, both addicted to and aware of the media's capacity for celebrity making, violence mongering, and sensationalism, its ideological power and seductive materialism. Pictures shaped their visual and critical viewpoints. Some, like the Pop artists before them, were employed by media companies—Barbara Kruger was chief designer for Condé Nast's *Mademoiselle* magazine, and Richard Prince was doing picture research for Time-Life. There they had firsthand exposure to the inner workings and materials of the mass media and soon incorporated photographs and photomechanical procedures into their art to redefine photography no less than art itself.

As influential as the commercial world was the California Institute of the Arts (CalArts) in Valencia, the training ground for many of these artists. Arguably the nation's most important art school in the seventies, it had been founded in 1961 by Walt Disney as a sort of interdisciplinary beehive that would feed his industry. With the establishment of Judy

450. **Duane Hanson**
Woman with Dog, 1977
Cast polyvinyl, poly-
chromed in acrylic with
cloth and hair, life size
Whitney Museum of
American Art, New York;
Purchase, with funds from
Frances and Sidney Lewis
78.6

Chicago and Miriam Schapiro's Feminist Art Program there in 1971 and the subsequent appointment of the Conceptual artists Douglas Huebler, Michael Asher, and John Baldessari to the faculty, CalArts became an avant-garde academy—an alternative art school, like the Nova Scotia College of Art and Design or the Whitney Museum of American Art Independent Study Program. The example of John Baldessari, who headed one of the innovative departments at CalArts, encouraged many students to trade in their paintbrushes for cameras—as he had done in 1967 (figs. 355, 451).

Photographic work of this generation often emphasized "making" a photograph rather than "taking" one, which subverted the conventional desire to capture the perfect composition in a single frame. The artists appropriated photographic imagery as available material for art making and transformed it through collage,

451. **John Baldessari**
Ashputtle, 1982
Eleven gelatin silver
prints, one silver dye
bleach print (Cibachrome),
and text panel, 84 x
72 in. (213.4 x
182.9 cm) overall
Whitney Museum of
American Art, New York;
Purchase, with funds from
the Painting and
Sculpture Committee
83.8a–m

452. David Salle
We'll Shake the Bag,
1980
Acrylic on canvas,
48 x 72 in. (121.9 x
182.9 cm)
Collection of Ellen Kern
© David Salle/Licensed by
VAGA, New York, NY

453. Richard Prince
*Untitled (3 Women
Looking in One Direction)*,
1980
Three chromogenic color
prints, 40 x 60 in.
(101.6 x 152.4 cm) each
Chase Manhattan Bank,
New York

Her statements—among them, "Everyone's work is equally important," "Private property created crime," "Money creates taste," and "Abuse of power comes as no surprise"—raised questions about control, authority, and subjugation and packed a punch in the urban spaces where they were often displayed.

All these artists probe stereotypes of desire and of female objectification by intervening in the process that creates them. Their work is inconceivable without feminism. But women were also leaders in this new generation because they gravitated naturally toward photography. There was, first of all, a long tradition of women working in the medium (Kruger studied with Diane Arbus, and Charlesworth studied with Lisette Model). Women, moreover, were quicker to recognize that the sociocultural definition of gender was not justified by any genetic determinants, but rather was constructed through photographic representation, whether in magazines, newspapers, billboards, or on television and movie screens. To Sherrie Levine, Sarah Charlesworth, Barbara Kruger, Cindy Sherman, and Laurie Simmons, photography itself was therefore the most potent means of deconstructing the gender stereotypes that it had helped create.

But there was another side to this complicity with populism: many of these same buildings triggered a complex discourse that stressed not the symbolic value of representation but its potential duplicitousness and instability. The very eclecticism and pastiche of postmodernism served as evidence of a new form of abstraction, where signs proliferated madly and promiscuously. The abandonment of the modernist box permitted theorists from many disciplines to focus on spatial conditions of unprecedented complexity and to use them to show that the certainties of the Enlightenment were giving way to a new, less teleological attitude of the present.

A unifying, though no less ironic, element of these opposing views of postmodernism is that architecture remained the touchstone of the debate for the culture at large. Indeed, a significant impact of postmodernism in architecture was the transformation of its successful practitioners into celebrities with star status. On television, in magazines, and as retailers and trendsetters, architects came to mingle with other "personalities"—personalities also invented by the media and by a popular desire for intimacy with public figures and a whiff of their power and success. This strange combination of nostalgia, fantasy, exploration, and money came together in the transformation of the Disney company from a simple producer of cartoons to a postmodern and corporate version of the Medici family of the Renaissance (fig. 465). As Graves, Stern, Frank Gehry, and a whole host of international architects were hired to give thematic substance to hotels, restaurants, and ever-proliferating theme parks, a new form of postmodern patronage was born. In the process, architecture assumed a cultural significance it had not enjoyed for decades, but lost more critical respect than it could perhaps afford. —S. L.

465. **Michael Graves**
Team Disney Building,
Burbank, California,
1986–91
Disney characters ©
Disney Enterprises, Inc.
Corbis/Robert Holmes

466. **Richard Prince**
Spiritual America, 1983
Chromogenic color print,
23½ x 15⅞ in.
(59.7 x 40.3 cm)
Whitney Museum of
American Art, New York;
Gift of an anonymous
donor 91.86.2

467. **Sherrie Levine**
*Barcham Green Portfolio
No. 5 (Walker Evans)*,
1986
Photogravure and
aquatint, 19 x 14¹⁵⁄₁₆ in.
(48.3 x 37.9 cm)
Whitney Museum of
American Art, New York;
Purchase, with funds from
the Print Committee
90.42

Not only can the reframing of found images show how representation shapes our perception of gender, but it again raises questions about uniqueness, authorship, and originality—just as the mechanical, reproductive imagery of Pop art had earlier challenged the role of the artist in traditional painting and sculpture. To some artists of the late 1970s and early 1980s, originality was nothing more than a socially constructed fiction of mastery, control, and empowerment. This fiction is made patently manifest in the "rephotography" of Richard Prince and Sherrie Levine, for instance, where found photographs from magazine spreads or illustrations of art objects are rephotographed with little alteration and signed as originals. By bringing the image into an art context, its social codes and peculiar unreality— what Richard Prince refers to as "social science fiction"—also become apparent.[135] Acting as an editor, Prince chose photographs of sunsets, biker chicks, hot rods, and female entertainers to rephotograph. He then made subtle alterations to produce strange or special hallucinatory effects, ranging from softened clarity in enlarged images to loving details in cropped photos (fig. 466). Though at first it seemed that his minimal intervention involved no thought or effort, the images were actually carefully chosen for form and content, and their transformation was significant.

Likewise, Sherrie Levine chose reproductions of works of art by earlier male masters of European modernism— Egon Schiele, Aleksandr Rodchenko, Kazimir Malevich, Fernand Léger, El Lissitzky, Piet Mondrian, and Joan Miró—as well as the classic American photographers Walker Evans and Edward Weston (fig. 467). Sometimes she rephotographed their works, and sometimes she faithfully copied them as intimate watercolors and drawings on the same scale as the reproductions from which they were taken. Though interpreted as a subversive commentary on originality, authorship, and ownership, the process enabled Levine to make those works hers. Ultimately, both Prince and Levine show that the personal and the social are necessarily intertwined and that they replace the heroic artist-subject with an unstable, ambiguous, and anti-heroic presence.

THE CRITICAL LEGACY OF POSTSTRUCTURALISM

The rise of distinctively postmodernist practices required a reconceptualization of the terms in which art was received and discussed. A new form of art history and criticism evolved, one that reflected the body of European critical and theoretical work known as poststructuralism. Poststructuralism developed in the intellectual and political climate of post-1968 France, especially in the writings of Roland Barthes, Jean Baudrillard, Jacques Derrida, Michel Foucault, and Jacques Lacan. They challenged the classical humanist division of knowledge into discrete fields such as art history, literature, and philosophy, arguing instead for a fluid, hybrid terrain called the human sciences. Although their writings fall into no single discipline—Lacan's work, for example, merges psychoanalysis and linguistics and is pertinent to literary criticism—all examine the participation of systems of representation in broad social and historical processes.

These works—including Barthes' *Critical Essays*, Foucault's *The Order of Things* and *Discipline and Punish*, and Derrida's *Of Grammatology*—were translated into English during the 1970s and disseminated to an American audience. By the late 1970s, poststructuralist approaches had entered the framework of American universities. Art history, traditionally considered an autonomous discipline, had been transformed sufficiently by the mid-1980s for the noted historian Norman Bryson to remark on the tendency in the "New Art History" to seek out relations with other fields and to adapt critical methods from them. Such crossovers also reflected an interest on the part of the new generation of artists and writers in the postwar media image world. New journals appearing on both sides of the Atlantic (*October* and *Representations* in the United States; *Screen*, *Block*, and *Word and Image* in England) published writing informed by poststructuralist concepts alongside English translations of Continental texts.

Poststructuralism has no single definition; as an ensemble of approaches, it should be distinguished from deconstruction, the specific analytical method that Derrida developed to dismantle the foundations of Western philosophy and literature. Nevertheless, all of poststructuralism shares a "deconstructive" aim of exposing representations as historical formations that not only occupy social space but also exercise power. The work of Foucault and Baudrillard, in particular, provides influential accounts of the ways in which dominant social orders use coded representations to consolidate and perpetuate their political power. In visual arts practices of the 1980s, representations were increasingly seen not as re-presentations of an existing reality but as reality's constitutive agent. The poststructuralist view that what we know as reality is produced through representations reflects the extent to which images and symbols intervene in our world, shaping attitudes and social norms.

Criticism in the 1980s took aim at the received ideas of modernism, at its institutions—studio, gallery, museum—and its art. Opposing the view of the art work as a bounded object produced by a creative subject, critics contested the notions of authorship, originality, "enduring meaning," and "eternal value." Emblematic of these concerns are Rosalind Krauss' influential collection of essays *The Originality of the Avant-Garde and Other Modernist Myths* (1985) and Douglas Crimp's *On the Museum's Ruins* (1993). As Walter Benjamin had predicted in the 1930s, photography played a role in

Manifestations such as rephotography and the examination of images as social constructs rather than as veristic views of reality presented a new group of critics with an opportunity to define a postmodernist art. Postmodernism, like modernism before it, does not concern a particular style or movement, but is rather a shift in attitude about what the value of art is, how it should be defined, what it should strive for, and what it can signify. To modernists, art was validated as the expression of individual creativity, and its disciplines—especially painting and sculpture—were supposed to be truthful to the essential properties of each medium. These were the underlying principles of twentieth-century modernism, including Clement Greenberg's formalist criticism and modernist art from Abstract Expressionism through Minimalism. But even Minimalism, as we have seen, questioned the idea of authorship, as sculptors used prefabricated industrial materials, or had their designs executed by others. Moreover, from the fifties on, new forms of art were introduced— Pop, Postminimalism, Conceptual, and performance, among others—that disintegrated the old boundaries between media and introduced "impure," nontraditional materials into art.

this critical project, its multiple, machine-made means serving to dislodge aesthetic assumptions of creative expression and artistic singularity. What Crimp termed "the photographic activity of postmodernism" was addressed in criticism by Krauss, Hal Foster, Craig Owens, and Abigail Solomon-Godeau, among others.

Yet, as Owens commented in 1983, it was a "specifically feminist consciousness" that placed "the politics of representation. . .on the agenda of contemporary art." Critics and artists alike argued that sexuality is a social construction, resulting from the widespread circulation of signs. Again, imported theory had a priming role, especially the work of the French feminists Hélène Cixous and Luce Irigaray; the French Marxist philosopher Louis Althusser; and the British-based film theorists Laura Mulvey and Stephen Heath, whose work was published in Screen. However, at the core were the psychoanalytic writings of Lacan. As early as 1958, he summarized the radical powers newly attributed to images, observing that "images and symbols for the woman cannot be isolated from images and symbols of the woman. . . .It is representation, the representation of feminine sexuality. . .which conditions how it comes into play." —K. L.

With the modernist criteria challenged, two kinds of postmodernism arose. The first was a popular, retrograde form found in much new architecture and the emerging Neo-Expressionist painting. This work used a pastiche of historical styles and decorative elements to declare art's independence from the modernist concept of stylistic unity. But the more profound form of postmodernism, as seen in the photographic work of Cindy Sherman, Sherrie Levine, Richard Prince, and their colleagues, deconstructed and reconstructed the very nature of representation.

A new generation of critics framed this postmodernism in terms derived from European philosophy and literary theories that had evolved into a general concept known as poststructuralism. Poststructuralism perceived all forms of art, visual or verbal, as a set of social signs or cultural codes. This theoretical proposition became the framework for an intellectually rigorous art criticism that focused—as the artists were doing—on the political and sexual nature of representation and on the systems of power that shaped it.

Although this critical theory eventually became rigid and self-limiting, failing to take into account the visual pleasures and psychological content that enriched the art, it did succeed in giving photography a privileged position in the postmodernist project. Artists and theorists both understood that the supposed truthfulness and naturalism of photography made it the principal agent of ideology.

Street Culture: Art and Community

While some artists were using media images to critique the media itself, others were employing media techniques to situate their messages in a public context. Taking to the streets, they created billboards, fly posters, graffiti, and other public signage. This engagement with "public address" intersected with a broader artistic movement toward grassroots community activism and a renewed interest in street life.

Much of this community-oriented art came out of New York City. The multiethnic street culture of the Lower East Side (which included the East Village), the South Bronx, or Times Square had great appeal to a new generation of artists, many of whom, having been priced out of SoHo, were living in these neighborhoods. Their reclamation of abandoned or tenement spaces was reminiscent of the loft movement in SoHo a decade earlier. And they, too, inadvertently created a dilemma for themselves: their very presence in these neighborhoods hastened the process of gentrification—and the consequent loss of the energetic cultural diversity that had nourished them.[136]

By the 1970s, the Lower East Side was an impoverished area, heavily infiltrated by junkies and drug pushers; it was also home to punk rockers, Hell's Angels, prostitutes, and many immigrant groups. Artists and musicians were drawn to a neighborhood that had become a twenty-four-hour carnival. Out of this heady street culture came a second wave of activist alternative groups, including the artist collectives Collaborative Projects (Colab) and Group Material on the Lower East Side, and Fashion Moda in the Bronx. These new groups—whose members insisted that they were not alternatives to anything—favored a nonchalant mix of art and popular culture. With their inclusive and democratic vision, these artists revolutionized curatorial practice and provided a new, less dogmatic model for the expression of social activism.

Colab was one of several artist collectives that emerged at the end of the 1970s, partly in response to the growing institutionalization of older alternative spaces, and partly because younger artists wanted to form their own groups. The activities of Colab were always provocative and embraced the community. Located in a storefront space called ABC No Rio (a name taken from a faded street sign), Colab specialized in dense hangings in atypical spaces (fig. 468). Founded initially as a way to funnel public grant money to individual artists, the group soon concentrated on generating publicly sited art projects that dealt with the social concerns of the artists and the community. Sometimes Colab illegally commandeered abandoned structures. In 1979, for instance, it took over an empty city-owned building on Delancey Street as a venue for the "Real Estate Show," which attacked New York's housing policies.[137] The group's activities extended to many media: *X Magazine*, which pioneered punk graphics, was a Colab publication, and several members of Colab started the New Cinema, a center for the emerging No Wave Super-8 film movement.

In 1980, Colab occupied a former massage parlor near Times Square and turned it into a temporary art venue. The "Times Square Show" was one of the first

468. Installation view of "Animals Living in Cities" at ABC No Rio, New York, 1980
Photograph © Andrea Callard 1980

NO WAVE CINEMA

Between 1978 and 1987, No Wave Cinema was a small, though ultimately influential, film movement that operated out of New York's East Village and owed its existence to a technological innovation. In the late 1970s, Kodak introduced and mass-marketed a new small-gauge film: Super-8 mm sound film. At $6.50 per three-minute roll, Super-8 afforded many artists, musicians, and performers the opportunity to explore the medium of filmmaking without the budgetary constraints of the more expensive 16 mm and 35 mm formats. Since most practitioners of Super-8 filmmaking were not formally trained in the craft, they developed their own shooting and editing language—frequently influenced by B movies of the 1950s. Of equal importance, however, was the high-contrast black-and-white or acidic color of the film, which gave No Wave Cinema its striking appearance. Thus the combination of experimental filmmaking techniques and a new film stock produced an innovative cinema aesthetic.

469. **Michael Oblowitz**
King Blank, 1983
16 mm film, black-and-white, sound; 73 min.
Courtesy Rosemary Hochschild

Super-8 mm sound film used a magnetic sound strip on the edge of the film stock to record sound—much like audiocassette tapes—which distinguished it from previous 8 mm films. The recorded sound tracks often included dialogue improvised by the actors or music produced by bands of the period, such as the Contortions, D.N.A., Mars, John Lurie and the Lounge Lizards, and Lydia Lunch's Teenage Jesus and the Jerks. Retaining the aggressive aural style of the punk movement, these bands employed a combination of scraping guitars, jazzlike improvisation, and accelerated vocals, showing no allegiance to any one particular musical style or "wave." They thus became known as No Wave bands. The films known as No Wave Cinema recorded their performances against settings of New York buildings and bleak interiors. Thematically, No Wave films were equally cutting edge, incorporating social issues pertinent to the East Village underground: rebellion against authority and against conservative sexual politics. By embracing these visual and aural aesthetics, challenging themes, and often frank and graphic portrayals, No Wave Cinema became a vanguard movement.

470. **Richard Kern**
Fingered, 1986 (featuring Lydia Lunch)
Super-8 mm film-to-videotape transfer, black-and-white, sound; 25 min.
© Richard Kern

Many of the filmmakers identified with it were also founders or members of the artist collective Colab. One of Colab's first projects was the New Cinema, which in 1978 began to regularly exhibit media works in a former Polish social club on East 8th Street. The New Cinema screened works by its founders Becky Johnston, Eric Mitchell, and James Nares, as well as those by Vivienne Dick and John Lurie. The screenings at the New Cinema were also distinguished by their presentation format: the films were transferred from Super-8 film to videotape and then projected with an Advent video projector. The New Cinema's bold repudiation of the accepted distinction between film and video—the latter long viewed by film advocates as inferior—marked an important step in the equalization of the two moving-image technologies.

hybrid pictorial language that combined graffiti with Pop, Surrealism, and other high-art styles. Keith Haring used universally legible signs in his simple cartoon-style line drawings, which could be executed quickly on empty advertising placards on the subway platform or on large tarp canvases in the studio. His images ranged from playful barking dogs and cavorting figures to the radiant child (his signature image) and apocalyptic explosions, as well as safe sex and anti-drug messages. Kenny Scharf likewise used a psychedelic cartoon style and Day-Glo palette to execute space-age images on canvas and customize everyday appliances. Jean-Michel Basquiat, who would soon rise to fame and stardom, became a casualty of the age when he died of a drug overdose at age twenty-eight in 1988. Basquiat's street tag was "Samo" with a crown over it. In his canvases, he created a blend of the sophisticated and the primitive rendered in de Kooning-style brushwork that merged images drawn from African culture and American popular culture with scratched-out words and phrases that formed a unique African American poetry (fig. 507).

507. **Jean-Michel Basquiat**
Hollywood Africans, 1983
Synthetic polymer and mixed media on canvas, 84 x 84 in. (213.4 x 213.4 cm)
Whitney Museum of American Art, New York; Gift of Douglas S. Cramer 84.23

Soon other commercial galleries started to open in the East Village. Most of them were owned and operated by artists, and they encompassed a broad aesthetic range—from Civilian Warfare, which featured expressionism and a contemporary junk aesthetic, to Gracie Mansion, who started out by showing intimately scaled art in her bathroom (fig. 508), to Nature Morte, International with Monument, and the Pat Hearn Gallery, all of which favored cool, Neo-Conceptual work. It wasn't long before museums and uptown galleries started to do "East Village Scene" shows and the neighborhood became an exotic location for museum tours and Sunday outings. By 1984, there were almost seventy storefront galleries on the Lower East Side, which together formed an entire "alternative" commercial art community.

508. Installation view of the "Famous Show" at the Gracie Mansion Gallery, New York, 1982

Market Power

The 1980s ushered in a growing conservative sentiment in the nation's social and political life. Many Americans had become increasingly disillusioned by the perceived inability of the Carter administration to lead the nation, revitalize the economy, or articulate a compelling vision for the future. In 1980, half the electorate failed to go to the polls, reflecting a general alienation from politics and government. But those who did vote elected Ronald Reagan, a Republican, in a landslide victory (fig. 509). With Reagan's election, however, came the right wing's ascent to power, and for community activists and protest artists, it was a crushing blow. In contrast to Carter, Reagan presented a new and clear conservative vision of America's future—one based on decentralized government, a return to "traditional" values, and an aggressive foreign policy, all of which perfectly suited the New Right, as it came to be called.

A former Hollywood actor, Reagan had campaigned under the slogan "Make America Proud Again," and his administration constantly invoked patriotism, faith in God, and freedom from government interference. As the decade progressed, these credos became weapons for the New Right in its war against liberal politics. Reagan's two-term tenure spurred the growth of right wing, single-issue groups, who had had enough of the radicalism and liberalism of the sixties and seventies, which they held responsible for the sexual revolution, Vietnam war protests, and the breakdown of the nuclear family. They galvanized their forces to defeat the Equal Rights Amendment in 1982 and wage strident campaigns against homosexuality and abortion.

Reagan wasted no time in shrinking the federal government, cutting taxes, and dismantling many of the social programs of the previous two decades. For the unskilled, the unemployed, or those dependent on government assistance, it was a bleak period. But Reagan's policies were good for American business. The tax cuts, combined with substantial increases in military spending, helped promote one of the largest economic expansions and stock market booms the country had ever seen. Those at the upper economic levels of society spent lavishly and enjoyed a high standard of living.

509. *President Ronald Reagan and First Lady Nancy Reagan at the White House*, 1980s

The booming economy had a trickle-down effect on the art world, which also prospered. With the rise of the New Right and the market boom came a resurgence of traditional forms of art: painting and sculpture that could be collected. The spectacular ascent of the young painter Julian Schnabel is emblematic of the mood that was sweeping the country. Schnabel, who had come from Brooklyn via Brownsville, Texas, burst upon the art scene in 1980 like a "bull in the china shop," said *Newsweek*—an allusion both to his aggressive self-confidence and the broken plates he painted on.[142] He soon teamed up with the young art dealer Mary Boone, whose unbridled ambition and energy matched Schnabel's boldness and brazen self-promotion. The two persuaded Leo Castelli to get on board, and so the venerable dealer took on his first new artist in over a decade. The prices for Schnabel's work quickly escalated.

Schnabel's paintings on broken crockery caused a sensation when they were shown (fig. 510). They made many critics apoplectic but reinforced the belief that painting could be lifted out of its supposed doldrums, even if through a combination of daring and arrogance. The fractured, dimensional surface of the works, which had precedents in 1970s Pattern painting, literally broke the flatness of the picture plane. Freely mixing figurative and abstract idioms, Schnabel went on to paint on velvet, linoleum, and theater backdrops, creating lush, decorative painting on an operatic scale and full of historical allusions. Schnabel invoked grand themes through his titles and made portraits of or dedicated works to a host of cultural, religious, and historical figures—among them Saint Ignatius Loyola, Saint Francis, Pope Pius IX, Malcolm Lowry, Antonin Artaud, and Maria Callas; to this pantheon, he also added family and friends.

Schnabel's intense, large-scale works spoke for a renewed belief in the power and possibility of painting. In this sense, they recalled the expansive confidence and heroics of Abstract Expressionism. Another brand of nostalgia also pervades Schnabel's art: with its pastiche of historical quotations from earlier masterworks and literary texts (any subject or image was fair game) and mix of high and low culture (fig. 511), it presented a postmodernist affection for appropriating older styles, as in the Chippendale-style top that caps Philip Johnson's 1984 AT&T Building in New York.

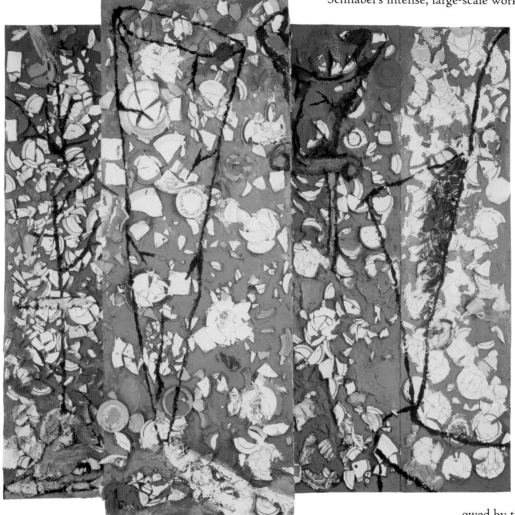

510. **Julian Schnabel**
The Patients and the Doctors, 1978
Oil, plates, and glue on wood, 96 x 108 x 12 in. (244 x 274 x 30.5 cm)
Private collection

In the late seventies, Schnabel's bold and dramatic style was also stimulated by his recognition of certain post-war European artists. Sigmar Polke, Anselm Kiefer, Jannis Kounellis, and Joseph Beuys, who had been at work since the sixties, were practically unknown in America at the time, having been overshadowed by the American avant-garde. They were all process-oriented and used unconventional materials (straw, tar, fat, felt, and minerals) in daring and expressive painting and sculpture. Some, like Polke, had pioneered the incompatible conjunctions of styles and superimpositions of images as a standard operating procedure, breaking with the imperative of stylistic consistency. Other Americans besides Schnabel started taking note of this important European art, prompted by, among other things, the memorable Beuys retrospective at the Guggenheim Museum in 1979.

In fact, the 1980s witnessed an influx of art from Europe, as Americans discovered that vanguard art was no longer an exclusively American affair. European imports had begun in the 1960s, with the Nouveaux Réalistes, for example, mostly to complement American developments. But this art was never understood in its own context. In the eighties, however, exhibitions and sales of Arte Povera works, those by Beuys, and younger Neo-Expressionist German painters and British sculptors, along with work by the new Italian painters known as Transavanguardia, brought European art to the forefront of American consciousness for the first time since World War II.

This new internationalism was signaled by a number of exhibitions in the early eighties that also focused on the revival of painting: "A New Spirit of Painting" at the Royal Academy of Arts, London (1981); "Zeitgeist" at the Martin-Gropius-Bau, Berlin (1982); and "The New Art" at the Tate Gallery, London (1983). These were just some of the shows that spotlighted young painters such as Schnabel, along with several of his American peers, among them David Salle, Eric Fischl, Susan Rothenberg, Jean-Michel Basquiat, and Robert Longo—alongside the European painters Sigmar Polke, Georg Baselitz, Francesco Clemente, Anselm Kiefer, Markus Lüpertz, Jörg Immendorff, Gerhard Richter, and A. R. Penck. The work of this group was often characterized as Neo-Expressionist, though like all appellations, the label never adequately described the art or the artists' intentions. Nevertheless, these artists did have certain characteristics in common: they embraced expression and sentiment to create an art of excess, one that was emotionally and physically charged.

Eric Fischl almost single-handedly infused life into narrative figuration with his genre paintings that revealed the psychosexual underside of the suburban American soul (figs. 514, 515). Susan Rothenberg, who had introduced figurative imagery in the 1970s in her horse paintings (fig. 429), continued in the next decade to explore abstract gesture and mark making around allusive figurative content. She was soon annexed to the Neo-Expressionist movement—and remained one of its few women. Robert Longo

511. **Julian Schnabel**
Exile, 1980
Oil and antlers on wood, 90 x 120 in. (228.6 x 304.8 cm)
Collection of Mrs. Barbara Schwartz

presented a rock 'n' roll, cinematic vision of corporate culture through images of ambivalent and alienated desires in his Men in the Cities series (fig. 513). In these monumental, larger-than-life works on paper, conceived by Longo but executed by a commercial illustrator, men and women dressed for success strike poses that alternately suggest pleasure or pain. Leon Golub weighed in with the strongest paintings of his career. His Mercenary series—paintings featuring men committing acts of brutality and aggression against other men—won him international recognition for the first time (fig. 512).

David Salle, a thoughtful provocateur, created paintings with a new kind of space inspired by film montage (figs. 516, 517). For many observers, these works, with their disjunctive spaces, stylistic variety, and unexpected combinations of imagery, came to epitomize postmodern painting. Salle pilfered fragments of images from numerous sources, from art and design to pornography, and then combined and layered them in moody, introverted paintings. The vibration of quotations and styles produced a visual buzz, even though the expression was emotionally neutral. Rather than presenting an image of reality, he was presenting the equivocal reality of images.

Some questioned Salle's right to use these scavenged images. The cartoonists Mike Cockrill and Judge Hughes brought suit against Salle for copyright infringement

512. **Leon Golub**
White Squad I, 1982
Synthetic polymer on
canvas, 120 x 184 in.
(304.8 x 467.4 cm)
Whitney Museum of
American Art, New York;
Gift of The Eli Broad
Family Foundation and
purchase, with funds from
the Painting and
Sculpture Committee
94.67

513. **Robert Longo**
Untitled, 1981
Charcoal, graphite,
silkscreen, ink, and tem-
pera on paper, 60 x 96 in.
(152.4 x 243.8 cm)
Collection of B.Z./Michael
Schwartz

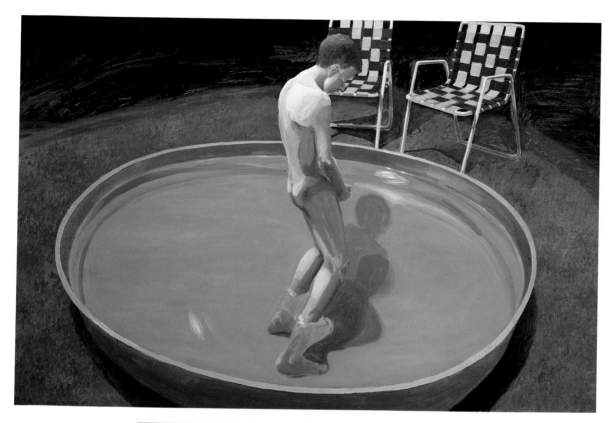

514. **Eric Fischl**
Sleepwalker, 1979
Oil on canvas, 72 x 108 in.
(182.9 x 274.3 cm)
Private collection

515. **Eric Fischl**
Birthday Boy, 1983
Oil on canvas, 84 x 108 in.
(213.3 x 274.3 cm)
Collection of Achille and
Ida Maramotti

Other artists made abstract objects that functioned as cultural signs. Peter Halley's simple geometric vocabulary of squares and rectangles stands for cells and conduits and suggests an architecture of circuitry for a new technological world (fig. 523). Allan McCollum's *Surrogates*, begun in 1981, were handmade Hydrocal objects made to look like small Minimalist paintings—black fields, surrounded by white mats, bordered by black frames (fig. 531). Though made by hand, they recalled mass-produced objects, and McCollum in fact turned them out by the hundreds, typically installing these *Surrogates* in big groupings of twenty to forty units. This

535. **Ashley Bickerton**
Le Art (Composition with Logos, #2), 1987
Mixed media, 34½ x 72 x 15 in. (87.6 x 182.3 x 38.1 cm)
Private collection; courtesy Sonnabend Gallery, New York

abstraction about art as commodity had its roots in Pop and Conceptual art and is not far removed from Richard Artschwager's earlier simulations of abstract paintings, where synthetic Formica wood grain stands for a picture of wood (fig. 296).

The quiet morbidity and surreal nature of these objects was taken to a hyperreal level by Jeff Koons, who used actual consumer goods as symbolic surrogates for the idea of art as commodity and the self as product. His vacuum cleaner encased in plexiglass, basketballs floating in fish tanks, or a stainless steel bunny cast from an inflatable toy are pristine objects, with the life squeezed out of them (figs. 533, 534). Koons, like the Pop artists, took consumer goods and transformed them through alterations in scale and material. By making them dysfunctional, he turned them into metaphoric artifacts. His brilliant series of sculptures engaged a wide range of consumer habits—from liquor consumption and pornography to sports and entertainment. The self-conscious awareness of the art object as commodity can also be seen in Ashley Bickerton's *Le Art*—a crafted, machinelike form covered in logos like a customized race car; the inclusion of the artist's signature in two highly visible places suggests a surrogate self-portrait (fig. 535).

These were the years when art became a big business. In 1980, a new price level was reached for the work of a living artist when Jasper Johns' *Three Flags* was sold to the Whitney Museum for $1 million. The financial stakes were suddenly raised, and artists began to take an active interest in the marketing of their works. No longer did artists think, as many had in the seventies, that selling was somehow equated with selling out. In fact, artists in the eighties often had waiting lists for work not yet made. Everyone was profiting from a booming economy. Dealers and collectors controlled market value. Critics were hired to write essays for catalogs underwritten by galleries; art advisers took the uninitiated by the hand and showed them what to buy and what works were likely to appreciate (taking a cut of the purchase price in the process); and curators and critics went free-lance, organizing shows for whomever would foot the bill.

A new generation of collectors also emerged, one that identified with the bold moves of the new artists. Charles Saatchi, Eli Broad, and Douglas Cramer established their own private museums to house their collections. Meanwhile, public

514. Eric Fischl
Sleepwalker, 1979
Oil on canvas, 72 x 108 in.
(182.9 x 274.3 cm)
Private collection

515. Eric Fischl
Birthday Boy, 1983
Oil on canvas, 84 x 108 in.
(213.3 x 274.3 cm)
Collection of Achille and
Ida Maramotti

museums were expanding at a frantic pace, with new buildings and wings for contemporary art breaking ground across the country. Art was not only fashionable and profitable, it was also considered a tangible commodity, and many banks started accepting art as collateral against loans. Art was fetching staggering prices; the bidding at auctions was frenzied and intoxicating. By the end of the decade, de Kooning's *Interchange* (1955) broke another record for a living artist, selling at auction to a private collector for $20.7 million in 1989.

The "big boys"—the Neo-Expressionist painters—got the most ink during the 1980s and soon became "art stars." They interacted with other celebrities and business tycoons, moving effortlessly between the world of art and the world of power, commerce, and fame. This Hollywoodization of the art world had been initiated by Andy Warhol, whose entrepreneurship and star-making abilities now enchanted a new generation of self-made stars. The monarch of the scene, Warhol fraternized with the younger artists, including Haring, Basquiat (with whom he collaborated), and Schnabel, to whom he was a role model and father figure (fig. 538).

THE NEW HOLLYWOOD: RISKY BUSINESS

In 1980, Ronald Reagan was elected president and *The Empire Strikes Back* (Irvin Kershner), the triumph of an authoritarian evil force over altruistic do-gooders, was the year's top-grossing film. The two events inaugurated an era of corporate and cultural raiders.

The following year witnessed the launch of the television show *Entertainment Tonight*, which promoted the logic that if a film made a lot of money, it must be good. Soon afterward came MTV, which purveyed videos of popular songs. MTV's lightning-paced edits, eroticized imagery, and fractured narratives influenced films such as *Flashdance* (1983, Adrian Lyne) and *Top Gun* (1986, Tony Scott).

In a nation long polarized by Vietnam, Watergate, and what to do about double-digit inflation, political and social consensus was elusive. The only thing most Hollywood films of the eighties could agree on was that, in the words of the Michael Douglas character in *Wall Street* (1987, Oliver Stone), "greed is good."

Movies about money made money. *Risky Business* (1983, Paul Brickman) introduced Tom Cruise as a teenage entrepreneur who makes a pile as a pimp. *Wall Street* profiled the rise and fall of a snaky moneyman (Michael Douglas) who preaches the gospel of greed and finds a young disciple (Charlie Sheen). Whereas seventies movies were about the corruption of youth by elders, in eighties movies youth could hardly wait to sell out. *The Big Chill* (1983, Lawrence Kasdan) celebrated the reunion of 1960s idealists turned 1980s capitalists.

Two action-adventure series, the Indiana Jones and Rambo cycles, introduced invincible heroes, embodied by, respectively, a bullwhip-cracking Harrison Ford and an Uzi-toting Sylvester Stallone, who arrived as if immunized from the self-doubt of the preceding decade. Although the Indiana Jones movies that began with *Raiders of the Lost Ark* (1981, Steven

540. Henry Thomas in *E.T.: The Extra-Terrestrial*, directed by Steven Spielberg, 1982 Universal Pictures

Spielberg, produced by George Lucas) are set on the eve of World War II and the Rambo pictures that began with *First Blood* (1982, Ted Kotcheff) are set after Vietnam, both purveyed the spectacle of war for a nation fighting the last battles of the Cold War.

Next to these fantasy heroes were reality heroines. There was Sissy Spacek as the country canary Loretta Lynn in *Coal Miner's Daughter* (1980, Michael Apted), Jessica Lange as Patsy Cline in *Sweet Dreams* (1985, Karel Reisz), Sigourney Weaver as the primatologist Dian Fossey in *Gorillas in the Mist* (1988, Michael Apted), and Meryl Streep as the nuclear whistle-blower Karen Silkwood in *Silkwood* (1983, Mike Nichols) and as the storyteller Isak Dinesen in *Out of Africa* (1985, Sydney Pollack). Weaver in *Aliens* (1986, James Cameron) and Linda Hamilton in *The Terminator* (1984, James

541. **Nam June Paik**
Fin de Siècle II, 1989
201 television sets and
four laser discs, 480 x
168 x 60 in. (1219.2 x
426.7 x 152.5 cm) overall
Whitney Museum of
American Art, New York;
Gift of Laila and Thurston
Twigg-Smith 93.139

Money spelled success for much of the "greed decade." It was the era of block-buster movies (*Jaws* had initiated the trend in 1975, but later action adventure movies such as *Raiders of the Lost Ark* [1981] took the phenomenon to a new high), and blockbuster art shows, beginning with "Treasures of Tutankhamen" at the Metropolitan Museum of Art in 1978. Drawing more than a million visitors, the exhibition was a portent of things to come and established new expectations for the gate. "What is loved is a hit. What is a hit is loved," said the writer George Trow.[143]

Michael Jackson's album *Thriller* topped the charts in 1983, and "Material Girl" Madonna emerged as a major pop star in 1984. The mistress of manufactured images for the camera, she created shifting personas to reflect ever-changing desires (fig. 539). Given the growing love affair between the entertainment industry and the art world, it comes as no surprise that several painters of the eighties, including Salle, Schnabel, and Longo, went on to direct Hollywood movies in the nineties.

Cameron)—both produced by Gale Anne Hurd—flexed their muscles in primal films about a woman fighting to rescue her surrogate or biological child. At the same time, the Terminator himself, a cyborg killer portrayed by Arnold Schwarzenegger, embodied the era's obsession with machismo, muscles, and machines.

The antidote to these high-testosterone and high-estrogen affairs was a trio of gender-bending comedies in which women pose as men to enjoy male prerogatives and vice versa. The fun of *Tootsie* (1982, Sydney Pollack), *Victor/Victoria* (1982, Blake Edwards), and *Yentl* (1983, Barbra Streisand) was in watching Dustin Hoffman, Julie Andrews, and Streisand explore how the other gender lived.

The defining film of the decade, *E.T.: The Extra-Terrestrial* (fig. 540), was virtually alone in suggesting that something besides money and success could fill the emotional void. Spielberg's inspirational movie about suburban kids adrift after the divorce of their parents has a wizened creature from another planet unify a broken family, involving its members in something larger than themselves. The film, which capitalized on marketing strategies such as product placement and merchandise tie-ins, was a spectacular commercial success and pop-cultural phenomenon. Many studios, misidentifying *E.T.*'s market as primarily young and male, started cranking out movies targeted at young boys. Only *E.T.*, however, whose audience was actually quite diverse, had widespread appeal.

Before the 1960s, movies were marketed to the broadest possible audience. By the 1980s, it was the rare film—for example, *The Untouchables* (1987, Brian De Palma), a romanticized account of how the federal agent Eliot Ness (Kevin Costner) cleaned up mobsters such as Al Capone (Robert De Niro) in Prohibition-era Chicago—that had wide appeal. Studio marketing departments had perfected the divide-and-conquer art of narrowcasting a movie to a target group. A film such as *The Color Purple* (1985, Steven Spielberg), tracing forty years in the life of a Southern black woman (Whoopi Goldberg), was pitched to African Americans. Comedies such as *Fast Times at Ridgemont High* (1982, Amy Heckerling), *Desperately Seeking Susan* (1985, Susan Seidelman), which featured the pop singer Madonna, and the John Hughes cycle starring Molly Ringwald— *Sixteen Candles*, *The Breakfast Club*, and *Pretty in Pink*—all zeroed in on the teenage market. *Platoon* (1986, Oliver Stone), a grunt's-eye view of Vietnam, was pitched to young and middle-aged males. In slicing up the audience, marketers reinforced the divisions in the American pie.

In 1989, George Bush was inaugurated president and *Batman* (Tim Burton), about the conflicted triumph of a plutocrat vigilante do-gooder (Michael Keaton) over the forces of anti-establishment evil (Jack Nicholson), was the year's top-grossing film. So blurred were distinctions between good and evil that it was increasingly hard to tell the heroes from the villains. —C. R.

The Culture Wars

The economic prosperity of the Reagan years gave the Republicans broad support among the electorate. When Reagan's term ended in 1988, George Bush, his vice president, was elected president in a landslide victory, in which the Republicans swept forty states. But the boom economy did not last. The first signs of weakness had appeared already toward the end of Reagan's second term. On October 19, 1987 ("Black Monday"), the stock market took a nosedive, dropping 22.6 percent in a single day. Although the market eventually recovered, a warning had been raised about the soundness of the American economy. Within three years, rising interest rates, which made it more expensive to borrow money, began to cripple domestic production and led to the collapse of the real estate market. A general decline in consumer spending, combined with the high interest rates, drove the economy into recession. Within a short time, many things that had come to signify the excesses of American life tumbled with the market: down went extravagant lifestyles, overextended savings and loan institutions, and real estate empires. By the end of the decade, the art market collapsed as well. The 1980s closed with a bad case of burnout and a need to reassess values.

542. **Robert Mapplethorpe**
Self-Portrait, 1988
Gelatin silver print, 24 x 20 in. (61 x 50.8 cm)
The Chase Manhattan Bank, New York
© The Estate of Robert Mapplethorpe

Not everyone, moreover, had enjoyed the privileges of wealth, comfort, and fame during the eighties. Among those who struggled with poverty, homelessness, AIDS, and racism, quiet despair and pent-up resentments turned into rage. The AIDS epidemic, which was identified and named in 1982, most graphically represents the other side of the 1980s.

The art world was ravaged by the AIDS epidemic. Scores of art professionals and artists—including Scott Burton, Keith Haring, and David Wojnarowicz—perished. During most of the Reagan years, right-wing groups blamed AIDS on immoral sexual behavior or drug addiction, and the government was slow to initiate research, treatment, and education programs. Gay activist groups such as ACT UP and Gran Fury raised increasingly strong voices of protest. The art world, united for the first time, helped raise millions of dollars for AIDS research (Art Against Aids), provided artists estate planning (Visual Aids), and produced art in direct response to the crisis. The art of David Wojnarowicz, who died in 1992, was among the strongest of these statements (fig. 543). In image- and text-packed, politically charged paintings and brooding photomontages, he empathized with powerlessness and vulnerability and expressed the antagonism between the organic and the mechanical, man and nature (fig. 492). He frankly depicted and wrote about gay sex, and his anger at being marginalized—or worse, demonized by institutionalized homophobia (fig. 545).

To neoconservatives, the AIDS crisis was a threat to the moral fabric of the nation just as Communism had once been. When the wall dividing the eastern and western sectors of Berlin—and, symbolically, East and West Germany—came down in 1989, it was the beginning of the end of the Cold War and the Communist peril. As America confronted mounting economic problems and social unrest, the reactionary right looked for a new scapegoat—and found it in progressive culture. Within this realm, any art that offended the standards of the moral majority was deemed "pornographic" or "obscene." Pornography and obscenity replaced Communism as the new bogeyman. The era of sexual McCarthyism, which culminated a decade later in President William Clinton's impeachment trials, had begun.

are Felix Gonzalez-Torres' conceptual texts and billboards (fig. 546), Keith Haring's ebulliently drawn safer-sex messages, Duane Michals' poetic serial photographs of handsome men enveloped in flowers, Nan Goldin's intimate photo documents of friends stricken with HIV, David Wojnarowicz's painted diatribes against the political system, and Masami Teraoka's images of condom-wielding geishas in the style of Japanese Ukiyo-e prints, to name just a few.

Some of the most influential AIDS art was public art produced by collectives and rarely seen in galleries and museums. Remarkably, the iconic images or symbols of the AIDS epidemic are not made-for-TV movies, photojournalistic pictures, or schmaltzy pop songs, but the NAMES Project Quilt, a community art work, and two logo-emblem images, Silence = Death (fig. 547) and the Red Ribbon (fig. 548), which were conceived by, respectively, the Silence = Death collective (some of whose members became the core of the Gran Fury collective), and the Artists' Caucus of Visual AIDS, the New York organization that in 1989 originated Day Without Art, the annual day of mourning and action in response to the AIDS crisis.

Gran Fury originally operated as the propaganda arm of the activist group ACT UP, exhibiting its work both in the streets and in galleries. The group gave visual form to the shocking statistics emanating daily from the federal Centers for Disease Control with graphic street works that married the methods of art, advertising, and education. One print offered the alarming news that one in sixty-one babies born in New York is HIV–positive and another wittily cajoled men to "Use Condoms or Beat It." The group's famous Benetton ad–inspired image of three interracial, homosexual, and heterosexual couples kissing above the caption "Kissing Doesn't Kill: Greed and Indifference Do" prompted one Chicago alderman to call the print ad "an incitement to homosexuality" when it was exhibited on the sides of buses in that city (fig. 544). Like everything touched by HIV, the art it spawned has been frequently controversial and often politicized. —R. A.

In 1989, a series of vicious attacks was launched against artists, cultural institutions, and the National Endowment for the Arts (NEA), intensifying into a heated public and political debate. Throughout the media, culture was assaulted with a force many never imagined possible. It was shocking and sobering to recognize that basic First Amendment rights to free expression were in fact fragile and required continual defense and vigilance.

548. **Visual AIDS**
The Red Ribbon, 1991

Warning signs of a conservative cultural backlash had appeared in 1980, when Reagan attempted to abolish the NEA or at least drastically slash its budget. But the public attitude toward government-funded art began to change with the highly publicized controversy that raged around Richard Serra's *Tilted Arc*, a permanent, site-specific sculpture commissioned in 1979 by the General Services Administration (GSA) for 26 Federal Plaza in Lower Manhattan (fig. 549). Though the work was selected by an NEA-appointed panel of experts and exhaustively reviewed by the GSA for two years before its installation in 1981, *Tilted Arc* aroused hostilities immediately after it went up. Many of the federal employees working in and around the building felt that Serra's work—a massive, curving, tilted plane of Cor-ten steel bisecting the outdoor plaza—was ugly, threatening, and mean-spirited, a rusting eyesore that obstructed freedom of movement and open views. They called the 12-foot-high and 120-foot-long arc an "iron curtain" and a "steel wall." Most of the art community, however, praised and passionately defended *Tilted Arc* on aesthetic

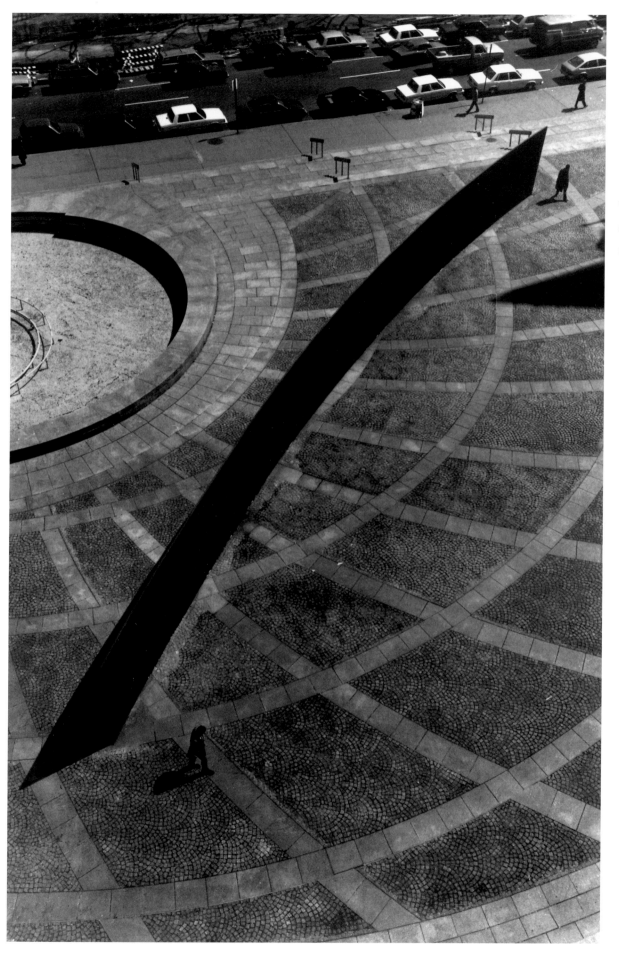

549. **Richard Serra**
Tilted Arc, 1981 (no longer exists)
Cor-ten steel, 144 x 1440 x 2½ in. (365.8 x 3657.6 x 6.4 cm)
Installed in Federal Plaza, New York

grounds, pointing out that challenging work often needs time before its artistic language can be appreciated and understood by a broader public.

Unwilling to try and close the gap between the art community and the public, and afraid to be the target of public acrimony, the GSA began to consider "relocating" the work. In 1985, after much petitioning and testimony on both sides in public hearings—presided over by the GSA and therefore hardly impartial—*Tilted Arc* was ordered removed. Serra argued that because *Tilted Arc* was commissioned as a permanent, site-specific work, its removal would be tantamount to destruction. Divorced from its intended context, the sculpture would lose all integrity as a work of art.

Public opinion and the GSA won out. But the decision to remove *Tilted Arc* set a dangerous precedent for government censorship of art and challenged the legitimacy of the art community's professional standing. It also posed larger questions: How should public money be spent on works of art and who should decide what is best for the "public"—specialists (i.e., art professionals), popular opinion, or government authorities?

There was even some public outcry against Maya Lin's *Vietnam Veterans Memorial* (fig. 550), now the most frequently visited place in Washington, D.C. Influenced by Earthworks and

550. **Maya Lin**
Vietnam Veterans Memorial, Washington, D.C., 1980–82
Granite, 450 ft. (137.2 m) length

Serra's confrontational site-specific sculptures, *Tilted Arc* in particular, Lin cut a wedge shape into the ground and buttressed it with polished black granite walls. You descend down the wedge to its low point, then up the other side, all the while reading the names of the dead soldiers inscribed on the walls. One of the most powerful public sculptures in America, the memorial is an enveloping tombstone and wailing wall that allows for private mourning in a public space. When it was installed, however, some Vietnam veterans groups objected to the abstraction of its conception. Why, they wondered, could there not be a representation of the heroism of the soldiers? Their lobbying efforts were successful, and a figurative tableau by Frederick Hart now stands in proximity to Lin's work.

The protesting veterans were accustomed to war memorials that showed brave, bronze-cast soldiers. Their objection to Lin's work, therefore, was less about its subject than its nonrepresentational form. *Tilted Arc*, in the meantime, was being denounced not for its abstract conception but for interfering in a public space. Both types of protest—against style and against function—were now joined by an outcry against content, this time from the extreme right. In the spring of 1989, just as *Tilted Arc* was being dismantled, the Reverend Donald Wildmon, an evangelical minister from Mississippi and head of the American Family Association (AFA), had a fateful encounter with a photograph. Wildmon had been noted for his attacks against films, such as *The Last Temptation of Christ*, and television, calling for sponsors of certain objectionable programs to withdraw their funding or face boycotts. In an Awards for the Visual Arts (AVA) exhibition catalog, supported by a grant from the NEA and the Equitable Life Assurance Society, Wildmon came across *Piss Christ*, a photograph by the Puerto Rican-born artist Andres Serrano that depicted a crucifix submerged in urine (fig. 551). Wildmon saw red, and the witch-hunt was on against Serrano, the NEA, and other "blasphemous" artists and their supporters. "Degenerate," he called them, the very term used by the Nazis in their purge of progressive culture in Germany. Wildmon organized a massive letter-writing campaign against Equitable, and after receiving several thousand complaints from policyholders, the company withdrew its decade-long sponsorship of the AVA program. Wildmon also alerted several friends in Congress, notably Senator Jesse Helms, a Republican from North Carolina.

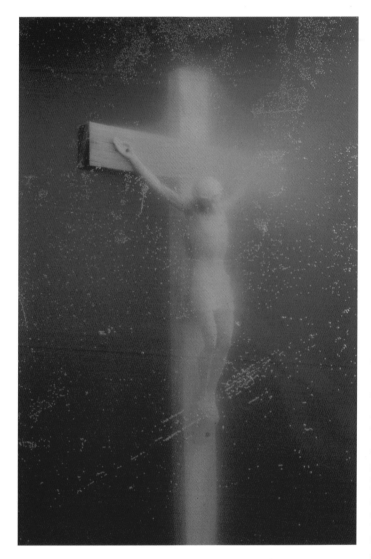

551. **Andres Serrano**
Piss Christ, 1987
Silver dye bleach print (Cibachrome), silicone, plexiglass, and wood frame, 60 x 40 in. (152.4 x 101.6 cm)
Collection of the artist

At about the same time, a young African American artist, Dread Scott, came under fire for an installation at the School of The Art Institute of Chicago that forced visitors to walk on the American flag as they entered the work. The State of Illinois cut support to the school, and President George Bush tried, unsuccessfully, to pass a constitutional amendment making flag desecration a federal offense.

The groundswell of hostility to culture was nowhere more evident than in the controversy that surrounded the now notorious exhibition "Robert Mapplethorpe: The Perfect Moment." The show of Mapplethorpe's technically classic but frankly erotic, homosexually oriented photographs (fig. 552) had been organized by the Institute of Contemporary Art at the University of Pennsylvania, Philadelphia, where it opened in December 1988; it then traveled to the Museum of Contemporary Art in Chicago. The next scheduled stop was The Corcoran Gallery of Art in Washington, D.C. But just a few days before the opening, the gallery's director, Christina Orr-Cahall, responding to the mood in Washington, decided to cancel the exhibition. The political firestorm ignited by her action culminated the following year in a showdown in Cincinnati, where museum director Dennis Barrie was indicted for hosting the Mapplethorpe exhibition at the Contemporary Arts Center. Mapplethorpe's work was used by Wildmon, Helms, Senator Alfonse D'Amato of New York, and others to illustrate their charges that decay and depravity permeated culture and that the NEA, in funding such "immoral trash," was flagrantly disregarding public decency.[144] A Wildmon AFA press release on Mapplethorpe offered the following denunciation: "The exhibit of photographs by Mapplethorpe, a homosexual who died of AIDS earlier this year, contains homoerotic photos that are nothing less than taxpayer-funded homosexual pornography."[145]

Wildmon's further attack on Mapplethorpe as a child molester, child pornographer, and sexual deviant was a fabrication that played on the public's fears about homosexuality and the spread of AIDS. A full-fledged sex panic was under way, allowing demagogues to exploit entrenched anxieties about change, difference, and the explicitly sexual.[146] And the panic was part of a larger right-wing attempt to regulate public expression of identity, deny freedom of choice, and diminish challenges to religious and governmental authority. Not surprisingly, it was gay, lesbian, black, and Hispanic artists who became the primary targets in this crusade against culture (fig. 544). The neoconservative position, which blamed the artists for not conforming to majority standards, was perhaps best summarized by Irving Kristol in a *Wall Street Journal* editorial: "What the 'arts community' is engaged in is a politics of radical nihilism. . . . What they do, in fact, is powerfully shaped by certain radical ideological currents; radical feminism, homosexual and lesbian self-celebration and black racism are among them."[147]

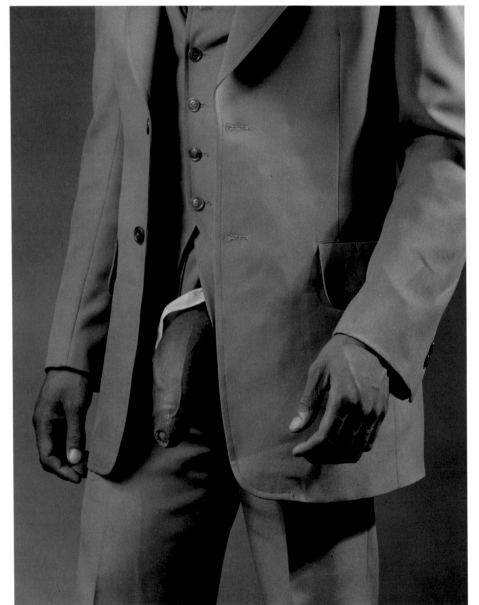

552. **Robert Mapplethorpe**
Man in Polyester Suit,
1980
Gelatin silver print, 40 x
30 in. (101.6 x 76.2 cm)
© The Estate of Robert
Mapplethorpe

In July 1989, one month after the Mapplethorpe show was canceled at the Corcoran, Jesse Helms took advantage of a sparsely attended Senate session to sneak through an amendment prohibiting the use of public funds (that is, NEA funds) for works that include "depictions of sadomasochism, homoeroticism, the sexual exploitation of children, or individuals engaged in sex acts and which, when taken as a whole, do not have serious literary, artistic, political, or scientific value." All 1990 NEA grant recipients were then required to sign this anti-obscenity pledge. In July 1990, John Frohnmayer, the head of the NEA, vetoed four grants by the lesbian, gay, and feminist performance artists Karen Finley, Holly Hughes, Tim Miller, and John Fleck for being "too political." The artists filed suit when their appeal was rejected in August. Three years later they settled the suit, winning reinstatement of the grants as well as damages for invasion of privacy and challenging the constitutionality of the "decency" pledge requirement of the NEA's 1990 guidelines.

These controversies weakened the NEA and threatened its credibility and existence. Many critics, like Kristol, argued that the agency should be abolished altogether. Others favored slashing the budget and imposing stricter content limitations on grants or restructuring the NEA and the peer panel review system. Still others wondered whether avant-garde art—which has traditionally assaulted mainstream values—should be funded by a government agency at all.

553. Cady Noland
The Big Shift, 1989
Pole, fittings, loops, flags,
handcuffs, miscellaneous
metal, bungee cord, key-
holder strap, bug sprayer,
and grill, 57 x 172 x 5 in.
(144.8 x 436.9 x 12.7 cm)
Collection of Jeffrey Deitch

In the fall of 1990, Congress reauthorized the NEA for a three-year term instead of the usual five-year term, but with no restrictions. It was decided that obscenity be determined by the courts and that any grantee convicted of obscenity be required to return the grant money. The NEA is still in existence, but its 1990 budget of $175 million has been cut in half and fellowships to individual artists were eliminated in 1995.

By 1990, vanguard artists found themselves not only embattled by reactionary forces but deprived of support from collectors and museums. The big money from corporate and private patrons that had funded exhibitions and brought prices to a near outrageous level was not available. Perhaps as a backlash against such excesses, many supporters of the arts turned to other causes. Art was no longer fashionable, and many galleries closed, while others retrenched, favoring safe artists with proven track records.

In retrospect, however, these crises served to raise important issues: Who decides what is art? What constitutes censorship? Throughout history, definitions of indecency and obscenity have shifted with the prevailing winds. In 1882, Walt Whitman's *Leaves of Grass* was banned in Boston; Theodore Dreiser's *An American Tragedy* was declared obscene by a Massachusetts court in 1930; and U.S. courts banned the sale of James Joyce's *Ulysses* until 1933. Two further questions emerged from the turbulence of the eighties: Is "quality" a relative, socially determined word—like "obscenity"? And, finally, how can the gap between art and the public's understanding of it be bridged? As a new global economy began to emerge in the nineties, new audiences for art had a vital interest in these questions.

Approaching
the Millennium
1990–2000

On the eve of the 1990s, dramatic political changes around the globe promised a "new world order." In 1989, thousands of pro-democracy demonstrators occupied Beijing's Tiananmen Square. Though violently suppressed by the Chinese government, this expression of dissent could not be completely silenced, and Beijing began to soften its hard-line rule. In the West, the collapse of the Berlin Wall heralded the end of Soviet domination in Central and Eastern Europe as well as the reunification of Germany. Within a short time, the Soviet Union itself was breaking up into independent, non-Communist states. At the start of the decade, the right-wing dictator Augusto Pinochet stepped down as president of Chile, while the South African parliament abrogated the country's racist apartheid laws. In the Middle East, Palestinians and Israelis were sitting together at the peace table.

The sense of optimism that greeted these auspicious events was not always fulfilled. The end of the Cold War, for example, created a vacuum of authority that unleashed long-repressed nationalist sentiments. Indeed, all over the world ethnic groups began to assert themselves in a drive for self-determination that has come to be identified with the 1990s. Throughout the nations in the former Communist bloc, such groups claimed the right to self-rule and self-expression—even when their populations were spread across established political borders. Serbs, Croats, Albanians, and smaller minorities in Yugoslavia had lived together, as Christians and Muslims, until liberation from the Communist yoke set off deadly internecine violence. Elsewhere, conflicts among different ethnic, religious, and political groups raged unabated in the post-Cold War era. Ethnic hostility erupted into genocide in Rwanda, endangering the stability of several Central African nations. Separatist and independence movements roiled India, Sri Lanka, Indonesia, and Ethiopia. Later in the decade, fragile peace accords reached in Israel and Northern Ireland threatened to unravel amid continuing factional strife.

In the United States, the idea of difference—racial, ethnic, sexual, and political—underwent a more positive evolution. It was a key element in the campaign and early administration of Bill Clinton, elected president in 1992 (and reelected in 1996). A liberal Democrat and baby boomer, Clinton rode to victory on a centrist platform of fiscal conservatism tempered with a progressive social agenda—health care reform, abortion rights, gun control, and inclusive policies toward people of color, women, gays and lesbians, and other groups that had been effectively disenfranchised during twelve years of Republican leadership. Clinton appointed more women and minorities to his cabinet than any previous president. He also met with gay and lesbian leaders in the White House and, early in his presidency, advocated an end to the ban on homosexuals in the military. Like his hero John F. Kennedy, Clinton understood the power of television, using nationally televised "town meetings" to debate issues such as the need to improve race relations in an effort to heal the discord among America's multicultural constituencies. And there was need for such debates. Despite the progressivism of the administration's policies, racial strife still lurked within American culture, sometimes emerging with appalling violence.

Clinton's call for national unity had wide appeal, and his administration eventually enjoyed a high approval rating. Much of Clinton's popularity, however, derived not from his social agenda but from the unprecedented economic upturn over which he presided. From 1992 to the end of the decade, the U.S. economy flourished, fueled in part by the lowest interest rates in a generation and the explosion of high-technology industries. Not surprisingly, the Clinton administration was also a strong advocate for the use of the Internet and other technological innovations in both education and business. The administration promoted an "Information Superhighway," linking individuals, communities, countries, and cultures, which would revolutionize education and trade. His forecast proved accurate: in 1993, the Internet linked 5 million people worldwide; at the end of the decade, about 100 million people were active online.

The Internet is but one part of a phenomenon known as globalization, which has produced a new, worldwide business and entertainment culture through the ubiquity and immediacy of modern telecommunications systems. Another part is represented by the international trade agreements that have been formulated in the 1990s—the North American Free Trade Agreement (NAFTA) between the United States and Mexico, the ongoing negotiations for the General Agreement on Tariffs and Trade (GATT), which involves countries around the world, and the Maastricht Treaty, signed by many European nations. These treaties, by reducing tariffs and other trade barriers and opening national borders, forged commercial and cultural links across the globe. Through such agreements and the proliferation of technology, diverse communities have been consolidating into a broad "global village" of trading and cultural partners. This new globalism naturally promoted the idea of cultural homogeneity. But such homogeneity also threatened a loss of individuality, of the characteristics that distinguish people, ethnic groups, and even nations. The desire to maintain and even assert these distinctions in an increasingly uniform world led people to search for new ways to be different, new ways to reinvent local and native traditions.

This sensitivity to difference within a global consciousness has had a dramatic effect on art and the mapping of its boundaries. We have started to look for innovation in art made outside the cultural "mainstream," whether in the diverse communities of America or in other areas of the world. Indeed, the definition of the word "mainstream" has undergone a radical revision, in part as a result of shifting demographics. Twenty years ago, for example, the population of Los Angeles was 70 percent Anglo; today it is just 40 percent Anglo. The increasingly articulate voices of different ethnic groups, nationally and globally, has moved the issue of personal identity to the forefront of political as well as aesthetic concerns. Identity

AMERICANIZATION: THE EXPORT OF AMERICAN CULTURE

Wherever you live in the world, whoever you may be, once the lights dim in a movie theater, or the screen lights up on your TV or PC, you become part of the American century. Many of the catchwords and concepts of twentieth-century political and cultural life have a peculiarly American provenance: the global market as the touchstone of capitalist "free" enterprise in the West; democratic capitalism as the rubric of the West's crusade against Communist or Socialist "empires of evil"; or, more recently, the catchword of global theorists, the "Coca-Cola-ization" of the world—which suggests that from a curvaceous bottle emerges the genie of the American dream—youth, entertainment, cool technologies, and hot financial markets.

The global spread of "America" as *the* quintessential cultural icon of the twentieth century, or as the "style" of *living* in the present (on-screen or on-line) and looking the part (jeans, Nikes, sweats), is about the triumph of an "image." The spread of Americanism as a cultural style comes from the capacity of American popular culture to translate its values, lifestyle, and products—its ideology—into consumable and reproducible images that can either be imitated or reinvented across the world, wherever Western-style "free" and "privatized" markets exist.

In the American century, then, a lifestyle can become an ideology in a way no other dominant "world" culture made possible for its subjects—to be an "anglicized" colonized person, for instance, was emphatically *not* to be British. If this century has been called the American century, it is not merely because of the feudal grip of Hollywood or Silicon Valley on the rest of the world, or even because Michael Jordan and Bill Gates bestride the world like colossi. What is distinctive about American cultural industries and icons is their ability to give "American" images a global relevance, an innate sense (however inappropriate) of belonging in various national and cultural locations.

Americanization, for instance, is not simply the creation of a global "youth" culture because MTV services "one quarter of the world's television households in 85 territories . . . tailored to the life-style and sensibilities of 12–34 year olds" (MTV Global fact sheet). The imaginative power of Americanization lies in persuading other cultures and nations to experience and commodify their own sense of modernity or postmodernity in an American style. That style, as a cultural commodity, is no longer the all-American "apple pie à la mode" of the fifties. The contemporary consumption of Americanized global culture is much more on the "take-out" model, where what is consumed may be "ethnic" but the style of consumption is still a version of the good ol' American drive-in. Global company logos illustrate this shift rather well. MTV's philosophy is "think globally, act locally," while the Ford Motor Company motto is "To be a multinational group, it is necessary to be national everywhere." What this means is that "Americanization" is less evident in the cultural "product" and more concerned with the process and the program. Americanization is now the "global" connectivity between national cultures that can reach their own peoples only through a cultural agency that is at once visible and invisible. What is "American" is neither simply the local nor the global but the economic and cultural linkage between the two. For instance, 85 percent of MTV Mandarin consists of music videos from China, while 75 percent of MTV India politics and the debates around multiculturalism and race in fact constitute one of the most important developments of the early nineties. Events such as the beating of Rodney King by officers of the Los Angeles Police Department, famously captured on videotape, which led to rioting in Los Angeles when the officers were acquitted, or the trial of O. J. Simpson, the former football star accused of murdering his white ex-wife, Nicole Brown Simpson, became lightning rods for race issues in America. In the arts, multiculturalism was evident in groundbreaking exhibitions such as "The Decade Show: Frameworks of Identity in the 1980s" at the New Museum of Contemporary Art, New York (1990), which highlighted artists of color who had been working throughout the eighties in relative obscurity. The 1993 Biennial at the Whitney Museum of American Art similarly featured "other" voices—of African Americans, Native Americans, and Asian Americans, as well as gays and lesbians. One of the most memorable contributions to the show was supplied by Los Angeles artist Daniel Martinez, who made buttons reading "I can't imagine ever wanting to be white" that were distributed at the museum entrance. The "Black Male" exhibition, also at the Whitney (1994), examined changing representations of black masculinity in America through art and film. These and other exhibitions, among them "Magiciens de la terre" (1989) at the Centre Georges Pompidou, Paris, which emphasized non-Western art and traditions in a fortress of Western culture, prompted a revaluation of what had previously been considered lesser places and cultures. Biennials in Johannesburg, Istanbul, Kwangju, and São Paulo caught the world's attention in the 1990s, as the demarcation line between margin and center blurred and shifted. The cultural relativity of terms such as "beauty" and "quality" was exposed, as it had been in the seventies by feminists and black activists.

Cultural diversity has awakened our understanding that the dominant aesthetic discourse has been Western, bourgeois, and male. The African American contribution to the nation's life and culture, for example, has long been undervalued. It is now foregrounded by the work and perspective of black

consists of Hindi music videos. Yet, says MTV Global, "each channel adheres to the overall style, programming philosophy and integrity of the MTV trademark while promoting local cultural tastes and musical talent." In this process, national cultures, once considered sovereign, are now downgraded to "local" tastes and talents.

Is Americanization nothing more than cultural imperialism dressed in the drag of digital technology, its tentacles twitching to the new rhythms of rockumentaries? To answer this question, we must look beyond the depredations of the icons and acronyms of Americanization—AOL, CNN, MTV, McDonald's, and Mickey Mouse. What then becomes apparent are two important aspects of the function of Americanization in contemporary conditions.

First, Americanization is frequently the "name" given to the anxious process of flux and confusion that accompanies moments when societies are in transformation and nations in transition. With the meltdown of the Soviet Union, and the emergence of genocidal nationalisms the world over, the very integrity of the nation-state as a political entity is in jeopardy as never before. It is little wonder, then, that in the midst of this historical trauma, the triumphalism frequently associated with the survival of the "American system" should be seen by many as a corporate takeover of other national cultures.

Second, the massive technological revolution that ends this century much as it began creates a deeper anxiety about who we are as a "people." Computer imaging, digitalization, cloning—these technological advances produce a deep fear that we will be turned from culture-respecting "individuals" to leisure-ravaging masses. Americanization is, then, the expression of an anxiety attributed to the standardization of taste and what Stefan Zweig called the "monotonization of the world" created by the global production of mass culture. At the end of the century, as nations lose some of their cultural sovereignty, and the supreme autonomy of the individual is wrested away by the power of intelligent machines, Americanization becomes the most salient sign of our precarious future.

The final irony of the American century may well be that what America has to teach the global world, at the dawn of the twenty-first century, is the lesson it has been struggling to learn, as a nation, throughout the present one. Despite the dispiriting statistics on race, poverty, crime, and the "culture wars" that bedevil America, there is scarcely another country more obsessed with the rights of minorities and the recognition of cultural diversity. Like all obsessions, American pluralism is prone to failure, defensiveness, overreaction, and fatigue. But it is nonetheless a magnificent obsession. It has infused the American century with a spirit of freedom and equality embodied in civil rights, women's rights, the needs of and obligations toward AIDS communities, the freedom of cultural and artistic expression, the care of the environment, and much else. If worldly ambition can fly on the wings of such a spirit of Americanization—with all its false starts and lost paths—then we may yet see a more equitable movement between one way of life and another, between oneself and the Other. —H. K. B.

Americans who have changed the mainstream—among them the sports hero Michael Jordan; pop music star Michael Jackson; film directors Spike Lee, John Singleton, and Julie Dash; author Toni Morrison; poet Maya Angelou; military leader General Colin Powell; Harvard professors of African American studies Henry Louis Gates, Jr., and Cornel West; talk show host Oprah Winfrey; and documentary filmmaker Henry Hampton. By defying clichés that limited the role of blacks in America, they have altered long-standing racial stereotypes.

A generation of visual artists have emerged in the nineties who also engage and challenge these stereotypes. Understanding that we all identify with the images through which the dominant culture represents us, they claim those representations in order to disclaim them—a process that forces a change in the viewer's consciousness. Kara Walker, for instance, imagines herself as a nineteenth-century slave girl in allegorical silhouette cycloramas (fig. 556). A police lineup is the subject of Gary Simmons' work, and the candidates for inspection are symbolized by a row of gold-plated basketball sneakers (fig. 557). In another work by Simmons, the

A NEW AVANT-GARDE IN ARCHITECTURE

In 1988, The Museum of Modern Art in New York held an exhibition entitled "Deconstructivist Architecture," which attempted to present as a consolidated entity an international group of architects, among them Zaha Hadid, Rem Koolhaas, Peter Eisenman, Daniel Libeskind, and Bernard Tschumi. The premise of the show was twofold: first, that this group of architects was engaged in a critical practice deploying strategies associated with the historical avant-gardes, especially Russian Constructivism; second, that this redeployment was informed by the tactics of theorists such as Jacques Derrida. While there was much controversy over whether deconstructivism was simply another style in the postmodern smorgasbord of styles or a categorically different form of practice—and perhaps even more debate over whether someone like Frank Gehry read philosophy at all—deconstructivism did register an architectural sea change (fig. 554). It helped invent a new and hybrid form of architect—part critic, part theorist, part professional—who pursued a fundamentally interdisciplinary practice that paralleled the emergence of new types of transmedia art forms. Moreover, many of the most prominent architects involved were European-born but located at least part of the time in the United States: the Dutch Koolhaas was at the Institute for Architecture and Urban Studies in New York when he wrote his influential *Delirious New York* in 1978 (fig. 555); Libeskind, born in Poland, taught for many years at the Cranbrook Academy of Art in Michigan; and Tschumi, trained at the École des Beaux-Arts in Paris, ultimately became dean of Columbia University's Graduate School of Architecture in New York.

This influx of people and ideas did a great deal to dismantle the sentimental patriotism of American postmodernism. Perhaps most important, the architects' appeal to theoretical rigor opened architecture to the critical voices of feminism, AIDS activism, postcolonialism, and other transformative intellectual and political developments. By the time the first major buildings of these architects were completed—Koolhaas' Kunsthalle in Rotterdam (1992), Tschumi's *Parc de la Villette* in Paris (1998), and Libeskind's Jewish Museum in Berlin (1998)— their earlier theoretical work had already contributed to a particularly American effort to establish a critical, even avant-garde, architectural practice for the late twentieth century. —S. L.

554. *Deconstructivist Architecture*, by Philip Johnson and Mark Wigley New York: The Museum of Modern Art, 1988

555. *Delirious New York: A Retroactive Manifesto for Manhattan*, by Rem Koolhaas, cover illustration by Madelon Vriesendorp New York: Oxford University Press, 1978

556. Kara Walker
The End of Uncle Tom and
the Grand Allegorical Tableau
of Eva in Heaven, 1995
(detail)
Cut paper, 10 x 40 ft.
(3 x 12.1 m) overall
Collection of Jeffrey Deitch

557. Gary Simmons
Lineup, 1993
Synthetic polymer on wood
with gold-plated basketball
shoes, 114 x 240½ x
18 in. (289.6 x 610.9 x
45.7 cm) overall
Whitney Museum of
American Art, New York;
Purchase, with funds from
the Brown Foundation, Inc.
93.65a–p

The element of anxiety and danger was always present in Chris Burden's work, but now it was embodied in densely compacted hanging spheres of metal and toy train tracks, which look like horrific post-apocalyptic detritus (fig. 570). Paul McCarthy, who in the seventies began staging grotesque and visceral performances (fig. 571), in the nineties made disturbing objects that involve mechanical performing figures in stage-set tableaux (fig. 572). Raymond Pettibon's eccentric drawings merge personal observations, literary history, and pop culture in a range of emotions, from the agitated to the lethargic (figs. 574, 575). Cast-off, rejected rag dolls found at flea markets are stitched together by Mike Kelley in works such as *More Love Hours Than Can Ever Be Repaid*, a disturbing reminder of child abuse or other painful childhood memories (fig. 573). In another work, *Lumpenprole*, the dolls are concealed under an afghan, their shapes creating a topography of repressed memories (fig. 576).

576. Mike Kelley
Installation view of "Mike Kelley" at the Musée d'Art Contemporain, Bordeaux, France, 1992
Foreground: *Lumpenprole*, 1991; background: *Ageistprop*, 1991

Although the work of Los Angeles artists can be interpreted in a regional context, the work of other artists across America also took a dark turn in the early nineties. Several exhibitions— "Dislocations" at The Museum of Modern Art, New York (1991), "Distemper: Dissonant Themes in the Art of the 1990s" at the Hirshhorn Museum and Sculpture Garden, Washington, D.C. (1996), and the international traveling show "Post Human" (1992–93)—have charted a growing sense of alienation, doom, and dystopia that may express the anxiety of a society awaiting the millennium. We have witnessed bizarre cultists committing mass suicide, terrorists blowing up airplanes and government buildings, the continuing AIDS plague, police brutality captured on videotape, and the moral breakdown of our most trusted and admired heroes. These strange events and the media's fixation and incessant replay of lurid disasters, criminal violence, and confessional spectacle has intensified our sense of wariness and fallibility.

In art, this unease has found palpable expression in the word-based paintings of Christopher Wool (fig. 532), the moody, scavenged-sign installations of Jack Pierson (fig. 577), and the abject images of Paul McCarthy, Mike Kelley, and Sue Williams (fig. 578). Indeed, an art of extreme vulnerability and fragility is one of the principal characteristics of the nineties, as is also seen in the work of Felix Gonzalez-Torres, Jim Hodges, Richard Prince, and Robert Gober.

Gober's work has long alluded to loving, dying, and waste, as well as to domestic dysfunction. Even his use of dismembered body parts, such as a single trousered leg protruding from the wall (fig. 580), is both tender and discomforting. The sinks he began to make as early as 1985 are nonfunctional domestic objects, lacking hardware and pipes and presented in repeated sequences or in stacked pairs in the serial form of Minimalism (fig. 579). But they are handmade and have a decidedly human

577. Jack Pierson
Desire, Despair, 1996
Metal, plastic, plexiglass,
and wood, 117½ x 56¼ in.
(298.5 x 142.9 cm)
Whitney Museum of
American Art, New York;
Purchase, with funds from
the Painting and Sculpture
Committee 97.102.2a–l

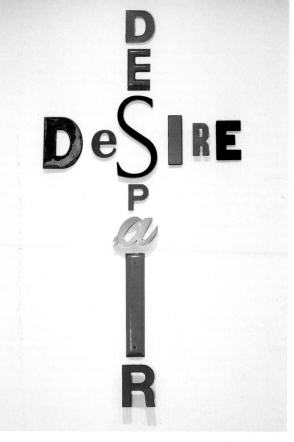

578. Sue Williams
Large Blue Gold and Itchy,
1996
Oil and synthetic polymer
on canvas, 96 x 108 in.
(243.8 x 274.3 cm)
Whitney Museum of
American Art, New York;
Purchase, with funds from
the Contemporary Painting
and Sculpture Committee
97.55

579. **Robert Gober**
The Ascending Sink, 1985
Plaster, wood, wire lath,
steel, and semigloss
enamel paint, two pieces
stacked, 30 x 33 x 27 in.
(76.2 x 83.8 x 68.6 cm)
each
Private collection

580. **Robert Gober**
*Untitled (Leg with
Candle)*, 1991
Wax, cloth, wood, leather,
and human hair, 13½ x
7 x 37½ in. (34.3 x
17.8 x 95.5 cm)
Whitney Museum of
American Art, New York;
Purchase, with funds from
Robert W. Wilson 92.6

581. **Felix Gonzalez-Torres**
Untitled (Portrait of Ross in L.A.), 1991
Continuously replenished supply of multicolored candies individually wrapped in cellophane, dimensions variable
Private collection; courtesy Andrea Rosen Gallery, New York

presence. Gober's work of this period, which reintroduced intimacy and directness through the handcrafted object, was a touchstone for artists in the nineties.

Felix Gonzalez-Torres, like Gober, emerged in the eighties, and his work is the antithesis of the overblown, hyperbolic statements dominant at that time. Gonzalez-Torres, who died of AIDS in 1996, produced art in a variety of media that confronted real and projected loss. Following his partner's death, he made a photographic billboard project depicting their empty bed (fig. 546). He is best known for his ephemeral works, such as endlessly replenishable piles of candy (fig. 581) or stacks of printed paper meant to be taken away by the audience, or the more permanent and elegant strings of illuminated light bulbs (fig. 582). Although Gonzalez-Torres' art consciously references the scatter art and Postminimal forms of the late sixties, he endowed it with a personal conceptual content (the amount of candy "spilled" might be equal to his partner's weight, for instance), mixed with the activist's sense of generosity and democracy (he was a member of Group Material for years).

Just as Pop art provided a model for many artists in the eighties, artists in the nineties looked back to seventies art—to its scatter, ephemerality, and heterogeneity. In both decades, no dominant style prevailed, no major movements were named, only a few art "stars" emerged, and no clear ideology held sway. Again, as in the

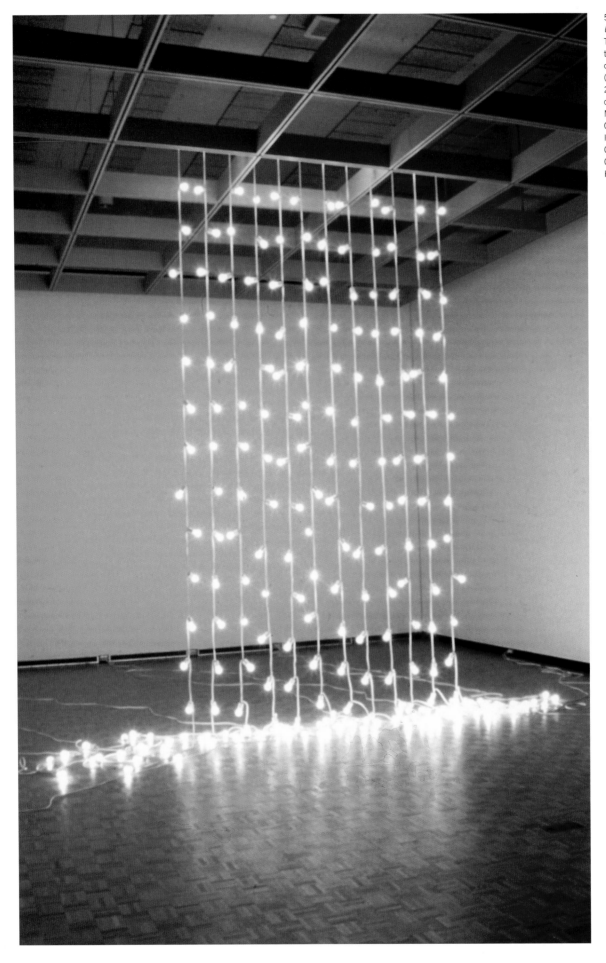

582. **Felix Gonzalez-Torres**
Untitled (North), 1993
Twenty-two light bulbs,
twelve strings, extension
cords, twelve parts, 270 in.
(685.8 cm) length, with
240 in. (609.6 cm) extra
cord each
Marieluise Hessel
Collection on permanent
loan to the Center for
Curatorial Studies, Bard
College, Annandale-on-
Hudson, New York

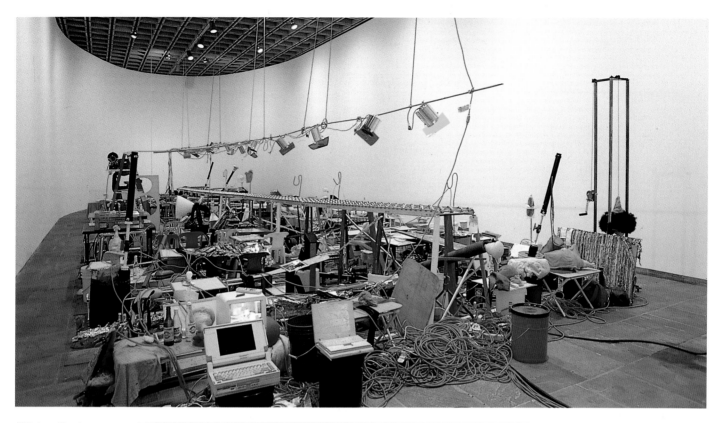

583. Jason Rhoades
Uno Momento/the theatre in my dick/a look to the physical/ephemeral, 1996
Mixed-media installation, approximately 25 x 70 ft. (7.6 x 21.3 m)
Hauser & Wirth, Zurich

584. Jim Hodges
On We Go, 1996
Silver-plated chain with pins, 57 x 48 x 22 in. (144.8 x 121.9 x 55.9 cm)
Collection of Eileen and Peter Norton

seventies, artists turned to ephemeral installations, film, performance, and photography. Their works employed modest materials and revealed an intimate touch and emotional life in a visually unheroic language. The materials in Jim Hodges' sculpture range from thin silver chains that form delicate spiderwebs (fig. 584) to synthetic flowers stitched together as sumptuous curtains. In Hodges' art, as in that of other young artists, beauty is precarious and humble attention is paid to craft. In stark contrast are the vast assemblage environments of Jason Rhoades, where objects are distributed across a large field in a seemingly random fashion (fig. 583). The arrangement, however, is actually a carefully considered structure that reveals the artist's interest in the typically male culture of tools, fix-it-yourself magazines, and home improvement projects.

A number of artists who had been at work for years came to prominence in the nineties. Among those we have already encountered are David Hammons, Mike Kelley, and Robert Gober, as well as Louise Bourgeois, Lari Pittman, and Kiki Smith. Their aesthetic, which had defied the hyperbolic spectacle of so much eighties art, became critical in defining that of the nineties. Bourgeois' career enjoyed something of a renaissance as she produced some of her strongest work in her eighties, proving that age has nothing to do with generative power. Her looming cast bronze spiders, "cells" or cage-like environments, and her wonderful assemblages of clothes saved over a lifetime provoked and enchanted audiences (fig. 586). Lari Pittman's work of the nineties draws on a range of ethnic traditions, high and low culture, and gay politics, inventing a unique style that is garishly beautiful, humble and bold, and that makes use of both modest language and epic scale. Kiki Smith started out as a member of Colab, making lowly and offbeat objects out of plaster, paper, fabric, and glass that usually referred to some part of the human anatomy, to body function, or to our relationship to the environment. In the nineties, her growing material inventiveness and lyricism were matched by an increasingly intense subject matter. Using life-size figures, Smith's work became bolder, more visceral, and more provocative in its graphic depictions of death, decomposition, waste, and regeneration (fig. 585).

Women have made some of the strongest contributions to art in the

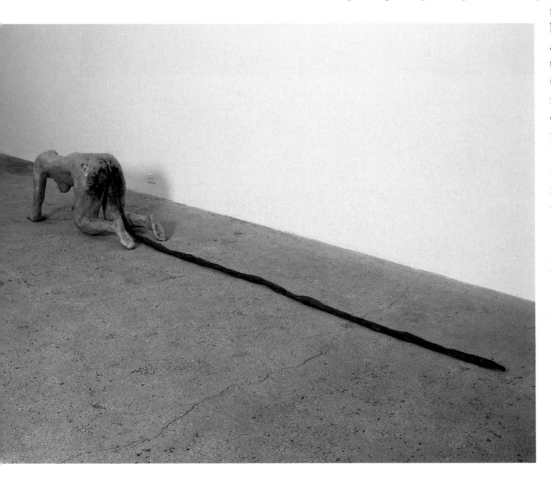

585. **Kiki Smith**
Tale, 1992
Wax, pigment, and papier-mâché, 23 x 160 x 23 in. (58.4 x 406.4 x 58.4 cm)
Collection of
Jeffrey Deitch

nineties. From Jennifer Pastor's elaborately researched and meticulously executed sculptural tableaux to Toba Khedoori's delicate monumental renderings of architectural structures to Shahzia Sikander's contemporary updatings of traditional Indian miniature painting and Kara Walker's powerful wall-scale silhouette cutouts, it is clear that women are expanding our visual vocabulary, often continuing to draw on and update craft traditions (fig. 556). Other significant contributions by women include Catherine Opie's and Sharon Lockhart's color photographs and Ann Hamilton's

586. Louise Bourgeois
Spider, 1997
Steel and mixed media,
175 x 262 x 204 in.
(444.5 x 665.5 x
518.2 cm)
Courtesy Cheim & Read,
New York
© Louise Bourgeois/
Licensed by VAGA,
New York, NY

587. **Ann Hamilton**
Mantle, 1996
Performance with shortwave
radio, table, and sixty
thousand flowers at Miami
Art Museum, Florida

588. **Janine Antoni**
Loving Care, 1992 (detail)
Performance with hair dye
at Anthony d'Offay Gallery,
London
Courtesy of the artist
and Luhring Augustine,
New York

589. **Catherine Opie**
Self-Portrait, 1993
Chromogenic color print, 39⅝
x 29⁹⁄₁₆ in. (100.6 x 76 cm)
Whitney Museum of
American Art, New York;
Purchase, with funds from
the Photography Committee
94.64

and Janine Antoni's tactile, performance-oriented sculptures and installations (figs. 588, 589), all of which convey a combination of toughness, delicate beauty, and sensuality.

The resurgence of the handmade and craft-related procedures in much nineties art is, in part, a reaction to the encroachment of technology on modern life and the distancing of human relations through the mediation of machines. New technologies such as video conferencing, online trading, cellular phones, virtual reality, and cybersex have diminished the need for personal contact. This has, in turn, allowed relationships to become infused with imagination and fantasy. One can project fantasies on the Internet, for instance, and even create imaginary surrogates of a different sex or age. Such merging of reality and fiction through new technologies has blurred the boundaries between the two. Today, we are more likely to wonder whether or not a photograph represents an actual reality, particularly since the computer can create seamless, lifelike scenes constructed (or enhanced) from real and/or fabricated imagery.

The construction of fictional realities has extended to the human form. People alter their appearance, sexuality, and identity—physically through bodybuilding, sex-change operations, plastic surgery; conceptually, through spin doctors. Michael Jackson and Ivana Trump have transformed their personas through plastic surgery. Face-lifts, breast implants, and liposuction are commonplace in our youth-obsessed, wrinkle-free world. The plastic, the artificial, and the non-natural reign. The sense that biology is no longer destiny has raised new moral issues. With the dawn of genetic engineering, biotechnology, and cloning, there is every indication that we may be moving into a "post-human" phase of evolution.

These new notions of the body and the self have stimulated a major revival and reinvention of figurative art, but now with a Conceptual orientation, from Paul McCarthy's mechanical figures (fig. 572) to Cindy Sherman's recent photographs, which construct hybrid figures from body parts, props, and prostheses (fig. 590), and to Robert Gober's installations of figures and body parts—pierced, dismembered, and submerged into the floor as components of strange tableaux (fig. 591).

Two important artists who gained attention in the

590. **Cindy Sherman**
Untitled (Mannequin),
1992
Silver dye bleach print
(Ilfochrome), 68⅛₆ x 45⅛ in.
(172.9 x 114.6 cm)
Whitney Museum of
American Art, New York;
Purchase, with funds from
the Wilfred P. and Rose J.
Cohen Purchase Fund and
the Photography Committee
92.76

1990s for their figurative works are Charles Ray and Matthew Barney. Ray, who during the 1980s made idiosyncratic abstract sculpture where things were not what they seemed, turned to figurative work at the beginning of the nineties (figs. 594, 595). Continuing to mine the strange in the familiar, he has made self-portraits that look like stiff, store mannequins or family ensembles that subtly distort scale to suggest dysfunction. With their human forms and mechanical appearance, Ray's works are strange hybrids that combine public and private, presence and absence. Matthew Barney's early performances, in which he scaled the wall of the gallery, took the art world by storm (fig. 592). In later works, he subjects himself to numerous

592. **Matthew Barney**
Blind Perineum, 1991
Videotape, color, silent;
87 min.
Barbara Gladstone Gallery,
New York
© 1991 Matthew Barney

593. **Matthew Barney**
Drawing Restraint 7, 1993
Videotape, color, silent;
13 min.; steel, plastic, and
fluorescent light fixtures in
room, 120 x 180 x 264 in.
(304.8 x 457.2 x 670.6 cm)
Whitney Museum of
American Art, New York;
Purchase, with funds from
the Painting and Sculpture
Committee 93.33
© 1993 Matthew Barney

594. **Charles Ray**
Puzzle Bottle, 1995
Glass, painted wood, and
cork, 13⅜ x 3¾ x 3¾ in.
(34 x 9.5 x 9.5 cm)
Whitney Museum of
American Art, New York;
Purchase, with funds from
the Contemporary Painting
and Sculpture Committee
and Barbara and Eugene
Schwartz 95.85a–b

595. **Charles Ray**
Fall '91, 1992
Mannequin and mixed
media, 96 x 36 x 26 in.
(243.8 x 91.4 x 66 cm)
The Broad Art Foundation,
Santa Monica, California

HOLLYWOOD: OF CANNIBALS AND KINGS

"The trouble with movies as a business is that they're an art; the trouble with movies as an art is that they're a business," quipped Charlton Heston, paraphrasing the ancient Hollywood paradox. During the last decade of the century that witnessed the birth of film as both business and art, filmmakers increasingly juggled the contradictory roles of businessman and artist.

Thus Steven Spielberg, who directed an immodest number of the most successful movies ever made, divided his output between profit and honor. For profit, he made the dinosaur theme park thrill rides *Jurassic Park* (1993) and its 1997 sequel, *The Lost World*. For honor, he made the serious dramas *Schindler's List* (1993), about the Nazi war profiteer who saves the lives of Jews working for him; *Amistad* (1997), about the 1839 slave mutiny; and *Saving Private Ryan* (1998), a World War II combat film about the glory and folly of losing lives to save lives. Spielberg's serious films were the most explicit products of the "culture of empathy" inaugurated with President Bill Clinton in 1992.

Similarly, the director Jonathan Demme, who scored a phenomenal success with the psycho-thriller *The Silence of the Lambs* (1991), starring Jodie Foster as the FBI trainee recruited to debrief the psychotic cannibal Hannibal Lecter (Anthony Hopkins), seemed determined to invest his talents in more empathic projects, such as *Philadelphia* (1993), about a homophobic black attorney (Denzel Washington) who defends an AIDS-stricken lawyer (Tom Hanks) fired from his firm and comes to recognize homophobia as a form of racism; and *Beloved* (1998), starring Oprah Winfrey and Danny Glover, from the Toni Morrison novel about traumatized former slaves after Emancipation.

Under the political watch of President George Bush, Communist regimes from Berlin to Moscow fell, as did the Berlin Wall. This had the immediate effect of robbing American films of the perennial bad guy, the Communist madman. The confusion about whether Communists were friends or enemies gave considerable dramatic tension to such films as *The Hunt for Red October* (1990, John McTiernan) and *Crimson Tide* (1995, Tony Scott).

The demise of America's historic enemy also prompted many Americans to look for the enemy within. The actor-director Kevin Costner's *Dances with Wolves* (1990) is the saga of a Civil War soldier who abhorred U.S. treatment of Native Americans and joined a Lakota Sioux tribe. Robert Redford's *Quiz Show* (1994), with Ralph Fiennes and John Turturro as the winner and loser of a rigged 1950s game show, explored how television sponsors exploited an unsuspecting public. *Jerry Maguire* (fig. 599) featured Tom Cruise as an amoral sports agent who learns from a football player (Cuba Gooding, Jr.) about values of the nonmonetary kind.

Like *Jerry Maguire*, *White Men Can't Jump* (1992, Ron Shelton), starring Woody Harrelson and Wesley Snipes as basketball hustlers, suggested that the one level playing field for black and white Americans was—the playing field. Only Denzel Washington seems to have found other arenas. Perhaps the first African American to

599. Tom Cruise and Cuba Gooding, Jr., in *Jerry Maguire*, directed by Cameron Crowe, 1996 Columbia Tri-Star Pictures

600. Denzel Washington and Angela Bassett in *Malcolm X*, directed by Spike Lee, 1992 Warner Brothers

transformations—from man to woman to mythological creature—with clothing and makeup and specifically crafted, special-effects prostheses (fig. 593). He has also elaborated his mythological narratives in an epic cycle of film works entitled *Cremaster*.

The confusion of the real and the imaginary qualifies almost every cultural art form of the decade. The "mockumentary," for instance, is a new form of film that looks like a documentary, but intentionally mixes fact and fiction. In his film *JFK* (1991), director Oliver Stone used black-and-white film segments to suggest found footage. The film, which weaves together found documentary footage, constructed documentary footage, and constructed fiction about the assassination of President Kennedy, focuses on a moment when many Americans began to question the official government account. In *The Truman Show* (1998), the protagonist is the unwitting star of a television series: every aspect of his life is staged, controlled, and invaded by the camera without his knowledge. When he finally discovers what is going on, he is not allowed to escape. The question "is it real?" is ever present today as virtual experiences such as travel and sex through the Internet, or the simulacra of Las Vegas, have become commonplace. In a total reversal of standards, anything that looks real must now be doubted, while anything announcing its artificiality is more trustworthy.

The rise of the artificial has been accelerated by digital technology, which has provided new imaging techniques that also expand the visual imagination. Artists can use the computer as a tool to visualize and study fractal formations, to freeze and retrieve frames from television and movies, as a visual encyclopedia, and as a means to manipulate images. They are also using the computer for archiving and storing images and as a preparatory tool. Terry Winters, for example, employs computer-generated forms as a basis for the linear networks of lines that give his new paintings an electronic buzz (fig. 601). Mathew Ritchie has evolved an elaborate creation myth in his paintings that is in part inspired by computer games and animation—and he has a website that serves as a corollary to the paintings.

play the everyman in Hollywood movies where race wasn't the subject, he starred as a journalist in *The Pelican Brief* (1993, Alan J. Pakula), a navy lieutenant in *Crimson Tide*, and an army officer in *Courage Under Fire* (1996, Edward Zwick)—in addition to his roles as a black Civil War soldier in *Glory* (1989, Edward Zwick) and as the eponymous political activist in *Malcolm X* (fig. 600).

Led by the prolific and prodigiously talented Spike Lee, who made the searing drama of racism *Do the Right Thing* (1989), the epic biography *Malcolm X*, and the Million Man March drama *Get on the Bus* (1996), African American filmmakers during the 1990s were able to break into Hollywood. John Singleton's *Boyz N the Hood* (1991) and Allen and Albert Hughes' *Menace II Society* (1993) were bleak dispatches from the war zone of South Central Los Angeles, films that led the critic Armond White to observe that "black kids see their teenage years in terms of survival, while white kids see theirs in terms of fun."

The exception to White's thesis may be *Clueless* (1995, Amy Heckerling), an update of Jane Austen's Emma as a Beverly Hills High sophomore, which boasted rich kids black and white. Heckerling was one of many women filmmakers to make their marks with romantic comedies. Others included Penny Marshall with *Big* (1988), starring Hanks as the boy in a man's body caught between his desire to be big and to remain a kid, and Nora Ephron with *Sleepless in Seattle* (1993).

Like an uncommon number of nineties hits, *Sleepless* starred Tom Hanks, the decade's most beloved common man, as the widower renewed by love. Hanks brought the human factor to films, whether as the AIDS-afflicted lawyer in *Philadelphia*, the coach in *A League of Their Own* (1992, Penny Marshall), the slow-witted witness to history in *Forrest Gump* (1994, Robert Zemeckis), the astronaut Jim Lovell in *Apollo 13* (1995, Ron Howard), or the squadron leader in *Saving Private Ryan*.

Among actresses, only Jodie Foster enjoyed a career as varied. As the spooked fed in *Silence of the Lambs*, the mother of a prodigy in *Little Man Tate* (1991), which she also directed, the cardsharp in *Maverick* (1994, Richard Donner), and the scientist who receives a message from extraterrestrials in *Contact* (1997, Robert Zemeckis), Foster made women the intellectual subject rather than the sexual object of films.

As military arsenals were downsized after the Cold War, a domestic war erupted over violence on screen. The two most controversial films were *Thelma and Louise* (1991, Ridley Scott) and *Pulp Fiction* (1994, Quentin Tarantino). The former starred Geena Davis as a runaway wife and Susan Sarandon as her pal who use a handgun in self-defense and, as fugitives, go on a shooting spree. *Pulp Fiction*, a stylized affair influenced by film noir, starred John Travolta and Samuel L. Jackson as hitmen-philosophers with a glib attitude toward killers and killing. Both films inflamed the national debate about screen violence, and both were very, very popular.

But the biggest debate at century's end is internal. In response to spectacles such as the very real-seeming velociraptors in *Jurassic Park* or the title character appearing in historic newsreel footage in *Forrest Gump*, the burning question is whether film technology is threatening to overwhelm film narrative. Not only is film an art and a business, it is also a storytelling and technological vehicle. —C. R.

601. **Terry Winters**
Parallel Rendering 2,
1996
Oil on linen, 96 x 120 in.
(243.8 x 304.8 cm)
Tate Gallery, London

602. **Gary Hill**
*Inasmuch As It Is Always
Already Taking Place,*
1990
16-channel video/sound
installation at The
Museum of Modern Art,
New York

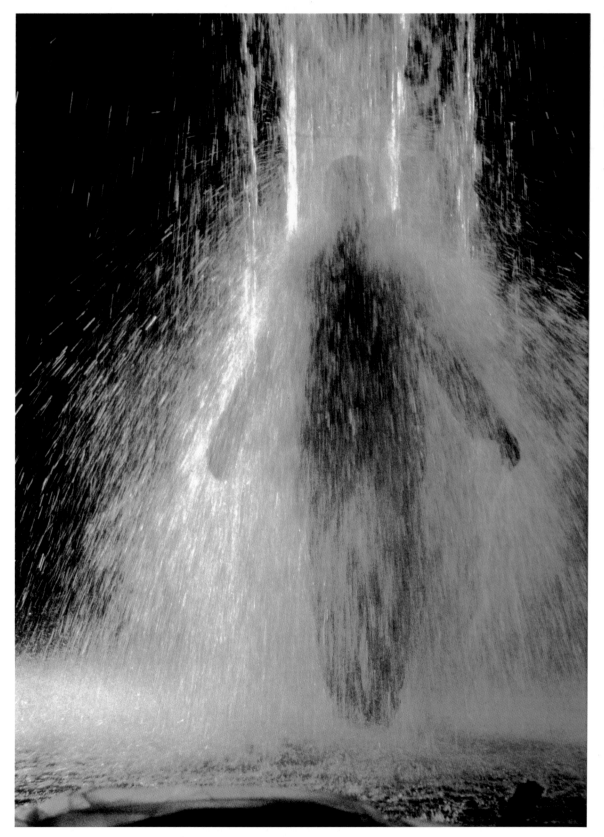

603. **Bill Viola**
The Crossing, 1996
Video/sound installation,
192 x 330 x 684 in.
(4.9 x 8.4 x 17.4 m)
The Bohen Foundation;
Promised gift to the
Solomon R. Guggenheim
Museum, New York
© 1999 Bill Viola

FILM AND VIDEO INSTALLATION IN THE 1980S AND 1990S

By the beginning of the eighties, performative, perceptual video installations had been replaced by theatrical environments, often shown in museums, in which the video monitor operated as a narrative element. As video editing grew more sophisticated and technology more widespread, two perennial subjects in American art—landscape and the urban environment—became major themes, in a range of videotapes and installations by Bill Viola, Doug Hall, Mary Lucier, Rita Myers, Juan Downey, Frank Gillette, Dara Birnbaum, Shigeko Kubota, Woody and Steina Vasulka, Susan Hiller, Nam June Paik, and Bruce and Norman Yonemoto. Woody and Steina Vasulka, pioneers of early video art, created a number of installations, including Steina's *The West* (1983),

604. **Mary Lucier**
Ohio at Giverny, 1983
(detail)
Seven monitors, dimensions variable, with two laser-discs, color, sound;
18½ min.
Whitney Museum of American Art, New York;
Purchase, with funds from the Louis and Bessie Adler Foundation, Inc., Seymour M. Klein, President and Mrs. Rudolph B. Schulhof
83.35a–j

a study of the New Mexican desert. Mary Lucier's *Ohio at Giverny* (fig. 604) evoked childhood memory through a luminous depiction of the French and American countryside, while Bill Viola's installations—such as *Room for St. John of the Cross* (1983)—framed the relationship between man, nature, and the physical landscape within an existential spirituality.

Many of these artists continued to make video installations through the 1980s and 1990s. In a period that saw the fall of the Berlin Wall and Communism in Europe, Dara Birnbaum's installations such as *Tiananmen Square* (1990–91) reflected a concern with the deep social and political changes taking place. Bruce Nauman's angst-ridden pieces, including *Clown Torture* (fig. 605), expressed strong feelings of alienation, disorientation, anxiety, and violence. The role technology played in this alienation had been underlined in Nam June Paik's ironic installations *Moon Is the Oldest TV* (1965–76), in which technology replaces nature. Tony Oursler's projective installations of the early nineties made visible technology's intrusiveness on a psychic level.

Video projection had been used by artists such as Nauman, Viola, and Peter Campus since the 1970s (fig. 419). Projection released the video image from the constriction of the television monitor and, in the work of Gary Hill, Oursler, and Viola, from any frame at all. Bill Lundberg, Robert Whitman, and Tony Conrad had projected film onto objects in the 1960s. Now the frameless image returned. In Hill's *Tall Ships*, sixteen black-and-white, ghostlike projections of people move interactively, according to the viewer's movements, in the darkness of a long corridor.

The widespread use of video projection in the 1990s led to a new, cinematic

For some artists, digital technologies have become a primary medium. Artists' websites have proliferated, as have works made specifically for the Web, which incorporate text, images, and quick-time sequences. Through the Internet, artists can distribute their work to millions of viewers at very little cost. Cyberspace has become a new public venue for artists to work in.

Artists making video installations, such as Gary Hill and Bill Viola (figs. 602, 603), have used digital technology to enhance their presentations or to create interactive works. Advanced digital resolution in the nineties has taken the video medium into a more sensual, sculptural, and experiential realm. Other technological advances permit a level of retinal stimulation and sensationalism that has supplanted the low-key, relatively drab video art of the past. New video works such as Hill's *Tall Ships* and Viola's *Tree of Knowledge* create zones or environments where the viewer can enter and interact with a magnified landscape of faces, body fragments, and other images. The extension of video into a physically interactive dimension—as in Diana Thater's rich, chromatic projections or

aesthetic, in which the languages of video and film began to merge. Diana Thater made a number of site-specific installations using different planes of projected video imagery that examined nature within the language of Hollywood film and Conceptual art (fig. 606). Artists working in other media—for example, Janine Antoni and Ann Hamilton in sculpture and performance (figs. 587, 588)—also began to make video installations.

Film asserted itself as a major medium and influence throughout the 1990s. Matthew Barney made the *Cremaster* series, a group of highly baroque films designed to be shown exclusively in movie theaters, and the imagery in his installations referenced forties Hollywood film. The narratives in Lorna Simpson's sumptuous black-and-white video projections evoked the stylized dramas of Hollywood film noir. By contrast, Liisa Roberts' installations used film as sculpture, inserting the plane of the projected film image into the gallery space in order to question our perceptions of time and memory. Just as the Internet had begun to break down the concept of art in physical space, film, the oldest time-based medium of all, used the moving image to reassert concrete spatial form. —C. I.

605. **Bruce Nauman**
Clown Torture: Dark and Stormy Night with Laughter, 1987
Video installation, color, sound, continuous loop; dimensions variable
Collection of Barbara Balkin Cottle and Robert Cottle

606. **Diana Thater**
The Bad Infinite, 1993
Three color laserdiscs,
three laserdisc players,
one sync box, three video
projectors, and film gels,
dimensions variable
Whitney Museum of
American Art, New York;
Purchase, with funds from
The Robert B. and Emilie
W. Betts Foundation
95.84a–j

607. **Tony Oursler**
Getaway #2, 1994
Mattress, cloth, video projector, laserdisc player,
and laserdisc, 16 x 117½ x
86 in. (40.6 x 298.5 x
218.4 cm) overall
Whitney Museum of
American Art, New York;
Purchase, with funds from
the Contemporary Painting
and Sculpture Committee
95.22a–h

Tony Oursler's hybrid talking heads (figs. 606–08)—has made the medium more challenging to artists and more engaging to viewers. Video has in fact finally been accepted as a serious art form. It is not only collected with growing enthusiasm but has been stealing the spotlight from other art forms at large international art exhibitions. Video has also become a familiar language thanks to the global pervasiveness of MTV, with its fast-cutting videos set to music—videos often made by independent video artists as a means of supporting themselves.

The expansive, diverse art of the past decade is still too close to be called history or to be viewed with sufficient perspective. As in earlier periods, it encompasses multiple and contradictory tendencies, and we can only speculate about what future generations will find of lasting consequence. One thing is clear, however, even up close: we are shedding the old chauvinistic attitudes that gave rise to the term "The American Century" and are recognizing the multiplicity of cultures that is, and probably always has been, America's greatest strength. Over the past five decades, a profound shift has occurred in our approach to both history and cultural practice. Revisionist art history and the influence of cultural studies have overturned many once cherished assumptions—about the purpose and development of the avant-garde, about the hierarchies upon which the foundations of modern art history have been built, and about fixed styles and national boundaries. Artists now consider almost anything a fit subject or material for art making, while a heterogeneous array of perspectives has enriched the ways we look at art. Despite these changes—and because of them—two old questions still have currency: What is art? And what is American?

608. **Tony Oursler**
Mother's Boy, 1996
Sony CPJ 200 projector,
VCR, videotape, and
acrylic on fiberglass,
18 in. (45.7 cm) diameter
Collection of Tom Peters

92. "The Artists Say: Dan Flavin," *Art Voices*, 4 (Summer 1965), p. 72.

93. Donald Judd, "Specific Objects" (1965), reprinted in *Donald Judd: Complete Writings, 1959–1975* (New York: New York University Press, 1975), pp. 181–89.

94. Clement Greenberg, "Recentness of Sculpture," *American Sculpture of the Sixties*, exh. cat. (Los Angeles: Los Angeles County Museum of Art, 1967), p. 25.

95. Maurice Berger, *Labyrinths: Robert Morris, Minimalism, and the 1960s* (New York: Harper and Row Publishers, 1989).

96. Lawrence Alloway, "Serial Forms," *American Sculpture of the Sixties*, p. 15.

97. Anna C. Chave, "Minimalism and the Rhetoric of Power," *Arts Magazine*, 64 (January 1990), pp. 44–63.

98. Gregory Battcock, "The Art of the Real: The Development of a Style, 1948–68," *Arts*, 42 (June 1968), p. 44.

99. See Robert Pincus-Witten, "Postminimalism: An Argentine Glance," *The New Sculpture, 1965–75: Between Geometry and Gesture*, exh. cat. (New York: Whitney Museum of American Art, 1990).

100. Lucy Lippard, "Eccentric Abstraction," *Art International*, 10 (November 1966), revised essay reprinted in Lippard, *Changing: Essays in Art Criticism* (New York: E. P. Dutton, 1971), p. 98.

101. Robert Morris, "Anti-Form," *Artforum*, 6 (April 1968), pp. 33–35.

102. Donald Judd, "Specific Objects," p. 187.

103. Max Kozloff, "9 in a Warehouse: An 'Attack on the Status of the Object,'" *Artforum*, 7 (February 1969), pp. 38–42.

104. Robert Pincus-Witten, "Postminimalism: An Argentine Glance," p. 25.

105. Richard Serra, quoted in Rosalind E. Krauss, *Passages in Modern Sculpture* (New York: Viking Press, 1977), p. 276.

106. See Rosalind E. Krauss, *Passages in Modern Sculpture* (New York: The Viking Press, 1977), chap. 6, pp. 201–42.

107. Michael Fried, "Art and Objecthood," *Artforum*, 5 (Summer 1967), pp. 12–23.

108. Tony Smith, quoted in Samuel Wagstaff, Jr., "Talking with Tony Smith," *Artforum*, 5 (December 1966), p. 19.

109. Robert Smithson, "The Monuments of Passaic," *Artforum*, 6 (December 1967), pp. 48–51.

110. Robert Smithson, "Entropy and the New Monuments," *Artforum*, 4 (June 1966), pp. 26–31.

111. Walter de Maria, "The Lightning Field: Some Facts, Notes, Data, Information, Statistics and Statements," *Artforum*, 18 (April 1980), p. 58.

112. Joseph Kosuth, "Art After Philosophy" (1969), in Gabriele Guercio, ed., *Art After Philosophy and After: Collected Writings, 1966–1990* (Cambridge, Massachusetts: MIT Press, 1991), p. 20.

113. Sol LeWitt, "Paragraphs on Conceptual Art," *Artforum*, 5 (Summer 1967), pp. 79–83.

114. Joseph Kosuth, "Art as Idea as Idea," in *Information*, exh. cat. (New York: The Museum of Modern Art, 1970), p. 69.

115. Seth Siegelaub, quoted in Charles Harrison, "On Exhibitions and the World at Large: A Conversation with Seth Siegelaub," *Studio International*, 178 (December 1969), reprinted in Gregory Battcock, *Idea Art: A Critical Anthology* (New York: E. P. Dutton, 1973), pp. 165–73.

116. Douglas Huebler, quoted in *January 5–31, 1969*, exh. cat. (New York: Seth Siegelaub, 1969), n.p.

117. See Jack Burnham, *Software*, exh. cat. (New York: The Jewish Museum, 1970).

118. Lucy Lippard and John Chandler, "The Dematerialization of Art," in Lippard, *Changing*, p. 255.

119. Robert Hughes, "The Decline and Fall of the Avant-Garde," *Time*, December 18, 1972, pp. 111–12.

120. Jon Hendricks and Jean Toche, *GAAG, the Guerrilla Art Action Group, 1969–1976: A Selection* (New York: Printed Matter, 1978).

121. A statement from these artists—John Dowell, Sam Gilliam, Daniel Johnson, Joe Overstreet, Melvin Edwards, Richard Hunt, and William T. Williams—was published in the "Politics" section in *Artforum*, 9 (May 1971), p. 12.

122. Victor Sorell, "Articulate Signs of Resistance and Affirmation in Chicano Public Art," in *Chicano Art: Resistance and Affirmation, 1965–1985*, exh. cat. (Los Angeles: Wight Art Gallery, University of California, Los Angeles, 1990), pp. 148–51.

123. Linda Nochlin, "Why Have There Been No Great Women Artists?," *Art News*, 69 (January 1971), pp. 22–39.

124. Grace Glueck, "Women Artists Demonstrate at Whitney," *The New York Times*, December 23, 1970, reprinted in *Cultural Economies: Histories from the Alternative Arts Movement, NYC* (New York: The Drawing Center), p. 23.

125. Andreas Huyssen, "Mapping the Postmodern," in *After the Great Divide: Modernism, Mass Culture, Postmodernism* (Bloomington: Indiana University Press, 1986), p. 185.

126. Clement Greenberg, "On the Role of Nature in Modernist Painting" (1949), reprinted in Greenberg, *Art and Culture*, p. 174.

127. Robert Venturi, *Complexity and Contradiction in Architecture* (1966; 2nd ed. New York: The Museum of Modern Art, 1977), p. 17.

128. Carolee Schneemann, quoted in Lucy R. Lippard, *Overlay: Contemporary Art and the Art of Prehistory* (New York: Pantheon Books, 1983), p. 67.

129. Dan Cameron, *Carolee Schneemann: Up To and Including Her Limits*, exh. cat. (New York: The New Museum of Contemporary Art, 1996), pp. 27–28.

130. Phil Patton, "Other Voices, Other Rooms: The Rise of the Alternative Space," *Art in America*, 65 (July–August 1977), pp. 80–89.

131. Vickie Goldberg, *The Power of Photography: How Photographs Changed Our Lives* (New York: Abbeville Press, 1991).

132. Douglas Crimp, *Pictures*, exh. cat. (New York: Artists Space; Committee for the Visual Arts, 1977), p. 3.

133. Craig Owens, quoted in Barbara Kruger and Sarah Charlesworth, "Glossalia," *Bomb*, 5 (Spring 1983), p. 61.

134. Jonathan Alter, "The Cultural Elite: The Newsweek 100," *Newsweek*, October 5, 1992, p. 37.

135. Richard Prince, quoted in Kristine McKenna, "On Photography: Looking for Truth Between the Lies," *Los Angeles Times*, May 19, 1985, p. 91.

136. Irving Sandler, "Tenth Street Then and Now," in Janet Kardon, *The East Village Scene*, exh. cat. (Philadelphia: Institute of Contemporary Art, University of Pennsylvania, 1984), pp. 10–19; Craig Owens, "East Village '84: Commentary, The Problem with Puerilism," *Art in America*, 72 (Summer 1984), pp. 162–63.

137. Lehmann Weichselbaum, "The Real Estate Show," *East Village Eye* (January 1980), reprinted in Alan Moore and Marc Miller, eds., *ABC No Rio Dinero: The Story of a Lower East Side Art Gallery* (New York: ABC No Rio with Collaborative Projects, 1985), pp. 52–53.

138. Jeffrey Deitch, "Report from Times Square," *Art in America*, 68 (September 1980), pp. 58–63.

139. Elizabeth Hess, "The People's Choice," *The Village Voice* (1981), reprinted in Moore and Miller, eds., *ABC No Rio Dinero*, p. 24.

140. For a detailed history of CBGB-OMFUG, see Roman Kozak, *This Ain't No Disco: The Story of CBGB* (Boston: Faber and Faber, 1988).

141. Edit deAk, "Urban Kisses/Slum Hisses" (1981), reprinted in Moore and Miller, eds., *ABC No Rio Dinero*, pp. 34–35.

142. Mark Stevens, "Bull in the China Shop," *Newsweek*, May 11, 1981, p. 79.

143. George W. S. Trow, *Within the Context of No Context* (Boston: Little, Brown and Company, 1981), p. 27.

144. Jesse Helms, quoted in Cathleen McGuigan, "Arts Grants Under Fire," *Newsweek*, August 7, 1989, p. 23.

145. Quoted in Richard Bolton, "The Cultural Contradictions of Conservatism," *New Art Examiner*, 17 (June 1990), p. 26.

146. Carol Vance has introduced the sex panic theory, most notably in "Reagan's Revenge: Restructuring the NEA," *Art in America*, 78 (November 1990), pp. 49–55.

147. Irving Kristol, "It's Obscene But Is It Art?" *The Wall Street Journal*, August 7, 1990, p. A8.

148. Lari Pittman, quoted in *Sunshine & Noir: Art in L.A. 1960–1997*, exh. cat. (Humlebaek, Denmark: Louisiana Museum of Modern Art, 1997), p. 202.

149. Joan Didion, *Slouching Towards Bethlehem* (New York: Dell Publishing, 1968), p. 65, quoted in Norman M. Klein, "Inside the Consumer-Built City: Sixty Years of Apocalyptic Imagery," in *Helter Skelter: L.A. Art in the 1990s*, exh. cat. (Los Angeles: The Museum of Contemporary Art, 1992), p. 27.

Selected Bibliography

General
Surveys: Art, History, and Culture

Albright, Thomas. *Art in the San Francisco Bay Area, 1945–1980: An Illustrated History* (exhibition catalog). Berkeley: University of California Press, 1985.

Armstrong, Tom, et al. *200 Years of American Sculpture* (exhibition catalog). New York: Whitney Museum of American Art, 1976.

Arnason, H. H. *History of Modern Art: Painting, Sculpture, Architecture, Photography*. 3rd ed. (revised and updated by Daniel Wheeler). New York: Harry N. Abrams, 1986.

Ashton, Dore. *American Art Since 1945*. New York: Oxford University Press, 1982.

Bearden, Romare, and Harry Henderson. *A History of African-American Artists: From 1792 to the Present*. New York: Pantheon Books, 1993.

Bois, Yve-Alain, and Rosalind E. Krauss. *Formless: A User's Guide* (exhibition catalog). Paris: Centre Georges Pompidou, 1996.

Brougher, Kerry, et al. *Hall of Mirrors: Art and Film Since 1945* (exhibition catalog). Los Angeles: The Museum of Contemporary Art, Los Angeles, 1996.

Brown, Milton W., et al. *American Art: Painting, Sculpture, Architecture, Decorative Arts, Photography* (1979). Reprt. Englewood Cliffs, New Jersey: Prentice-Hall; New York: Harry N. Abrams, 1988.

Burnham, Jack. *Beyond Modern Sculpture: The Effects of Science and Technology on the Sculpture of This Century* (1968). Reprt. New York: George Braziller, 1982.

Crane, Diana. *The Transformation of the Avant-Garde: The New York Art World, 1940–1985*. Chicago: University of Chicago Press, 1987.

Fineberg, Jonathan. *Art Since 1940: Strategies of Being*. New York: Harry N. Abrams, 1995.

Forty Years of California Assemblage (exhibition catalog). Los Angeles: Wight Art Gallery, University of California, Los Angeles, 1989.

Frascina, Francis, et al., *Modernism in Dispute: Art Since the Forties*. New Haven: Yale University Press in association with The Open University, 1993.

Geldzahler, Henry. *New York Painting and Sculpture: 1940–1970* (exhibition catalog). New York: The Metropolitan Museum of Art, 1969.

Hughes, Robert. *American Visions: The Epic History of Art in America*. New York: Alfred A. Knopf, 1997.

Hunter, Sam, ed. *An American Renaissance: Painting and Sculpture Since 1940* (exhibition catalog). Fort Lauderdale, Florida: Museum of Art, 1986.

Joachimides, Christos M., and Norman Rosenthal, eds. *American Art in the 20th Century: Painting and Sculpture, 1913–1993* (exhibition catalog). Berlin: Martin-Gropius-Bau; London: Royal Academy of Arts and the Saatchi Gallery, 1993.

Krauss, Rosalind E. *Passages in Modern Sculpture*. New York: Viking Press, 1977.

Leja, Michael. *Reframing Abstract Expressionism: Subjectivity and Painting in the 1940s*. New Haven: Yale University Press, 1993.

Lucie-Smith, Edward. *American Art Now*. New York: William Morrow and Company, 1985.

Patton, Sharon F. *African American Art*. New York: Oxford University Press, 1998.

Plagens, Peter. *Sunshine Muse: Contemporary Art on the West Coast*. New York and Washington, D.C.: Praeger Publishers, 1974.

Powell, Richard J. *Black Art and Culture in the 20th Century*. New York: Thames and Hudson, 1997.

Rose, Barbara. *American Art Since 1900* (1967). Rev. ed. New York and Washington, D.C.: Praeger Publishers, 1975.

Rosenthal, Mark. *Abstraction in the Twentieth Century: Total Risk, Freedom, Discipline* (exhibition catalog). New York: Solomon R. Guggenheim Museum, 1996.

Senie, Harriet F. *Contemporary Public Sculpture: Tradition, Transformation, and Controversy*. New York: Oxford University Press, 1992.

Smith, Richard Candida. *Utopia and Dissent: Art, Poetry, and Politics in California*. Berkeley: University of California Press, 1995.

Warren, Lynne, et al. *Art in Chicago, 1945–1995* (exhibition catalog). Chicago: Museum of Contemporary Art, 1996.

Wheeler, Daniel. *Art Since Mid-Century: 1945 to the Present*. New York: Vendome Press, 1991.

Criticism and Theory

Ashton, Dore. *Out of the Whirlwind: Three Decades of Arts Commentary*. Ann Arbor, Michigan: UMI Research Press, 1987.

Berger, Maurice, ed. *Modern Art and Society: An Anthology of Social and Multicultural Readings*. New York: Icon Editions/HarperCollins Publishers, 1994.

Bois, Yve-Alain. *Painting as Model* (1990). Reprt. Cambridge, Massachusetts: October/MIT Press, 1995.

Bryson, Norman, ed. *Calligram: Essays in New Art History from France*. New York: Cambridge University Press, 1988.

Buettner, Stewart. *American Art Theory: 1945–1970*. Ann Arbor, Michigan: UMI Research Press, 1981.

Burgin, Victor. *The End of Art Theory: Criticism and Postmodernity*. Atlantic Highlands, New Jersey: Humanities Press International, 1986.

Calas, Nicolas. *Transfigurations: Art Critical Essays on the Modern Period*. Ann Arbor, Michigan: UMI Research Press, 1985.

Crimp, Douglas. *On the Museum's Ruins*. Photographs by Louise Lawler. Cambridge, Massachusetts: MIT Press, 1993.

Crow, Thomas. *Modern Art in the Common Culture*. New Haven: Yale University Press, 1996.

Danto, Arthur C. *Beyond the Brillo Box: The Visual Arts in Post-Historical Perspective*. New York: Farrar, Straus & Giroux, 1992.

Warhol, Andy, and Pat Hackett. *POPism: The Warhol '60s*. New York: Harcourt Brace Jovanovich, 1980.

Whiting, Cecile. *A Taste for Pop: Pop Art, Gender, and Consumer Culture*. New York: Cambridge University Press, 1997.

America at the Crossroads, 1964–1976

Armstrong, Richard, and Richard Marshall, eds. *The New Sculpture, 1965–1975: Between Geometry and Gesture* (exhibition catalog). New York: Whitney Museum of American Art, 1990.

Ault, Julie, ed. *Cultural Economies: Histories from the Alternative Arts Movement, NYC* (exhibition catalog). New York: The Drawing Center, 1996.

Battcock, Gregory, ed. *Idea Art: A Critical Anthology*. New York: E. P. Dutton, 1973.

——, ed. *The New Art: A Critical Anthology* (1966). Reprt. New York: E. P. Dutton, 1973.

Beardsley, John. *Probing the Earth: Contemporary Land Projects* (exhibition catalog). Washington, D.C.: Hirshhorn Museum and Sculpture Garden, Smithsonian Institution, 1977.

Broude, Norma, and Mary D. Garrard, eds. *The Power of Feminist Art: The American Movement of the 1970s, History and Impact*. New York: Harry N. Abrams, 1994.

Goldstein, Ann, and Anne Rorimer. *Reconsidering the Object of Art, 1965–1975* (exhibition catalog). Los Angeles: The Museum of Contemporary Art, 1995.

Griswold del Castillo, Richard, Teresa McKenna, and Yvonne Yarbro-Bejarano, eds. *Chicano Art: Resistance and Affirmation, 1965-1985* (exhibition catalog). Los Angeles: Wight Art Gallery, University of California, Los Angeles, 1990.

Hess, Thomas B., and Elizabeth C. Baker, eds. *Art and Sexual Politics: Women's Liberation, Women Artists, and Art History* (1973). Reprt. New York: Collier Books, 1975.

Jones, Amelia, ed. *Sexual Politics: Judy Chicago's "Dinner Party" in Feminist Art History* (exhibition catalog). Los Angeles: UCLA at the Armand Hammer Museum of Art and Cultural Center, 1996.

Kardon, Janet. *The Decorative Impulse* (exhibition catalog). Philadelphia: Institute of Contemporary Art, University of Pennsylvania, 1979.

Lippard, Lucy R. *From the Center: Feminist Essays on Women's Art*. New York: E. P. Dutton, 1976.

——. *Get the Message? A Decade of Art for Social Change*. New York: E. P. Dutton, 1984.

——. *The Pink Glass Swan: Selected Essays on Feminist Art*. New York: New Press, 1995.

——, ed. *Six Years: The Dematerialization of the Art Object from 1966 to 1972* (1973). Berkeley: University of California Press, 1997.

Lucie-Smith, Edward. *Art in the Seventies*. Ithaca, New York: Cornell University Press, 1980.

Marshall, Richard. *New Image Painting* (exhibition catalog). New York: Whitney Museum of American Art, 1978.

Masheck, Joseph. *Historical Present: Essays of the 1970s*. Ann Arbor, Michigan: UMI Research Press, 1984.

McShine, Kynaston, ed. *Information* (exhibition catalog). New York: The Museum of Modern Art, 1970.

Meyer, Ursula. *Conceptual Art*. New York: E. P. Dutton, 1972.

Monte, James, and Marcia Tucker. *Anti-Illusion: Procedures/Materials*. New York: Whitney Museum of American Art, 1969.

Morgan, Robert C. *Art into Ideas: Essays on Conceptual Art*. New York: Cambridge University Press, 1996.

Nochlin, Linda. *Women, Art, and Power and Other Essays*. New York: Icon Editions/Harper & Row, 1988.

Pincus-Witten, Robert. *Postminimalism*. New York: Out of London Press, 1977.

——. *Postminimalism into Maximalism: American Art, 1966–1986*. Ann Arbor, Michigan: UMI Research Press, 1987.

Pollock, Griselda. *Vision and Difference: Femininity, Feminism, and Histories of Art*. New York: Routledge, 1988.

Raven, Arlene, Cassandra L. Langer, and Joanna Frueh, eds. *Feminist Art Criticism: An Anthology*. Ann Arbor, Michigan: UMI Research Press, 1988.

Robins, Corinne. *The Pluralist Era: American Art, 1968–1981*. New York: Icon Editions/Harper & Row, 1984.

Rose, Bernice. *Drawing Now* (exhibition catalog). New York: The Museum of Modern Art, 1976.

Sonfist, Alan, ed. *Art in the Land: A Critical Anthology of Environmental Art*. New York: E. P. Dutton, 1983.

Szeeman, Harald. *Live in Your Head: When Attitudes Become Form. Works, Concepts, Processes, Situations, Information* (exhibition catalog). London: The Institute of Contemporary Arts, 1969.

Tiberghien, Gilles A. *Land Art*. Translated by Caroline Green. New York: Princeton Architectural Press, 1995.

Wilding, Faith. *By Our Own Hands: The Women Artist's Movement, Southern California, 1970-1976*. Santa Monica, California: Double X, 1977.

Restoration and Reaction, 1976–1990

Atkins, Robert, and Thomas W. Sokolowski. *From Media to Metaphor: Art about AIDS* (exhibition catalog). New York: Independent Curators, 1991.

Belli, Gabriella, and Jerry Saltz. *American Art of the '80s* (exhibition catalog). Trento and Rovereto: Museo d'Arte Moderna e Contemporanea, 1991.

Bois, Yve-Alain, et al. *Endgame: Reference and Simulation in Recent Painting and Sculpture* (exhibition catalog). Boston: The Institute of Contemporary Art, 1986.

Carrier, David. *The Aesthete in the City: The Philosophy and Practice of American Abstract Painting in the 1980s*. University Park: Pennsylvania State University Press, 1994.

Crimp, Douglas. *Pictures: An Exhibition of the Work of Troy Brauntuch, Jack Goldstein, Sherrie Levine, Robert Longo, Philip Smith* (exhibition catalog). New York: Artists Space, 1977.

The Decade Show: Frameworks of Identity in the 1980s (exhibition catalog). New York: Museum of Contemporary Hispanic Art/The New Museum of Contemporary Art/The Studio Museum in Harlem, 1990.

Felshin, Nina, ed. *But Is It Art? The Spirit of Art as Activism*. Seattle: Bay Press, 1995.

Fox, Howard N. *Avant-Garde in the Eighties* (exhibition catalog). Los Angeles: Los Angeles County Museum of Art, 1987.

Frank, Peter, and Michael McKenzie. *New, Used, and Improved: Art for the '80s*. New York: Abbeville Press, 1987.

Ghez, Susanne, ed. *CalArts: Skeptical Belief(s)* (exhibition catalog). Chicago: The Renaissance Society at the University of Chicago; Newport Beach, California: Newport Harbor Art Museum, 1988.

Goldstein, Ann, and Mary Jane Jacob. *A Forest of Signs: Art in the Crisis of Representation* (exhibition catalog). Los Angeles: The Museum of Contemporary Art, 1989.

Halbreich, Kathy. *Culture and Commentary: An Eighties Perspective* (exhibition catalog). Washington, D.C.: Hirshhorn Museum and Sculpture Garden, Smithsonian Institution, 1990.

Heartney, Eleanor. *Critical Condition: American Culture at the Crossroads*. New York: Cambridge University Press, 1997.

Heiferman, Marvin, and Lisa Phillips, with John G. Hanhardt. *Image World: Art and Media Culture* (exhibition catalog). New York: Whitney Museum of American Art, 1989.

Joachimides, Christos M., and Norman Rosenthal, eds. *Zeitgeist: Internationale Kunstausstellung Berlin 1982* (exhibition catalog). Berlin: Martin-Gropius-Bau, 1982.

Joachimides, Christos M., Norman Rosenthal, and Nicholas Serota, eds. *A New Spirit in Painting* (exhibition catalog). London: Royal Academy of Arts, 1981.

Kardon, Janet. *The East Village Scene* (exhibition catalog). Philadelphia: Institute of Contemporary Art, University of Pennsylvania, 1984.

Levin, Kim. *Beyond Modernism: Essays on Art from the '70s and '80s*. New York: Icon Editions/Harper & Row, 1988.

Linker, Kate, et al. *Difference: On Representation and Sexuality* (exhibition catalog). New York: The New Museum of Contemporary Art, 1985.

Lucie-Smith, Edward. *Art in the Eighties*. New York: Phaidon/Universe, 1990.

McShine, Kynaston. *An International Survey of Recent Painting and Sculpture* (exhibition catalog). New York: The Museum of Modern Art, 1984.

Moore, Alan, and Marc Miller, eds. *ABC No Rio Dinero: The Story of a Lower East Side Art Gallery.* Foreword by Lucy R. Lippard. New York: ABC No Rio with Collaborative Projects, 1985.

Saltz, Jerry. *Beyond Boundaries: New York's New Art.* Essays by Roberta Smith and Peter Halley. New York: Alfred van der Marck Editions, 1986.

Schjeldahl, Peter. *The Hydrogen Jukebox: Selected Writings of Peter Schjeldahl, 1978–1990.* Introduction by Robert Storr. Berkeley: University of California Press, 1991.

Siegel, Jeanne, ed. *Art Talk: The Early '80s.* New York: DaCapo Press, 1988.

———, ed. *Artwords 2: Discourse on the Early '80s.* Ann Arbor, Michigan: UMI Research Press, 1988.

Taylor, Paul. *After Andy: SoHo in the Eighties.* Portraits by Timothy Greenfield-Sanders. Introduction by Allan Schwartzman. Melbourne: Schwartz City, 1995.

———, ed. *Post-Pop Art.* Cambridge, Massachusetts: MIT Press, 1989.

Tomkins, Calvin. *Post- to Neo-: The Art World of the 1980s.* New York: Henry Holt and Company, 1988.

Approaching the Millennium, 1990–2000

Benezra, Neal, and Olga M. Viso. *Distemper: Dissonant Themes in the Art of the 1990s* (exhibition catalog). Washington, D.C.: Hirshhorn Museum and Sculpture Garden, Smithsonian Institution, 1996.

Clearwater, Bonnie, ed. *Defining the Nineties: Consensus-Making in New York, Miami, and Los Angeles.* North Miami: Museum of Contemporary Art, 1996.

Curiger, Bice. *Birth of the Cool* (exhibition catalog). Zurich: Kunsthaus Zürich; Hamburg: Deichtorhallen Hamburg, 1996.

Deitch, Jeffrey. *Post Human* (exhibition catalog). Pully/Lausanne, Switzerland: FAE Musée d'Art Contemporain; et al.

Golden, Thelma. *Black Male: Representations of Masculinity in Contemporary American Art* (exhibition catalog). New York: Whitney Museum of American Art, 1994.

Grynsztejn, Madeleine. *About Place: Recent Art of the Americas* (exhibition catalog). Essay by David Hickey. Chicago: The Art Institute of Chicago, 1995.

Schimmel, Paul. *Helter Skelter: L.A. Art in the 1990s* (exhibition catalog). Los Angeles: The Temporary Contemporary of The Museum of Contemporary Art, 1992.

Storr, Robert. *Dislocations* (exhibition catalog). New York: The Museum of Modern Art, 1991.

Sussman, Elisabeth, et al. *1993 Biennial Exhibition* (exhibition catalog). New York: Whitney Museum of American Art, 1993.

Wallace, Michele. *Black Popular Culture: A Project.* Dia Center for the Arts Discussions in Contemporary Culture, no. 8. Seattle: Bay Press, 1992.

Zelevansky, Lynn. *Sense and Sensibility: Women Artists and Minimalism in the Nineties.* New York: The Museum of Modern Art, 1994.

Performing Arts: Dance, Theater, and Music

Anderson, Jack. *Art without Boundaries.* Iowa City: University of Iowa Press, 1997.

Auslander, Philip. *American Experimental Theater: A Critical Introduction.* New York: University Arts Resources, 1993.

———. *From Acting to Performance: Essays in Modernism and Postmodernism.* New York: Routledge, 1997.

Banes, Sally. *Dancing Women: Female Bodies on Stage.* New York: Routledge, 1998.

———. *Democracy's Body: Judson Dance Theater, 1962–1964.* Ann Arbor, Michigan: UMI Research Press, 1983.

———. *Greenwich Village 1963: Avant-Garde Performance and the Effervescent Body.* Durham, North Carolina: Duke University Press, 1993.

———. *Writing Dancing in the Age of Postmodernism.* Hanover, New Hampshire: Wesleyan University Press/University Press of New England, 1994.

Battcock, Gregory, and Robert Nickas, eds. *The Art of Performance: A Critical Anthology.* New York: E. P. Dutton, 1984.

Bennington College Judson Project. *Judson Dance Theater, 1962–1966.* Bennington, Vermont: Bennington College, 1981.

Biner, Pierre. *The Living Theatre.* New York: Horizon Press, 1972.

Carr, C. *On Edge: Performance at the End of the Twentieth Century.* Hanover, New Hampshire: University Press of New England, 1993.

Chinoy, Helen Krich, and Linda Walsh Jenkins, eds. *Women in American Theatre: Careers, Images, Movements.* New York: Crown, 1981.

Cohen, Selma Jeanne, ed. *International Encyclopedia of Dance.* New York: Oxford University Press, 1998.

Cooke, Mervyn. *The Chronicle of Jazz.* New York: Abbeville Press, 1998.

Goldberg, RoseLee. *Live Art Since 1960.* New York: Harry N. Abrams, 1998.

Henry, Tricia. *Break All Rules! Punk Rock and the Making of a Style.* Ann Arbor, Michigan: UMI Research Press, 1989.

Little, Stuart W. *Off-Broadway: The Prophetic Theater.* New York: Coward, McCann and Geoghegan, 1972.

Livet, Anne, ed. *Contemporary Dance: An Anthology of Lectures, Interviews, and Essays with Many of the Most Important Contemporary American Choreographers, Scholars, and Critics.* New York: Abbeville Press in association with The Fort Worth Art Museum, 1978.

Morrissey, Lee, ed. *The Kitchen Turns Twenty: A Retrospective Anthology.* New York: The Kitchen Center for Video, Music, Dance, Performance, Film, and Literature, 1992.

Outside the Frame: Performance and the Object. A Survey History of Performance Art in the USA Since 1950 (exhibition catalog). Cleveland: Cleveland Center for Contemporary Art, 1994.

Perkins, William Eric, ed. *Droppin' Science: Critical Essays on Rap Music and Hip Hop Culture.* Philadelphia: Temple University Press, 1996.

Roudane, Matthew C. *American Drama Since 1960: A Critical History.* New York: Twayne, 1996.

Sayre, Henry M. *The Object of Performance: The American Avant-Garde Since 1970.* Chicago: University of Chicago Press, 1989.

Schwarz, K. Robert. *Minimalists: 20th-Century Composers.* London: Phaidon Press, 1996.

Shank, Theodore. *American Alternative Theater.* New York: Grove, 1982.

Siegel, Marcia B. *The Tail of the Dragon: New Dance, 1976–1982.* Durham, North Carolina: Duke University Press, 1991.

Photography

Blessing, Jennifer. *Rrose Is a Rose Is a Rose: Gender Performance in Photography* (exhibition catalog). New York: Solomon R. Guggenheim Museum, 1997.

Coke, Van Deren, ed. *One Hundred Years of Photographic History: Essays in Honor of Beaumont Newhall.* Albuquerque: University of New Mexico Press, 1975.

Davis, Keith F. *An American Century of Photography: From Dry-Plate to Digital. The Hallmark Photographic Collection.* Foreword by Donald J. Hall. Kansas City, Missouri: Hallmark Cards, Inc., in association with Harry N. Abrams, 1995.

Greenough, Sarah, et al. *On the Art of Fixing a Shadow: One Hundred and Fifty Years of Photography* (exhibition catalog). Washington, D.C.: National Gallery of Art; Chicago: The Art Institute of Chicago, 1989.

Grundberg, Andy. *Crisis of the Real: Writings on Photography, 1974–1989.* New York: Aperture, 1990.

Grundberg, Andy, and Kathleen McCarthy Gauss. *Photography and Art: Interactions Since 1946* (exhibition catalog). Fort Lauderdale, Florida: Museum of Art; Los Angeles: Los Angeles County Museum of Art, 1987.

Hall-Duncan, Nancy. *The History of Fashion Photography* (exhibition catalog). Rochester, New York: International Museum of Photography, George Eastman House, 1977.

Livingston, Jane. *The New York School Photographs, 1936–1963.* New York: Stewart, Tabori & Chang, 1992.

Newhall, Beaumont. *The History of Photography from 1839 to the Present Day.* Rev. ed. New York: The Museum of Modern Art, 1982.

Petruck, Peninah R., ed. *The Camera Viewed: Writings on Twentieth-Century Photography.* Vol. 2, *Photography after World War II.* New York: E. P. Dutton, 1979.

Smith, Joshua P., and Merry A. Foresta. *The Photography of Invention: American Pictures of the 1980s* (exhibition catalog). Washington, D.C.: National Museum of American Art, Smithsonian Institution, 1989.

Solomon-Godeau, Abigail. *Photography at the Dock: Essays on Photographic History, Institutions, and Practices.* Foreword by Linda Nochlin. Media & Society, no. 4. Minneapolis: University of Minnesota Press, 1991.

Sontag, Susan. *On Photography.* New York: Farrar, Straus & Giroux, 1977.

Squiers, Carol, ed. *The Critical Image: Essays on Contemporary Photography.* Seattle: Bay Press, 1990.

Steichen, Edward. *The Family of Man* (exhibition catalog). Prologue by Carl Sandburg. New York: The Museum of Modern Art, 1955.

Szarkowski, John. *Photography Until Now* (exhibition catalog). New York: The Museum of Modern Art, 1989.

Turner, Peter, ed. *American Images: Photography 1945–1980* (exhibition catalog). London: Barbican Art Gallery, 1985.

Willis, Deborah, ed. *Picturing Us: African American Identity in Photography.* New York: New Press, 1994.

Film, Video, and Sound

The American New Wave, 1958–1967 (exhibition catalog). Minneapolis: Walker Art Center; Buffalo: Media Study/Buffalo, 1982.

Battcock, Gregory, ed. *New Artists Video: A Critical Anthology.* New York: E. P. Dutton, 1978.

Cook, David A. *A History of Narrative Film* (1981). 2nd ed. New York: W. W. Norton & Company, 1990.

Delehanty, Suzanne. *Video Art* (exhibition catalog). Philadelphia: Institute of Contemporary Art, University of Pennsylvania, 1975.

Frampton, Hollis. *Circles of Confusion: Film, Photography, Video. Texts, 1968–1980.* Foreword by Annette Michelson. Rochester, New York: Visual Studies Workshop Press, 1983.

Hall, Doug, and Sally Jo Fifer, eds. *Illuminating Video: An Essential Guide to Video Art.* New York: Aperture in association with the Bay Area Video Coalition, 1990.

Hanhardt, John G., ed. *Video Culture: A Critical Investigation.* Layton, Utah: Peregrine Smith Books in association with Visual Studies Workshop Press, 1986.

A History of the American Avant-Garde Cinema (exhibition catalog). New York: The American Federation of Arts, 1976.

James, David E. *Allegories of Cinema: American Film in the Sixties.* Princeton: Princeton University Press, 1989.

Korot, Beryl, and Ira Schneider, eds. *Video Art: An Anthology.* New York: Harcourt Brace Jovanovich, 1976.

Lander, Dan, and Micah Lexier, eds. *Sound by Artists.* Toronto: Art Metropole; Banff, Canada: Walter Phillips Gallery, 1990.

MacDonald, Scott. *A Critical Cinema: Interviews with Independent Filmmakers.* Berkeley: University of California Press, 1988.

Sitney, P. Adams. *The Avant-Garde Film.* Anthology Film Archives Series, no. 3. New York: New York University Press, 1978.

———. *Visionary Film: The American Avant-Garde.* 2nd ed. New York: Oxford University Press, 1979.

Architecture and Design

Banham, Reyner. *Los Angeles: The Architecture of Four Ecologies.* New York: Harper & Row, 1971.

Betsky, Aaron, ed. *Icons: Magnets of Meaning* (exhibition catalog). San Francisco: San Francisco Museum of Modern Art, 1997.

De Long, David, Helen Searing, and Robert A. M. Stern, *American Architecture: Innovation and Tradition.* New York: Rizzoli, 1986.

Diamonstein, Barbaralee. *American Architecture Now* (1980). Foreword by Paul Goldberger. New York: Rizzoli, 1985.

Dilr, Elizabeth, and Ricardo Scofidio. *Flesh: Architectural Probes.* Essay by Georges Teyssot. New York: Princeton Architectural Press, 1994.

Dreyfuss, Henry. *Designing for People.* New York: Simon and Schuster, 1955.

Eisenman, Peter, et al. *Five Architects: Eisenman, Graves, Gwathmey, Hejduk, Meier.* New York: Oxford University Press, 1975.

Hayden, Dolores. *The Grand Domestic Revolution: A History of Feminist Designs for American Homes, Neighborhoods, and Cities.* Cambridge, Massachusetts: MIT Press, 1981.

Hitchcock, Henry-Russell, and Arthur Drexler, eds. *Built in USA: Post-War Architecture.* New York: The Museum of Modern Art in association with Thames and Hudson, 1952.

Jacobs, Jane. *The Death and Life of Great American Cities.* New York: Random House, 1961.

Jencks, Charles. *The Language of Post-Modern Architecture.* 6th ed. New York: Rizzoli, 1991.

Johnson, Philip, and Mark Wigley. *Deconstructivist Architecture* (exhibition catalog). New York: The Museum of Modern Art, 1988.

Kirkham, Pat. *Charles and Ray Eames: Designers of the Twentieth Century.* Cambridge, Massachusetts: MIT Press, 1995.

Koolhaas, Rem. *Delirious New York: A Retroactive Manifesto for Manhattan.* New York: Monacelli Press, 1994.

McCoy, Esther. *Case Study Houses, 1945–1962.* 2nd ed. Los Angeles: Hennessey & Ingalls, 1977.

Mertins, Detlef, ed. *The Presence of Mies.* New York: Princeton Architectural Press, 1994.

Neutra, Richard Joseph. *Survival through Design.* New York: Oxford University Press, 1954.

Ockman, Joan, ed., in collaboration with Edward Eigen. *Architecture Culture, 1943–1968: A Documentary Anthology.* New York: Columbia University Graduate School of Architecture, Planning, and Preservation and Rizzoli, 1993.

Scully, Vincent. *American Architecture and Urbanism.* Rev. ed. New York: Henry Holt and Company, 1988.

———. *Modern Architecture: The Architecture of Democracy* (1961). Rev. ed. New York: George Braziller, 1975.

Smith, Elizabeth A. T., et al. *Blueprints for Modern Living: History and Legacy of the Case Study Houses* (exhibition catalog). Los Angeles: The Museum of Contemporary Art, 1989.

Soja, Edward W. *Postmodern Geographies: The Reassertion of Space in Critical Social Theory.* New York: Verso, 1989.

Stern, Robert A. M. *New Directions in American Architecture* (1969). Rev. ed. New York: George Braziller, 1977.

Torre, Susana, ed. *Women in American Architecture: A Historic and Contemporary Perspective* (exhibition catalog). New York: The Architectural League of New York, 1977.

Tschumi, Bernard. *Event-Cities: Praxis.* Cambridge, Massachusetts: MIT Press, 1994.

Upton, Dell. *Architecture in the United States.* New York: Oxford University Press, 1998.

Venturi, Robert. *Complexity and Contradiction in Architecture.* Introduction by Vincent Scully. 2nd ed. New York: The Museum of Modern Art in association with the Graham Foundation for Advanced Studies in the Fine Arts, 1966.

Venturi, Robert, Denise Scott Brown, and Steven Izenour. *Learning from Las Vegas: The Forgotten Symbolism of Architectural Form* (1972). Rev. ed. Cambridge, Massachusetts: MIT Press, 1977.

Whitaker, Craig. *Architecture and the American Dream.* New York: Clarkson N. Potter, 1996.

Wiseman, Carter. *Shaping a Nation: Twentieth-Century American Architecture and Its Makers.* New York: W. W. Norton & Company, 1998.

Literature

Hellmann, John. *Fables of Fact: The New Journalism as New Fiction.* Urbana: University of Illinois Press, 1981.

Howard, Richard. *Alone with America: Essays on the Art of Poetry in the United States since 1950.* New York: Atheneum, 1969.

Kerrane, Kevin, and Ben Yagoda, eds. *The Art of Fact: A Historical Anthology of Literary Journalism.* New York: Scribner, 1997.

Mailer, Norman. *The Armies of the Night: History as a Novel, the Novel as History.* New York: New American Library, 1968.

Wolfe, Tom, and E. W. Johnson, eds. *The New Journalism.* New York: Harper & Row, 1973.

Notes on Contributors

Robert Atkins is a New York-based art historian and research fellow at the Studio for Creative Inquiry, Carnegie Mellon University. He is the author of *ArtSpoke: A Guide to Modern Ideas, Movements, and Buzzwords, 1848–1944* (1993), and *ArtSpeak: A Guide to Contemporary Ideas, Movements, and Buzzwords, 1945 to the Present* (1997, rev. ed.).
In 1991 he co-curated "From Media to Metaphor: Art About AIDS," the first major traveling group exhibition about AIDS.

Philip Auslander is associate professor in the School of Literature, Communication, and Culture at Georgia Institute of Technology. He is the author of *The New York School Poets as Playwrights: O'Hara, Ashbery, Koch, Schuyler, and the Visual Arts* (1989); *Presence and Resistance: Postmodernism and Cultural Politics in Contemporary American Performance* (1992); *From Acting to Performance: Essays in Modernism and Postmodernism* (1997); and *Liveness: Performance in a Mediatized Culture* (1999).

Sally Banes is the Marian Hannah Winter Professor of Theater History and Dance Studies at the University of Wisconsin-Madison. She has written extensively on dance, performance, and theater. Her books include *Democracy's Body: Judson Dance Theater, 1962–1964* (1993, reprt.); *Greenwich Village 1963: Avant-Garde Performance and the Effervescent Body* (1993); *Dancing Women: Female Bodies on Stage* (1998); and *Subversive Expectations: Performance Art and Paratheater in New York, 1976–1985* (1998).

Maurice Berger is senior fellow of the Vera List Center for Art & Politics, New School for Social Research. He is the author of numerous books and essays, including *White Lies: Race and the Myths of Whiteness* (1999); *How Art Becomes History* (1992); and *Labyrinths: Robert Morris, Minimalism, and the 1960s* (1989). He is also the editor of *The Crisis of Criticism* (1998).

Homi K. Bhabha is the Chester D. Tripp Professor in the Humanities at the University of Chicago and Visiting Professor in the Humanities at University College, London. He has delivered several honorary lectures and has recently been awarded a fellowship from Wissenschaftskolleg zu Berlin. Bhaba is the author of *The Location of Culture* (1994) and editor of the essay collection *Nation and Narration* (1990). He is currently at work on *A Measure of Dwelling*, a theory of vernacular cosmopolitanism.

John Carlin is the co-founder and president of Funny Garbage, a new media design and production company. He is also the founder and president of The Red Hot Organization, a not-for-profit production company that raises money and awareness for the fight against AIDS through such recording projects as "Stolen Moments" and "Red Hot + Rio." Also a curator, Carlin co-organized "The Comic Art Show" at the Whitney Museum of American Art, Downtown Branch, in 1983.

Tom Finkelpearl worked as a curator at P.S.1 Contemporary Art Center from 1981 to 1990. He was director of the Percent for Art in New York City program from 1990 to 1996, and executive director of the Skowhegan School of Painting and Sculpture program from 1996 to 1999. In 1999 he returned to P.S.1 as program director. His book on public art is in press.

Hilene Flanzbaum is associate professor of twentieth-century American literature and director of creative writing at Butler University. She was general editor of and a contributor to *The Americanization of the Holocaust* (1999) and managing editor of *Jewish-American Literature: A Norton Anthology* (1999).

Paula Geyh is assistant professor of English at Southern Illinois University. She has published numerous articles on postmodern literature, twentieth-century American literature, and literary theory in newspapers and scholarly publications. She was a co-editor of *Postmodern American Fiction: A Norton Anthology* (1997).

RoseLee Goldberg is adjunct professor in the Department of Art at New York University. She was formerly a curator at The Kitchen Center for Video, Music, Dance, Performance, Film, and Literature in New York City. She is the author of *Performance: Live Art since 1960* (1998), a history of performance art over the past four decades, and *Performance Art: From Futurism to the Present* (1988, rev. ed.). She is a frequent contributor to *Artforum* and is currently working on a monograph on Laurie Anderson.

Jeremy Green is assistant professor of English at the University of Colorado, Boulder, where he teaches courses in modern, contemporary, and postmodern American literature. He is currently working on a book, *The Fiction of Don DeLillo: Postmodernism and the American Imaginary*.

Chrissie Iles is curator of film and video at the Whitney Museum of American Art. She curated the film and video component for *The American Century: Art & Culture 1950-2000*, and is now working on a major survey exhibition of video and film installation in America from 1965 to 1975 for the Whitney Museum. She was previously head of exhibitions at the Museum of Modern Art, Oxford, in England. She has lectured widely and published many texts on film and video installation and on the history of performance.

Sylvia Lavin is chair of the Department of Architecture and Urban Design at UCLA. She has received numerous honors and fellowships, including the Getty Center for the History of Art and the Humanities Fellowship (1989-90). She writes extensively on modern and contemporary architecture in journals, magazines, and catalogs. She is the author of *Quatrèmere de Quincy and the Invention of a Modern Language of Architecture* (1992).

Andrew Levy is Edna Cooper Chair in English at Butler University, where he teaches American literature. He is currently working on a book, *American Revolutions*, and he is the author of *The Culture and Commerce of the Short Story* (1993). He co-edited *Postmodern American Fiction: A Norton Anthology* (1997) and *Creating Fiction* (1994).

Kate Linker is a New York-based critic who teaches postmodern theory and practice in the MFA Photography and Related Media program at the School of Visual Arts. Her articles and essays have been published in numerous international magazines and exhibition catalogs, and she is the author of the books *Love for Sale: The Words and Pictures of Barbara Kruger* (1990) and *Vito Acconci* (1994).

Carrie Rickey, film critic of *The Philadelphia Inquirer*, has written about art and film for such publications as *Artforum*, *Art in America*, *American Film*, and *The New York Times*. Her essays are collected in various anthologies, among them *The Rolling Stone Illustrated History of Rock and Roll* (1992, rev. ed.); *Produced and Abandoned* (1990); and *The Triumph of Feminist Art* (1993).

Eugenie Tsai is senior curator at the Whitney Museum of American Art, where she is currently organizing a Robert Smithson retrospective. Previously she curated "Lee Mingwei: Way Stations" (1998); "Gazing Back: Shigeko Kubota and Mary Lucier" (1995); and, for the Whitney Museum at Philip Morris, one-artist exhibitions of the work of Ik-Jung Kang, Byron Kim, Christian Marclay, Shirin Neshat, Carrie Mae Weems, and Lynne Yamamoto. She is the author of the Choice Award-winning book, *Robert Smithson Unearthed* (1991).

Steven Watson is a cultural historian of the group dynamics of the twentieth-century American avant-garde. He has written about the first American avant-garde—the Harlem Renaissance—and about the Beat Generation. His most recent book is *Prepare for Saints: Gertrude Stein, Virgil Thomson, and the Mainstreaming of American Modernism* (1999), and he is currently working on a book about Andy Warhol's Factory.

Matthew Yokobosky is an exhibition designer and curator specializing in film, video installation, and performance. At the Whitney Museum of American Art, he designed "Joseph Stella" (1994) and "The 1995 Biennial Exhibition" (1995) and curated "No Wave Cinema, '78–'87" (1996), which toured internationally. He was the design consultant and film and video curator for *The American Century: Art & Culture 1900-1950*. Currently, he is the exhibition designer of the Brooklyn Museum of Art.

Acknowledgments

A book of this scope requires the contributions of many people. Over the past two years, I have received valuable advice and suggestions from the following friends and colleagues who served as advisers for the exhibition: Maurice Berger, Homi K. Bhabha, Anna Chave, Francis Colpitt, Tom Crow, Stuart Ewen, Leon Falk, Coco Fusco, Joseph Giovaninni, RoseLee Goldberg, Thyrza Goodeve, David Joselit, Michael Kammen, Liz Kotz, Sylvia Lavin, Michael Leja, Greil Marcus, Robert Pincus-Witten, Ralph Rugoff, Allan Schwartzman, Robert Sklar, Rebecca Solnit, Carol Squiers, Mary Anne Staniszewski, Kristine Stiles, Henry Urbach, and Brian Wallis. Some of these advisers also wrote essays for this book, as did other scholars and critics. I am grateful to them all for their contributions, which have immeasurably enriched the volume.

This book would not have been possible without the Publications and New Media Department at the Whitney Museum and Jim Mairs of W. W. Norton. Katy Homans applied her prodigious talent to the design of the volume, while Maurice Berger and Alexandra Shelley gave incisive comments and editorial advice on the manuscript. A generous gift from Susan and Edwin Malloy enabled the publication to proceed. Although everyone mentioned was critical to the book, I am most indebted to Susan Harris, associate curator for *The American Century* project, who coordinated the volume. She has devoted nearly a full year to it with grace, dedication, and perseverance. Ongoing research, documentary material, and back-breaking clerical support were provided by Alpesh Patel, Hyon Su Kwon, Shana Rosengart, Jean Shin, and Adrienne Gagnon. Their conscientious devotion to this project has been remarkable. Some of the people that deserve special mention for their exceptional assistance in obtaining images and research materials are the staffs of Cheim & Reid, the Paula Cooper Gallery, Metro Pictures, Robert Miller Gallery, John Weber Gallery, the Addison Gallery of American Art, and the San Francisco Museum of Modern Art; Emily Abernathy, Jane Austrian, Miles Bellamy, Red Burns, Mary Corey, Laura Cottingham, Virginia Dwan, Janis Ekdahl, Thomas Erben, Nina Felshin, Tom Finkelpearl, Peter Freeman, Diana Gongora, Judith Green, Sara Greenough, Anna Halprin, Pat Hearn, Rob Hooper, Glenn Horowitz, Lillian Kiesler, Barbara Moore, Richard Oram, Ed Rider, Rick Rossin, Emily Russell, Susanna Singer, Tom Staley, Sloane Tanen, David Vaughn, and Joan Washburn.

At the Whitney Museum, a curatorial team was instrumental in developing the exhibition—furnishing ideas, research, and refining structural details that in turn helped define this publication. The team included former curators Adam D. Weinberg, Elisabeth Sussman, and Thelma Golden, and present curators Eugenie Tsai and Chrissie Iles. *The American Century* has truly been a collective endeavor at the Museum, with all the departments straining hard to realize this ambitious project—which includes not only the publication and exhibition but a website and public programs. In addition to the team of in-house curators and committee of advisers, Susan Harris and Karl Willers, also an associate curator for *The American Century* project, helped to research and select objects and then, with intelligence and discernment, saw the exhibition through after my departure from the Whitney Museum. Chrissie Iles, Maurice Berger, and Stephen Vitiello contributed their considerable expertise by curating specific sections of the exhibition. For the design of the exhibition, a talented team was brought in: Christian Hubert, architect, and his associate Jill Leckner met every expectation in their insightful design for a complex project with an overwhelming number of works; Nigel Smith worked with the curators and designers to create an imaginative and complementary graphic design conception. Kathyrn Potts oversaw the public programs, and Melissa Phillips took charge of the website. Willard Holmes, chief operating officer at the Museum, provided steady leadership through many transitions.

The collaboration with Intel has been unprecedented and rewarding, enabling the Museum to conceive and realize an exhibition on this scale. I am grateful to Andrew S. Grove, chairman of Intel, for his vision, and to his staff—Dana Houghton, Kevin Teixeira, Ralph Bond, Vince Thomas, and Ciaran Doyle—for their interest, enthusiasm, curiosity, and commitment to bringing *The American Century* to new audiences through the Internet—and bringing us into the twenty-first century.

Finally, for their support and faith in the importance of this project, I would like to thank the Whitney Board of Trustees, in particular Leonard A. Lauder, chairman; David A. Ross, former director of the Whitney Museum, who initiated the project; and Maxwell L. Anderson, director, who guided it through to completion. —L. P.

PHOTOGRAPH AND
REPRODUCTION CREDITS

Front cover Geoffrey Clements **Frontispiece** Photograph © Gianfranco Gorgoni **Back cover** (clockwise from top left): Figs. **534, 207, 79, 23, 455, 566, 431**

America Takes Command, 1950–1960
1 © 1998 Museum Associates, Los Angeles County Museum of Art. All Rights Reserved. © Estate of Hans Hofmann/Licensed by VAGA, New York, NY. **2/3** Ezra Stoller © Esto. **4** © 1999 Pollock-Krasner Foundation/ Artists Rights Society (ARS), New York; photograph Steven Sloman. **5** © 1999 Pollock-Krasner Foundation/ Artists Rights Society (ARS), New York; photograph © 1998 The Metropolitan Museum of Art, New York. **6** © 1991 Hans Namuth Estate. Courtesy Center for Creative Photography, The University of Arizona. **7** © 1999 Willem de Kooning Revocable Trust/Artists Rights Society (ARS), New York; photograph Ricardo Blanc. **8/9** © 1999 Willem de Kooning Revocable Trust/Artists Rights Society (ARS), New York; photograph Steven Sloman. **10** Steven Sloman. **11** Photograph © 1999 The Museum of Modern Art, New York. © Dedalus Foundation/Licensed by VAGA, New York, NY. **12** © Estate of Theodore Roszak/Licensed by VAGA, New York, NY; photograph Geoffrey Clements. **13** Sandak, Inc. **14/15** Geoffrey Clements. **16/17** © Estate of David Smith/Licensed by VAGA, New York, NY; photograph Jerry L. Thompson. **18** © 1999 Kate Rothko Prizel and Christopher Rothko/Artists Rights Society (ARS), New York. **19** © 1999 Kate Rothko Prizel and Christopher Rothko/Artists Rights Society (ARS), New York; photograph Steven Sloman. **20/21** Steven Sloman. **22** Julius Shulman. **23** Sandak/Macmillan Company, Connecticut. Courtesy Eames Office, Venice, California. **24** UPI/Corbis-Bettmann. **25** Courtesy Photofest. **26** Courtesy Brown Brothers, Sterling, Pennsylvania. **27** UPI/Corbis-Bettmann. **28** Archive Photos. **29** Photograph © Fred W. McDarrah. **30** Nina Leen/*Life* Magazine © Time Inc. **31** *Life* Magazine © Time Inc. Photographs © Arnold Newman. Art work © 1999 Pollock-Krasner Foundation/Artists Rights Society (ARS), New York. **32** Courtesy *Vogue*, © 1951 (renewed 1978) Condé Nast Publications, Inc. Art work © 1999 Pollock-Krasner Foundation/Artists Rights Society (ARS), New York. **33/34/35** The Kobal Collection. **36** UPI/Corbis-Bettmann. **37** AP/Wide World Photos. **38** UPI/Corbis-Bettmann. **39** Courtesy Charles Brittin and The Craig Krull Gallery. **40** Archive Photos. **41** City Lights Bookstore, San Francisco. Courtesy Robert Miller Gallery, New York. © Al Held/Licensed by VAGA, New York, NY. **43** Matthew Marks Gallery, New York. **44** Ezra Stoller © Esto. **45** Michael Marsland. **©** Yale University. All Rights Reserved. **46** Geoffrey Clements. **47** © 1954 Morris Louis. Courtesy Barbara Schwartz, Inc; photograph Earl Ripling. **48** Photograph © Fred W. McDarrah. **49** Courtesy Cheim & Read, New York. © Louise Bourgeois/ Licensed by VAGA, New York, NY. **50** © 1999 Pollock-Krasner Foundation/Artists Rights Society (ARS), New York; photograph courtesy Robert Miller Gallery, New York. **51** Courtesy the artist and ACA Galleries, New York. **52** Geoffrey Clements. **53** Robert E. Mates. **54** © 1999 The Estate of Sam Francis/Artists Rights Society (ARS), New York; photograph © 1999 The Museum of Modern Art, New York. **55** © Alex Katz/Licensed by VAGA, New York, NY; photograph Bill Jacobson. **56/57** Geoffrey Clements. **58** © Larry Rivers/Licensed by VAGA, New York, NY; photograph © 1999 The Museum of Modern Art, New York. **59** Photograph © 1999 The Museum of Modern Art, New York. **61** Robert E. Mates. **62** Geoffrey Clements. **63** Courtesy the artist. **64** UPI/Corbis-Bettmann; photograph John Springer. **65** UPI/Corbis-Bettmann. **66** John Wulp/ Living Theatre Archives. **67** © 1999 Barnett Newman Foundation/Artists Rights Society (ARS), New York; photograph Steven Sloman. **68** © 1999 Estate of Ad Reinhardt/Artists Rights Society (ARS), New York; photograph Robert E. Mates. **70** Geoffrey Clements.

Redefining the American Dream, 1950–1960
71/72 UPI/Corbis-Bettmann. **73** Archive Photos. **74** The Kobal Collection. **75** Art work © 1999 Pollock-Krasner Foundation/Artists Rights Society (ARS), New York; photograph Sheldan C. Collins. **76** Courtesy William S. Wilson. **77** Photofest. **78** © Bruce Roberts 1993/Photo Researchers, Inc., New York. **79** Sony Legacy Recordings; photograph Sheldan C. Collins. **80** Photofest. **81** Reproduced by permission of Sterling Lord Literistic, Inc. © 1985 by John Sampas, Literary Rep. **82** © Allen Ginsberg Trust; courtesy Fahey Klein Gallery, Los Angeles. **83** Copyright 1957 by Grove Press, Inc. Cover photograph Fred Lyon. **84** Photograph Harry Redl; courtesy City Lights Bookstore, San Francisco. **85** © 1967 Larry Keenan. **86** Copyright

© 1956, 1974, renewed 1984 by Saul Bellow. Used by permission of Viking Penguin, a division of Penguin Putnam Inc. Jacket design by Bill English. **87** Copyright 1945, 1946, 1951 by J. D. Salinger. Used by permission of Little, Brown and Company. Jacket design by Michael Mitchell. **88** Copyright © 1959, renewed 1987 by Philip Roth. Reprinted by permission of Houghton Mifflin Co. All Rights Reserved. Jacket illustration by Sanford Roth. **89** Anthology Film Archives, New York. **90** Copyright Robert Frank; courtesy Anthology Film Archives, New York. **91/92** Anthology Film Archives, New York. **93** Geoffrey Clements. **94** Sheldan C. Collins. **96** Ben Blackwell. **97** George Hixson. **98** Geoffrey Clements. **99** George Hixson. **100** Julius Shulman. **101** © 1999 Estate of Jay DeFeo/Artists Rights Society (ARS), New York; photograph Ben Blackwell. **102** © 1999 Estate of Louise Nevelson/Artists Rights Society (ARS), New York; photograph Jerry L. Thompson. **103** Geoffrey Clements. **104** © 1999 John Chamberlain/Artists Rights Society (ARS), New York; photograph Jerry L. Thompson. **105** Jerry L. Thompson. **107** Geoffrey Clements. **109** Courtesy Barbara Schwartz. **110** Photograph © 1999 The Art Institute of Chicago. All Rights Reserved. **112** Photograph © 1999 The Museum of Modern Art, New York. **113/115** Geoffrey Clements. **116** © Robert Rauschenberg/Licensed by VAGA, New York, NY. **117** Squidds & Nunns. **118** © Robert Rauschenberg/ Licensed by VAGA, New York, NY. **119** SKM 1996/Per Anders Allsten. **120** Michael Tropea. **121** © Robert Rauschenberg/ Licensed by VAGA, New York, NY. **122** © 1999 Artists Rights Society (ARS), New York/ADAGP, Paris/Estate of Marcel Duchamp. **123** © Robert Rauschenberg/Licensed by VAGA, New York, NY. **124** Geoffrey Clements. **125** © 1999 Artists Rights Society (ARS), New York/ADAGP, Paris/Estate of Marcel Duchamp; color transparency Graydon Wood, 1996. **126** Louis A. Stevenson, Jr. Courtesy Cunningham Dance Foundation. **127** © Robert Rauschenberg/Licensed by VAGA, New York, NY. **128** Courtesy Cunningham Dance Foundation. **129** Paul Fusco/Magnum Photos, Inc. **130/131** © Jasper Johns/Licensed by VAGA, New York, NY; photograph © 1999 The Museum of Modern Art, New York. **132** © Jasper Johns/Licensed by VAGA, New York, NY; photograph Hickey-Robertson, Houston. **133** Courtesy Leo Castelli Gallery, New York. **134** © Robert Rauschenberg/ Licensed by VAGA, New York, NY; photograph Walter Russell. **135** © Jasper Johns/Licensed by VAGA, New York, NY; photograph Geoffrey Clements. **136** © Jasper Johns/Licensed by VAGA, New York, NY. **137** © Jasper Johns/Licensed by VAGA, New York, NY. Courtesy Philadelphia Museum of Art. **138** © Jasper Johns/ Licensed by VAGA, New York, NY; photograph Paula Goldman. **139** Courtesy Lillian Kiesler. **140** Geoffrey Clements. **141/142** © Robert R. McElroy/Licensed by VAGA, New York, NY. Getty Research Institute, Research Library, 980063; courtesy Norton Simon Museum Archives, Pasadena, California. **143** Courtesy Claes Oldenburg and Coosje van Bruggen. **145** Photograph Scott Hyde. Courtesy Getty Research Institute, Research Library, 980063. **146** Photograph Martha Holmes. Courtesy Claes Oldenburg and Coosje van Bruggen. **147** © Robert R. McElroy/Licensed by VAGA, New York, NY. Courtesy Claes Oldenburg and Coosje van Bruggen. **148** © Robert R. McElroy/Licensed by VAGA, New York, NY. **149** Martha Holmes. **150** Max Baker. **151** © The Estate of Peter Moore/Licensed by VAGA, New York, NY. **152** © 1999 Artists Rights Society (ARS), New York/ADAGP, Paris; photograph © Harry Shunk. **153** © Robert R. McElroy/ Licensed by VAGA, New York, NY. **154** © DPA/IPOL. **155** Courtesy Cunningham Dance Foundation. **156** Robert E. Mates. **157** Photograph courtesy Museum of Modern Art, Ludwig Foundation, Vienna. **158** Brad Iverson. **160** © The Estate of Peter Moore/Licensed by VAGA, New York, NY.

New Frontiers, 1960–1967
161 Magnum Photos, Inc./© 1963 Bob Adelman. **162** AP/Wide World Photos. **163** UPI/Corbis-Bettmann. **164** © Robert Frerck/Woodfin Camp & Associates. **165/166** Courtesy Procter & Gamble Archives, Cincinnati. **167** Fred R. Tannery. **168** Jim Strong. **169** UPI/Corbis-Bettmann. Art work © 1999 Andy Warhol Foundation for the Visual Arts/Artists Rights Society (ARS), New York. **170** © 1999 Andy Warhol Foundation for the Visual Arts/Artists Rights Society (ARS), New York; photograph Jim Strong. **171** © Robert Rauschenberg/Licensed by VAGA, New York, NY. **172** © George Segal/Licensed by VAGA, New York, NY. **173** Eric Pollitzer. **174** © Marisol/ Licensed by VAGA, New York, NY; photograph Robert E. Mates. **175** © Alex Katz/Licensed by VAGA, New York, NY; photograph Geoffrey Clements. **176** © 1999 Andy Warhol Foundation for the Visual Arts/Artists Rights Society (ARS), New York; photograph Billy Name. Courtesy Gavin Brown's Enterprise, New York. **177** © James Rosenquist/ Licensed by

VAGA, New York, NY. **179** © 1999 Andy Warhol Foundation for the Visual Arts/Artists Rights Society (ARS), New York; photograph Rainer Crone. **181** © 1999 Willem de Kooning Revocable Trust/Artists Rights Society (ARS), New York; photograph © 1991 The Metropolitan Museum of Art, New York. **182** Rudolf Nagel. **183** © 1999 Richard Artschwager/Artists Rights Society (ARS), New York; photograph Adam Reich. Courtesy Mary Boone Gallery, New York. **184** © 1999 Andy Warhol Foundation for the Visual Arts/Artists Rights Society (ARS), New York; photograph Hickey-Robertson, Houston. **185** © 1999 Andy Warhol Foundation for the Visual Arts/Artists Rights Society (ARS), New York; photograph Art Resource, New York. **186** © 1999 Andy Warhol Foundation for the Visual Arts/Artists Rights Society (ARS), New York; photograph Rudolph Burckhardt. **187** © 1999 Andy Warhol Foundation for the Visual Arts/Artists Rights Society (ARS), New York. **188** © 1999 Andy Warhol Foundation for the Visual Arts/Artists Rights Society (ARS), New York; photograph Geoffrey Clements. **189** © Stephen Shore. Courtesy PaceWildensteinMacGill. **190** Ugo Mulas, Milan. **191** Photograph © Gerard Malanga. **192** Jim Strong. Courtesy Sidney Janis Gallery, New York. **193** © Estate of Roy Lichtenstein; photograph Robert McKeever. **195/196** © Tom Wesselmann/Licensed by VAGA, New York, NY; photograph Geoffrey Clements. **197** © James Rosenquist/ Licensed by VAGA, New York, NY; photograph Photothèque des collections du Mnam/Cci. **198** © Jasper Johns/ Licensed by VAGA, New York, NY; photograph Rheinisches Bildarchiv, Cologne. **199** © 1999 Andy Warhol Foundation for the Visual Arts/Artists Rights Society (ARS), New York; photograph Geoffrey Clements. **200/201** © 1967, The Andy Warhol Museum, Pittsburgh, A Museum of Carnegie Institute. **202** Photograph © Fred W. McDarrah. **203** *Interview* magazine, vol. 1, no. 1, 1969, reprinted by permission of Brant Publications, Inc.; photograph courtesy The Archives of The Andy Warhol Museum, Pittsburgh. **204** Anthology Film Archives, New York, and Arthouse, Inc. **205/206** Anthology Film Archives, New York. **207** © Estate of Roy Lichtenstein. **208** Copyright © 1998 Los Angeles County Museum of Art. All Rights Reserved. **209** Steven Sloman. **210** Bliss Photography. **211/212** Geoffrey Clements. **213** Courtesy L.A. Louver Gallery, Venice, California. **214** © The Mark Shaw Collection/Photo Researchers, Inc., New York. **215** Magnum Photos, Inc./© 1963 Danny Lyon, from *Memories of the Southern Civil Rights Movement* (Chapel Hill: Published for the Center for Documentary Studies, Duke University, by the University of North Carolina Press, 1992). **216** AP/Wide World Photos. **217** © Estate of Roy Lichtenstein; photograph Rheinisches Bildarchiv, Cologne. **218** © James Rosenquist/Licensed by VAGA, New York, NY. **219** Sandak, Inc. **220** © 1999 Robert Indiana/Morgan Art Foundation/Artists Rights Society (ARS), New York; photographs Camerarts Inc., New York. **221** © Romare Bearden Foundation/Licensed by VAGA, New York, NY. **222** © 1999 Andy Warhol Foundation for the Visual Arts/Artists Rights Society (ARS), New York; photograph © 1998 Museum Associates, Los Angeles County Museum of Art. **223** © 1999 Andy Warhol Foundation for the Visual Arts/Artists Rights Society (ARS), New York; photograph Art Resource, New York. **224** © 1999 Andy Warhol Foundation for the Visual Arts/Artists Rights Society (ARS), New York. **225** © 1999 Andy Warhol Foundation for the Visual Arts/Artists Rights Society (ARS), New York; photograph Art Resource, New York. **226** UPI/Corbis-Bettmann. **227** Courtesy Venturi, Scott Brown and Associates, Inc.; photograph George Pohl. Copyright © 1972 The Massachusetts Institute of Technology. **229** Robert E. Mates. **230** © 1999 Robert Mangold/Artists Rights Society (ARS), New York; photograph Sandak, Inc. **231** © 1999 Frank Stella/Artists Rights Society (ARS), New York; photograph Geoffrey Clements. **232** Geoffrey Clements. **233** © 1999 Estate of Ad Reinhardt/Artists Rights Society (ARS), New York; photograph Geoffrey Clements. **234** © 1999 Frank Stella/Artists Rights Society (ARS), New York; photograph Rudolph Burckhardt. **235** Geoffrey Clements. **236** © 1999 Sol LeWitt/Artists Rights Society (ARS), New York; photograph courtesy PaceWildenstein, New York. **237** Copyright © 1973 La Monte Young & Marian Zazeela; photograph Robert Adler, courtesy Mela Foundation. **238** © 1969 Whitney Museum of American Art. Photographs of Steve Reich by Robert Fiore. **239** Paula Court. **240** © 1999 Estate of Dan Flavin/Artists Rights Society (ARS), New York; photograph Rudolph Burckhardt. **241** © 1999 Estate of Dan Flavin/ Artists Rights Society (ARS), New York. Courtesy Leo Castelli Gallery, New York. **242/243** © Carl Andre/Licensed by VAGA, New York, NY. **244** © Carl Andre/Licensed by VAGA, New York, NY; photograph courtesy Tate Gallery Publishing Ltd. **245** © Estate of Donald Judd/Licensed by VAGA, New York, NY; photograph Rudolph Burckhardt.

246 © Estate of Donald Judd/ Licensed by VAGA, New York, NY; photograph Ellen Page Wilson, courtesy PaceWildenstein, New York. 247 © Estate of Donald Judd/Licensed by VAGA, New York, NY; photograph © Todd Eberle. 248 © Estate of Donald Judd/Licensed by VAGA, New York, NY; photograph Lee Stalsworth. 249 © Estate of David Smith/Licensed by VAGA, New York, NY; photograph © Dan Budnik/Woodfin Camp & Associates. All Rights Reserved. 250 Jerry L. Thompson. 251 Photograph The Jewish Museum, New York/Art Resource, New York. Art work by Robert Morris © 1999 Robert Morris/Artists Rights Society (ARS), New York; art work by Donald Judd © Estate of Donald Judd/ Licensed by VAGA, New York, NY. 252 © 1999 Estate of Tony Smith/Artists Rights Society (ARS), New York; photograph Geoffrey Clements. 253 © 1999 Estate of Tony Smith/Artists Rights Society (ARS), New York; photograph courtesy The Corcoran Gallery of Art, School of Art Archives. 254/255/256 Anthology Film Archives, New York. 257 Photograph © The Estate of Peter Moore/Licensed by VAGA, New York, NY; photograph Barbara Moore. 258/259/260 Photograph © The Estate of Peter Moore/ Licensed by VAGA, New York, NY. 261 © 1999 Robert Morris/Artists Rights Society (ARS), New York. Art work by Sol LeWitt © 1999 Sol LeWitt/Artists Rights Society (ARS), New York; photograph Bill Jacobson. 262 Photograph © The Estate of Peter Moore/Licensed by VAGA, New York, NY; courtesy Solomon R. Guggenheim Foundation, New York. Performance © 1999 Robert Morris/Artists Rights Society (ARS), New York. 263 Photograph © The Estate of Peter Moore/Licensed by VAGA, New York, NY. Performance © 1999 Robert Morris/Artists Rights Society (ARS), New York. 264 Jerry L. Thompson. 265 Courtesy PaceWildenstein, New York. 266 Bill Jacobson. 267 © 1999 Brice Marden/Artists Rights Society (ARS), New York; photograph Ben Blackwell. 268 Steven Sloman. 269 Courtesy Pace-Wildenstein, New York. 270 Geoffrey Clements. 271 © 1999 Barnett Newman Foundation/ Artists Rights Society (ARS), New York; photograph Paul Macapia. 272 Jerry L. Thompson. 273 © 1999 Robert Irwin/Artists Rights Society (ARS), New York; photograph Geoffrey Clements. 274 L.A. Louver Gallery, Venice, California.

America at the Crossroads, 1964–1976
275 UPI/Corbis-Bettmann. 276 Photograph © Ron Bennett/UPI/Corbis-Bettmann. 277 UPI/Corbis-Bettmann. 278 John Filo. 279 UPI/Corbis-Bettmann. 280 © Marc Riboud/Magnum Photos, Inc. 281/282 UPI/Corbis-Bettmann. 283/284 Photofest. 285 The Kobal Collection. 286 © Bonnie Freer/Photo Researchers, Inc., New York. 287 © 1999 Robert Morris/Artists Rights Society (ARS), New York; photograph Rudolph Burckhardt. 288 © Fotex/R. Drechsler/Shooting Star. 289 Photofest. 290 Joel Axelrad/Michael Ochs Archives, Venice, California. 291 The Everett Collection. 292 © Louise Bourgeois/ Licensed by VAGA, New York, NY; courtesy Cheim & Read, New York. 293 © Estate of H. C. Westermann/Licensed by VAGA, New York, NY. 294 Jerry L. Thompson. 295 Sheldan C. Collins. 296 © 1999 Richard Artschwager/ Artists Rights Society (ARS), New York; photograph Steven Sloman. 297 © The Estate of Eva Hesse; courtesy Robert Miller Gallery, New York. 298 © Louise Bourgeois/ Licensed by VAGA, New York, NY; photograph © 1999 The Museum of Modern Art, New York. 299 Jerry L. Thompson. 300 Bill Baron; courtesy the artist. 301 Jerry L. Thompson. 302 Courtesy Barbara Gladstone Gallery, New York; photograph Larry Lamé. 303 Art work by Bruce Nauman: © 1999 Bruce Nauman/Artists Rights Society (ARS), New York; photograph Harry Shunk. 304 © 1999 Bruce Nauman/ Artists Rights Society (ARS), New York; photograph courtesy Leo Castelli Gallery, New York. 305/306 © 1999 Richard Serra/Artists Rights Society (ARS), New York; photograph Peter Moore. 307 © 1999 Richard Serra/Artists Rights Society (ARS), New York; photograph Shunk-Kender. 308 Ralph Lieberman. 309 Copyright © 1969 by Kurt Vonnegut, Jr. Used by permission of Delacorte Press, a division of Random House, Inc. Jacket design by Paul Bacon. 310 Copyright © 1973 by Thomas Pynchon. Used by permission of Viking Penguin, a division of Penguin Putnam Inc. Jacket design by Marc Getter. 311 © 1999 Richard Serra/Artists Rights Society (ARS), New York; photograph Peter Moore. 312 © 1999 Richard Serra/Artists Rights Society (ARS), New York; photograph Geoffrey Clements. 313 © 1999 Richard Serra/Artists Rights Society (ARS), New York; photograph Geoffrey Clements. 314 Geoffrey Clements. 315 © 1999 Bruce Nauman/Artists Rights Society (ARS), New York; photograph Geoffrey Clements. 316 © Lynda Benglis/Licensed by VAGA, New York, NY. 317 © Estate of Robert Smithson/Licensed by VAGA, New York, NY; photograph Fred Scruton. Courtesy John Weber Gallery, New York. 318 © 1999 Robert

Morris/Artists Rights Society (ARS), New York; photograph Geoffrey Clements. 319 Jerry L. Thompson. 320 © The Estate of Eva Hesse; photograph © 1998 The Detroit Institute of Arts. 321 © The Estate of Eva Hesse; photograph courtesy Robert Miller Gallery, New York. 322 © The Estate of Eva Hesse; photograph Geoffrey Clements. 323 Copyright © 1968 and copyright renewed © 1996 by Tom Wolfe. Reprinted by permission of Farrar, Straus & Giroux, Inc; photograph Sheldan C. Collins. Jacket design by Milton Glaser. 324 Copyright © 1968 by Norman Mailer. Used by permission of Dutton Signet, a division of Penguin Putnam Inc. Jacket by Paul Bacon Studio. 325 Geoffrey Clements. 326 Jerry L. Thompson. 327 © Estate of Robert Smithson/Licensed by VAGA, New York, NY. 328 © Estate of Robert Smithson/Licensed by VAGA, New York, NY; photograph Geoffrey Clements. 329 Courtesy Skidmore, Owings & Merrill LLP. 330 Courtesy Barbara Gladstone. 331 © 1999 Robert Morris/Artists Rights Society (ARS), New York; photograph Walter Russell. © Solomon R. Guggenheim Foundation, New York/Robert Morris Archives. 332 Courtesy the artist. 333 John Cliett. All Reproduction Rights Reserved. © Dia Center for the Arts. 334/335/336/337 Courtesy the artist. 338 © Estate of Robert Smithson/Licensed by VAGA, New York, NY; photograph © Gianfranco Gorgoni. 339 John Cliett; courtesy Dia Center for the Arts, New York. 340 © Christo 1969; photograph Harry Shunk. 341 Sheldan C. Collins. 342/343 Courtesy Holly Solomon Gallery, New York. 344 Courtesy Eisenman Architects. 345 © Tim Street-Porter/ Esto. All Rights Reserved. 346 Courtesy Frank O. Gehry & Associates. 347 © 1999 Bruce Nauman/Artists Rights Society (ARS), New York; courtesy Sperone Westwater, New York. 348 © 1999 Lawrence Weiner/ Artists Rights Society (ARS), New York. 349 © 1999 Joseph Kosuth/ Artists Rights Society (ARS), New York; photograph Geoffrey Clements. 350 © 1999 Joseph Kosuth/Artists Rights Society (ARS), New York. 351 Courtesy the artist. 352 Courtesy Marian Goodman Gallery, New York. 354 © Geoffrey Clements. 355 Douglas M. Parker Studio, Los Angeles; courtesy Margo Leavin Gallery, Los Angeles. 356 Geoffrey Clements. 357 © 1999 Hans Haacke/Artists Rights Society (ARS), New York/VG Bild-Kunst, Bonn; courtesy the artist. 358 © 1999 Estate of Douglas Huebler/Artists Rights Society (ARS), New York; courtesy Darcy Huebler/Estate of Douglas Huebler. 359 Geoffrey Clements. 360 Clem Fiori; courtesy the Wooster Group. 361 © 1998 David Burnett/Contact Press Images. 362 Fred S. Prouser/Liaison Agency, Inc. 363 © 1972 Paramount Pictures Corporation. All Rights Reserved. 364 S.S. Archives/Shooting Star International. © All Rights Reserved. 365 The Kobal Collection. 366 David Reynolds; courtesy Jack Tilton Gallery, New York. 367 Photograph © Ka Kwong Hui; courtesy Jon Hendricks. Copyprint by Oren Slor, 1995. 368 Copyright © 1998 Museum Associates, Los Angeles County Museum of Art. All Rights Reserved. 369 © Betye Saar; courtesy Michael Rosenfeld Gallery, New York. 370 Courtesy Phyllis Kind Gallery, New York. 371 Linda Eber; courtesy SPARC. 372 © Don Carl Steffen; courtesy Rapho/Photo Researchers, Inc. 373 UPI/Corbis-Bettmann. 374 Kelly Barrie. 375 Christopher Burke; courtesy Cheim & Read, New York. 376 D. James Dee; courtesy Ronald Feldman Fine Arts, New York. 377 David Reynolds; courtesy Jack Tilton Gallery and P.P.O.W., New York. 378 © Miriam Schapiro; photograph D. James Dee. Courtesy Steinbaum Krauss Gallery, New York. 379 © 1979 Judy Chicago; photograph © Donald Woodman. 380 Orcutt & van der Putten; courtesy Alexander and Bonin, New York. 381 Geoffrey Clements. 382 Harry Shunk; courtesy the artist and DC Moore Gallery, New York. 383 John Stoel. 384 Geoffrey Clements. 385 Courtesy Phyllis Kind Gallery, New York. 386 Courtesy the artist. 387 © 1999 Frank Stella/Artists Rights Society (ARS), New York. 388 © Jasper Johns/Licensed by VAGA, New York, NY. 389 © 1999 Christie's Images, New York. © 1999 Sol LeWitt/Artists Rights Society (ARS), New York. © 1974 Virgin Music (Publishers) Ltd. Photograph Geoffrey Clements. 390 © 1999 Sol LeWitt/Artists Rights Society (ARS), New York; courtesy Susanna Singer. 391 Erró; courtesy the artist. 392 Minoru Niizuma; courtesy LenOno Photo Archive, New York. 393 Anthony McCall; courtesy the artist. 394 George Macunias. 395/396 © The Estate of Ana Mendieta; courtesy Galerie Lelong, New York. 397 Courtesy George and Betty Woodman. 398 Courtesy the artist. 399 Geoffrey Clements. 400 Courtesy Thomas Erben Gallery. 401 Photograph © 1972, Babette Mangolte. All Rights of Reproduction Reserved; courtesy Trisha Brown Company. 402 © 1993 Beatriz Schiller. 403 Kathy Dillon; courtesy Barbara Gladstone. 404 Michael Kirby; courtesy the Estate of Scott Burton. 405 Charles Hill; courtesy the artist. 406 Alfred Lutjeans. 407 Barbara Burden; courtesy the artist. 408 © 1999 Artists Rights Society (ARS), New York/VG Bild-Kunst, Bonn; photograph

Ute Klophaus. 409 Perry Hoberman. 410 Copyright © 1976, 1995, Babette Mangolte. All Rights of Reproduction Reserved. 411 Paula Court. 412 © 1999 Bruce Nauman/Artists Rights Society (ARS), New York. 413 © 1999 Bruce Nauman/Artists Rights Society (ARS), New York. 414 Photograph © The Estate of Peter Moore/Licensed by VAGA, New York, NY. 415 Courtesy the artist. 416 Courtesy the artist. 417/418 Courtesy Electronic Arts Intermix, New York. 419 Photothèque des collections du Mnam/Cci. 420 © 1999 Bruce Nauman/Artists Rights Society (ARS), New York; photograph © Giorgio Colombo, Milan. 421 Geoffrey Clements. 422 Robert E. Mates. 423 Sheldan C. Collins. 424 Courtesy McKee Gallery, New York. 425 Photograph © 1986 Douglas M. Parker, Los Angeles. 426 © Nancy Graves Foundation/Licensed by VAGA, New York, NY. 427 Robert E. Mates. 428 Courtesy Paula Cooper Gallery, New York. 429 © 1999 Susan Rothenberg/Artists Rights Society (ARS), New York; photograph Charles W. Crist. 430 © Jennifer Bartlett; courtesy Robert Miller Gallery, New York. 431 Steven Sloman. 432 Squidds & Nunns. 433 © 1999 Bryan Hunt/Artists Rights Society (ARS), New York; photograph Jerry L. Thompson.

Restoration and Reaction, 1976–1990
434 UPI/Corbis-Bettmann. 435 Used by permission of Whole Earth Magazine, San Rafael, California. 436 Courtesy NASA. 437 Geoffrey Clements. 438/439 © William Eggleston/A + C Anthology; transparency © 1999 The Museum of Modern Art, New York. 440 Geoffrey Clements. 441 © 1976 Richard Misrach; courtesy Robert Mann Gallery, New York. 442/443/444/445 Geoffrey Clements. 446 © Ezra Stoller/Esto. All Rights Reserved. 447 Marvin Rand; courtesy Cesar Pelli & Associates, Inc. 448/449 Geoffrey Clements. 450 Jerry L. Thompson. 451 Sheldan C. Collins. 452 © David Salle/Licensed by VAGA, New York, NY; courtesy Gagosian Gallery, New York. 453 Courtesy Chase Manhattan Bank. 454 Courtesy the artist. 455/456/457 Courtesy the artist and Metro Pictures, New York. 458 Geoffrey Clements. 459 Courtesy Mary Boone Gallery, New York. 460 © Zindman/Fremont; courtesy Mary Boone Gallery, New York. 461 © Jenny Holzer; photograph Jenny Holzer. 462 © Jenny Holzer; photograph Lisa Kahane. 463 © Jenny Holzer; courtesy Jenny Holzer. 464 © Norman McGrath/Esto. All Rights Reserved. 465 Corbis/Robert Holmes; used by permission of Disney Enterprises, Inc. 466 Geoffrey Clements. 467 © Walker Evans Archives/The Metropolitan Museum of Art, New York; photograph Geoffrey Clements. 468 © 1980 Andrea Callard. 469 Courtesy Rosemary Hochschild. 470 Photograph © Richard Kern. 471/472 © 1980 Andrea Callard. 473/474 Geoffrey Clements. 475 Courtesy Mary Boone Gallery, New York. 476 James A. Steinfeld/Shooting Star. 477/478 Bob Gruen. 479 © 1977 Ebet Roberts. 480 © 1975 The Estate of Robert Mapplethorpe. 481 © 1978 The Estate of Robert Mapplethorpe. 482 © 1980 The Estate of Robert Mapplethorpe. 483/484/485/486/487/488 All photographs © Nan Goldin; courtesy Matthew Marks Gallery, New York. 489 Geoffrey Clements. 490 © The Estate of Peter Hujar; photograph © 1999 D. James Dee. 491 Geoffrey Clements. 492 Courtesy The Estate of David Wojnarowicz and P.P.O.W., New York. 493 Courtesy Electronic Arts Intermix, New York. 494/495/496 © Andé Whyland. 497/498 The Everett Collection. 499 Courtesy Ronald Feldman Fine Arts, New York; photograph Jennifer Kotter. 500 © The Estate of Keith Haring; photograph Chantal Regnault. 501 © The Estate of Keith Haring; photograph Klaus Wittman. 502 © 1999 Kenny Scharf/Artists Rights Society (ARS), New York; photograph Geoffrey Clements. 503 © 1999 Artists Rights Society (ARS), New York/ADAGP, Paris (Jean-Michel Basquiat); photograph Geoffrey Clements. 504 Martha Cooper, from Subway Art, by Martha Cooper and Henry Chalfant (London: Thames and Hudson Ltd., 1984). 505/506 Henry Chalfant, from Subway Art, by Martha Cooper and Henry Chalfant (London: Thames and Hudson Ltd., 1984). 507 © 1999 Artists Rights Society (ARS), New York/ADAGP, Paris (Jean-Michel Basquiat); photograph Bill Jacobson Studio. 508 Timothy Greathouse; courtesy Gracie Mansion. 509 Archive Photos. 510/511 Courtesy the artist. 512 Courtesy Leon Golub. 513 Courtesy the artist and Metro Pictures, New York; photograph Lisa Kahane. 514 Courtesy Mary Boone Gallery, New York. 516 © David Salle/Licensed by VAGA, New York, NY; courtesy Ludwig Forum für Internationale Kunst, Aachen, Germany. 517 © David Salle/ Licensed by VAGA, New York, NY; courtesy Gagosian Gallery, New York. 518 Geoffrey Clements. 519 © 1999 Andy Warhol Foundation for the Visual Arts/Artists Rights Society (ARS), New York; photograph Art Resource, New York. 520 Transparency © 1998 Museum of Fine Arts, Boston. All Rights Reserved. 521 Courtesy Mary Boone Gallery, New York. 522 Courtesy Gagosian Gallery, New York. 523 © Fred Scruton; courtesy the artist. 524/525

This publication was coordinated by Lisa Phillips, Director, The New Museum of Contemporary Art, New York, and former Curator of Contemporary Art, Whitney Museum, and Susan Harris, Associate Curator, with the assistance of Hyon Su Kwon, former Senior Curatorial/Research Assistant, and Alpesh Patel, Research Assistant.

This publication was produced by the Publications and New Media Department at the Whitney Museum and W. W. Norton & Company.

Whitney Museum of American Art
Mary E. DelMonico, Head, Publications and New Media; *Production*: Nerissa Dominguez Vales, Production Manager; Jennifer Cox, Publications and New Media Assistant; *Editorial*: Sheila Schwartz, Editor; Dale Tucker, Associate Editor; Jennifer Bernstein, Producer Editor; Susan Richmond, Production Coordinator/Editorial Assistant; *Design*: Deborah Littlejohn, Senior Graphic Designer; Roy Brooks, Graphic Designer; *Rights and Reproductions*: Anita Duquette, Manager, Rights and Reproductions; Jennifer Belt, Photographs and Permissions Coordinator; Jane Austrian, Volunteer; Judy Greene, Volunteer.

W. W. Norton & Company
James L. Mairs, Vice President; Nancy Palmquist, Managing Editor; Otto Sonntag, Copy Editor; Nina Gielen, Editorial Assistant

Catalog design: Katy Homans
Printing: Balding + Mansell
Printed and bound in Great Britain